Learning through Play:

CURRICULUM AND ACTIVITIES FOR THE INCLUSIVE CLASSROOM

T5-AFC-751

Learning through Play:

CURRICULUM AND ACTIVITIES FOR THE INCLUSIVE CLASSROOM

KATHLEEN J. DOLINAR
CANDACE BOSER
ELEANOR HOLM
ILLUSTRATIONS BY CANDACE BOSER

Delmar Publishers Inc.™

I T P

NOTICE TO THE READER

Publisher does not warrant or guarantee any of the products described herein or perform any independent analysis in connection with any of the product information contained herein. Publisher does not assume, and expressly disclaims, any obligation to obtain and include information other than that provided to it by the manufacturer.

The reader is expressly warned to consider and adopt all safety precautions that might be indicated by the activities described herein and to avoid all potential hazards. By following the instructions contained herein, the reader willingly assumes all risks in connection with such instructions.

The publisher makes no representations or warranties of any kind, including but not limited to, the warranties of fitness for particular purpose or merchantability, nor are any such representations implied with respect to the material set forth herein, and the publisher takes no responsibility with respect to such material. The publisher shall not be liable for any special, consequential, or exemplary damages resulting, in whole or in part, from the readers' use of, or reliance upon, this material.

The authors and staff at Delmar Publishers wish to express their appreciation to the reviewers of this manuscript who contributed many thoughtful and constructive suggestions: Tanya L. Collins; Jeanne Goodwin; Faye Murphy; Kate Murray; Mary Jo Pollman; and Rebecca Reid.

Cover design by Westhouse Design

Delmar Staff
    Associate Editor: Erin J. O'Connor
    Project Editor: Andrea Edwards Myers
    Production Coordinator: James Zayicek
    Art and Design Coordinator: Karen Kunz Kemp

For information, address Delmar Publishers Inc.
3 Columbia Circle, Box 15–015
Albany, New York 12212-5015

COPYRIGHT © 1994
BY DELMAR PUBLISHERS INC.
The trademark ITP is used under license.

All rights reserved. No part of this work covered by the copyright hereon may be reproduced or used in any form or by any means—graphic, electronic, or mechanical, including photocopying, recording, taping, or information storage and retrieval systems—without written permission of the publisher.

Printed in the United States of America
published simultaneously in Canada
by Nelson Canada,
a division of The Thomson Corporation

1 2 3 4 5 6 7 8 9 10 XXX 00 99 98 97 96 95 94

Library of Congress Cataloging-in-Publication Data
Dolinar, Kathleen J.
    Learning through play : curriculum and activities for the
inclusive classroom / Kathleen J. Dolinar, Candace Boser, Eleanor
Holm.
        p.   cm.
    Includes bibliographical references (p.) and index.
    ISBN 0-8273-5653-6
    1. Handicapped children—Education (Preschool—Curricula.
2. Education, Preschool—Activity programs. 3. Play. I. Boser,
Candace. II. Holm, Eleanor. III. Title.
LC4019.2.D65   1994
371.9'0472—dc20   93-25976
                                         CIP

Contents

Section II Lessons / 49

Section I

Overview

part one
Introduction

You can use this **flexible**, interactive **curriculum** with children from three to six years of age. This curriculum highlights activities for the inclusion of preschoolers with handicaps. We have included various adaptations and activities for inclusion of all children in your classroom. While no one could address all of the possible changes that could be made for more participation, a procedure and framework have been developed to address these modifications and adaptations. However, all teachers—including nursery school, day-care, and preschool—will find this curriculum beneficial. Because you can modify or adapt many of the activities in this guide, this unique curriculum helps you integrate preschoolers with handicaps into your preschool setting. Furthermore the lesson plans allow you the flexibility to follow the children's lead. While no curriculum could address all of the possible changes that should be made to meet individual needs, we believe we have developed a framework and procedure to address modifications and adaptations.

This curriculum enables you to work with children for a four-day week. You use the fifth day of the week for assessment, *home visits*, and curriculum expansion. However, if your district utilizes a five-day, student-contact week, you can use the fifth day to review the week's activities. Or you can choose from the list of "Additional Activities" that follows each unit of study within this manual.

This manual contains twenty-six units of study. Eighteen units provide activities for four days or one week; seven units ("Autumn," "Winter," "Insects and Fish," "Spiders," "Christmas," "Easter," and "Antless Picnic") provide activities for eight days or two weeks; and one unit ("Thanksgiving") provides activities for three days. Thus the manual provides material for thirty-three weeks of study. Through the use of the "Additional Activities" you can extend this time.

The activities within each of the twenty-six units provide you with a framework to follow. However, as you are aware, in the preschool classroom the children must lead the direction of the learning situation. You must allow all preschoolers, whether or not they have special physical needs, to take responsibility for their own learning. The child, the adult, and the **environment** must come together as partners in learning. As an active partner the child can assume responsibility for her or his own learning. Various learning stations will further enhance a child's natural curiosity. Mastery is not the expectation. The process, not the product, is the focus.

This curriculum focuses on children, who are the catalyst for your instruction. You observe and enter play at their level. Be aware that when children experience meaningful interaction with adults, they are better able to experience meaningful interaction with other children. This curriculum allows children to grow in their ability to trust and to become friends in a cooperative setting that enhances their self-worth. Moreover, through utilizing language in meaningful ways in interactive play, the children will grow in their communication skills.

Learning is a process that continues throughout a person's life. Allowing the children to explore their environment through play at this early age will aid them in becoming more active participants in future integrated settings. Play can encompass any part of the child's day, whether child or teacher initiated.

Setting Up the Room

Set up the following stations around your room:

1. *Quiet*   In this area have pillows or beanbag chairs. Also have available a **variety** of books and stuffed animals for the children to read and hold as they sit and relax.
2. *Play*   Include in this area a play stove, dishes, pots, pans, dolls, dishes, and so on.
3. *Toy*   In this area have toys that the children remove from the shelves for play: trucks, blocks, puzzles, beads, and so on.
4. *Snack*   Prepare this area as a place where the children can come together for their daily snack. Make snack time an interactive time in which you introduce a variety of food to the children and provide time for them to socialize. Note that children with feeding problems may need assistance during this time.
5. *Art*   Equip this area with art supplies and small easels.
6. *Story*   In this area you will read stories to the children. You may also want to use this area for music. Have available a record player, cassette recorder, tapes, records, and rhythm instruments.

Make your room kid-oriented by placing all toys at the children's level for play. Distribute materials from all stations throughout the classroom to enhance the integration of learning. Put out of sight those toys the children may not play with during free play. Child-size furniture encourages sitting and working behavior. It is important to create an atmosphere of trust and support for the children. Their play will reflect the tone you have created in the classroom. Plan your schedules in a way that allows for the children's needs and does not create time pressures. Lastly, value and acknowledge the personal styles of each individual child.

Varied Activities

This manual provides you with a wide array of activities that will appeal to your preschoolers. As you prepare for art, music, and story reading, try to do the following:

1. *Art*   Make art a time for children to explore different media and express themselves. Because art is a process, you do not focus on a final product. Instead encourage each child's unique creativity throughout the entire process.
2. *Music*   Consider music as an opportunity to get together with the children and have fun with songs and instruments. Because some children may not want to participate immediately, allow them to enter into musical activities when they are ready.
3. *Books*   Remember that books are complex, **open-ended materials** that children can read, view for pictures, listen to, or simply manipulate for the enjoyment of their hingelike quality. Be aware that reading to preschoolers prepares them for later reading instruction and provides them with an enriching experience they might not have at home.

Learning Environment

When creating a space where children are to learn and play, care must be taken that the group's needs are met. These questions should be asked:

Who will use this space?
What are their needs?
How can those needs be met in this particular setting?
What are the goals and objectives of the program?

A good environment considers the needs of all involved in the program: children, teachers, **paraprofessionals**, and parents.

The size of the building and playground, the equipment and materials, and the way the space is used and organized are all parts of the physical setting. A *creative playground* stimulates a child's creativity and imagination and is a valuable piece of equipment for the preschooler. Successful program planning must also consider the health and safety of all children. A safety checklist may include:

- Person responsible for supervision
- Knowledge of emergency procedures
- Children knowing the rules in the classroom
- Toys being in good order and put away when not in use
- Things the children are not to use being put away

Understanding how young children grow, develop, and learn is very important. When planning space, adults should use a child's perspective. Equipment chosen should be appropriate for a wide range of skills and involve many senses. When arranging centers, balance the quiet and the noisy activities.

Play

Children go through various stages of play in their development. Children change immensely in their social development in the preschool years. Generally the stages of play children go through are the following:

1. Children play by one another, but do not interact (parallel play).
2. Children tend to want to play with the same object as another child.
3. Play is based on a common activity rather than who the playmate is.
4. Children engage in **cooperative play**.

It is important to make the environment one that makes the child feel good. A child who has difficulty interacting with the other children must be guided through play by an adult. Remember to enter at the child's level and interact during play. Success is a big factor in the learning environment. Positive comments on what you liked about what the child was doing are very important. Trust is very important between you and the child.

Sharing is not a skill that children are born with. It is important for the teacher to teach sharing. Placing a time limit on a toy another child wants is a beginning step to the sharing process. For example, say to Jason, "After two more songs on the tape recorder, you must give it to John." It is important for teachers to guide children through play situations. This leads to successful social development.

Mainstreaming

Mainstreaming has been controversial since the passage of P.L. 94-142 in 1975. Regular education has had a history of being reluctant to meet the needs of all children. The intent of the law was to place differently-abled children in the **least restrictive environment**. Likewise with the passage of P.L. 99-457 in 1986, preschoolers with disabilities would also have their needs addressed through the public education system.

According to Stainback and Stainback (1984), energy should be put forward to merge both regular educational and special education settings. Ysseldyke and Algozzine (1982) feel that with careful planning it should be possible to meet the unique needs of all students within one unified system of education—a system that does not deny differences but rather recognizes and makes accommodations for those differences.

The time is now for all educators to pool their resources in an effort to provide the best educational environment for all children. Just as children learn from one another, teachers can learn from each other. Reynolds (1988) emphatically stated that it is time for renegotiation of educational relationships, so that the needs of children who are differently-abled will be met as an integral part of the total education enterprise.

There is danger of thinking of a blind child or a deaf child or a retarded child because one tends to think of the handicap first and the child second. What must be kept in mind is that children are first and foremost children (Elkind 1979).

There obviously are differences, and sometimes they can be extreme. It is also clear that because of these differences some children need modifications and adaptations in their school experience. Differently-abled children who are mainstreamed with their peers have a setting that is a microcosm of real world experiences. This is the setting in which children can be prepared to cope with future life situations. Parker (1987) emphasizes that children in an integrated classroom setting enjoy the benefits of a skill-oriented program, the companionship of neighborhood children, and the opportunity to be responsible for their own behavior in a group setting of their peers.

Integration is not only necessary, it was also inevitable. Integration at the preschool level is presently being practiced whenever possible. Some examples would be Headstart, school district early childhood/special education classes, and preschools. Esposito (1988) has concluded that the best educational practice is to integrate differently-abled preschoolers in order to provide them with the benefits of appropriate models, more-complex communication, more-sophisticated play strategies, realistic reinforcements, and greater variations within the preschool environment. Consequently Huefner (1988) summarizes that the major purpose of integration is to ensure that children can learn from one another in the least restrictive environment. Success in a mainstreamed setting depends on the comfort level of the teacher, the availability of support staff, and the acceptance of the differently-abled children by their peers.

Gartner (1988) stated that P.L. 94-142 assured placement in the least restrictive environment; now we must get on with the unfinished work and integrate. The same is true for preschoolers with the passage of P.L. 99-457. The differently-abled let us know that they do not need restraint, but rather instruction, support, and companionship (Sirvis 1988). It is now our professional responsibility to educate ourselves to meet a child's individual needs.

References

Elkind, David. 1979. The affective classroom and children with special needs. In Meisels, S. J., ed., *Special Education and Development.* Baltimore, MD: University Park Press.

Esposito, Beverly G. 1987. The Effects of Preschool Integration on the Development of Nonhandicapped Children. *Journal of the Division for Early Childhood,* 12(1):31–44.

Gartner, Alan. 1988. Response to the January Executive Commentary: No More Noses to the Glass. *Exceptional Children,* 54(5):391.

Huefner, Dixie Snow. 1988. The Consulting Teacher Model: Risks and Opportunities. *Exceptional Children* Vol. 54, #5. pp. 403–14.

Parker, Lura G. 1987. *Educational Programming.* In Eugene T. McDonald, ed., Treating Cerebral Palsy For Clinicians by Clinicians. pp. 239–54. Texas: PRO-ED.

Reynolds, M.C. 1988. Response to the January executive commentary: No more noses to the glass. *Exceptional Children* 54(5):391.

Sirvis, B. 1988. Students with special health care needs. *Teaching Exceptional Children* 20(4):40–44.

Stainback, W., and S. Stainback. 1984. A rationale for the merger of special and regular education. *Exceptional Children* 51(2):102–10.

Ysseldyke, J.E., and B. Algozzine. 1982. *Critical Issues in Special and Remedial Education.* Boston: Houghton-Mifflin.

Recommended Readings

Salend, Spencer J. 1984. Factors Contributing to the Development of Successful Mainstreaming Programs. *Exceptional Children* 50(5):409–12.

Schleichkorn, J. 1983. *Coping with cerebral palsy.* School of Allied Health Professions. State University of New York at Stony Brook. Texas: PRO-ED.

Special Education at the Preschool Level

In 1986, P.L.94-142 was amended to include P.L. 99-457. This amendment to the Education of the Handicapped Act expanded and improved services for infants, toddlers, and preschoolers with special needs. The individual states then needed to develop their service models.

Initially, there is usually a referral to **early childhood special education** services. This referral may be made by the hospital at birth, so the child can begin receiving services right away in a home program. Or the child may be referred because of **developmental delays** observed by either parent or day-care provider. Physicians may make referrals because a child does not achieve **developmental milestones** at appropriate times. Preschool screening is also an alternative method in which children can be identified for early intervention services before kindergarten. The DIAL•R is an example of a screening tool used at preschool screening.

Once a child has been referred, a plan of **assessment** is determined by a team of educators and the child's parents. After the assessment is completed, it is determined if the child qualified for special education services according to the criteria set down by the state or your local school district.

The law requires that every child who qualifies for special education services have an Individualized Family Service Plan. This is also known as an IFSP. Some states have their own form, and districts throughout the state use this form. Your own local district may have their own plan to meet the needs of the individual child. The IFSP is designed to meet the needs of the child from birth to three years of age.

The IFSP is designed to coordinate services to the child and to assist the family in meeting the needs of their child. It may support the family in finding day care, support groups, other families whose children have similar needs, or respite. Respite is designed to give families relief from the every day care of the differently-abled child. Respite may offer the family assistance within their home or it may offer the family time away from the child in another setting, usually a home in which the person is trained to work with the differently-abled child. It may be for overnight, a week-end, or longer. The IFSP must be written annually and should be reviewed every six months.

The IFSP should include the following:

1. Current health and medical status.
2. Basic senses including hearing and vision.
3. Communication (speech and language development).
4. Social, emotional, and **behavior** development.
5. Physical and motoric development.
6. Cognitive development.
7. Self-help skills.
8. Academic performance, when appropriate.

At the age of three it may be decided that the child should begin services in a school setting. The setting would be through early childhood special education. At this time, the team at the early childhood special education site would develop an IEP, which is the individualized education plan. The IEP is a year-long plan of service to the child. Parents must be included in the planning of the IEP. It should be remembered that the parents know their child best and can give valuable input as to how their child can be successful.

Information on the IEP includes:

1. Child's name, address, and phone number.
2. Parents' names, address, and phone number.
3. Names of the IFSP planing team.
4. Date of the meeting.
5. Information that should be looked at:
   • Cognitive development
   • Present achievement
   • Communication skills
   • Motor development
   • Vision and hearing screening
   • Health and medical
   • Emotional development
   • Functional skills
   • Family needs or concerns
   • Health concerns
   • Social services needed
6. After looking at the above information, the team notes strengths/weaknesses and begins planning for the child's educational plan.
7. Goals and objectives are developed. These must be measurable. Also there is a review date noted to check if there is progress, usually in the fall and spring.
8. The team must look at what modifications will be needed in the curriculum. They must also consider what equipment the child will need to be successful. A behavior plan will be developed for those children who need one.

9. All services the child may need will be listed on the IEP. People responsible for these services are also listed. A case manager is determined, so that this plan is carried out and the necessary paperwork is current.

10. The IEP must also address the least restrictive environment for the child. This is necessary as P.L. 94-142 speaks to the time that the child is with his or her age peers in mainstream classrooms. If a child is not spending any time in a mainstream classroom, it needs to be explained why this educational option is best for the child.

The Physically Challenged Child in the Classroom

The child with **cerebral palsy** is a physically challenged child, whose needs may require minimal to maximum modifications. Special consideration must be given to the physically challenged child because of the amount of support staff, equipment, and adaptations needed in the classroom. *Handling techniques* must be developed for the safety of the child and also for adults involved. Mainstream preschool teachers need in-service training to meet the emotional, physical, educational, and psychological needs of the child with cerebral palsy.

Children with cerebral palsy have often been isolated from motor experiences because motorically they are unable to interact with the environment in the same manner as children who are not physically challenged. Teachers need to develop strategies and techniques to set up situations of success for all children in their classrooms.

There are a variety of ways to meet the needs of the child with cerebral palsy in a preschool setting. Specialists, like the **occupational therapist, physical therapist** and **speech-language pathologist**, could serve the child in the regular preschool setting. By serving the child in the classroom, the physically challenged child's learning potential is maximized with correct **positioning** and correct modifications and adaptations, as the child interacts in the curriculum. This model provides the preschool teacher with techniques that can assist the child. Sometimes it is necessary to have a paraprofessional assigned to help the physically challenged child. There are a number of possibilities for the **integrated curriculum**. Team members can brainstorm to meet the individual needs of the child in the mainstreamed classroom.

Many times a child with cerebral palsy needs special **adaptive equipment** like a **wedge**, a **bolster**, or a **corner chair** in the classroom for positioning or a wheelchair for mobility. Traffic patterns need to be considered for this child. It is also important to position the child correctly to maximize learning. The classroom must be barrier free.

Feeding may be another concern for the physically challenged child. It is important to keep in mind individual needs when determining snack. **Self-help skills**, like feeding oneself or holding onto a spoon, are a necessary part of the child's school day.

Speech and language may be another area where a child with cerebral palsy may need services. He/she may need a communication system, feeding techniques, or speech therapy to effectively communicate with peers. It is important that the other children be supportive and help the child communicate his or her needs. Children can be wonderful facilitators in helping each other modify the verbal environment.

Perception may be another area of need for the child with cerebral palsy. Learning for this child is uneven. He/she may have poor body awareness because of a lack of experience with his/her environment. Eye-hand coordination is especially difficult. Fingerplays, rhymes, clay activities, block building, and bead activities can help the child in this area.

It must be remembered that positioning and adaptations are a primary concern for the child with cerebral palsy to participate fully in an integrated setting. It is our professional responsibility to educate ourselves to meet a child's individual needs.

Recommended Readings

Reynolds, M.C. 1980. Response to the January executive commentary: No more noses to the glass. *Exceptional Children* 54(5):391.
Salend, S.J. 1984. Factors contributing to the development of successful mainstreaming programs. *Exceptional Children* 50(5):409–12.
Schlleichkorn, J. 1983. *Coping with cerebral palsy.* Texas: PRO-ED.
Sirvis, B. 1988. Students with special health care needs. *Teaching Exceptional Children* 20(4):40–44.
Stainback, W. and S. Stainback. 1984. A rationale for the merger of special and regular education. *Exceptional Children* 51(2):102–10.
Ysseldyke, J.E., and B. Algozzine. 1982. *Critical issues in special and remedial education.* Boston: Houghton-Mifflin.

Disability Areas

On the following pages we have included the categories of disabilities as reported by the federal government after the implementation of P.L. 94–142. We discuss the disability, then include various adaptations, activities, and recommended readings for further study.

The categories are as follows:

*   Speech and language disorders
*   Learning disabled or developmentally delayed children
*   Mentally handicapped children
*   Multiple disabilities
*   Emotional disturbances
*   Hearing losses and hearing impairments
*   Health impairments
*   Blindness and vision impairments

Speech and Language Disorders

Speech and language disorders include **articulation** problems, oral motor function, and voice problems. A child with an articulation problem cannot produce sounds correctly and often his/her intelligibility is affected, as well as the child's ability to understand and use language in a functional manner. It must be remembered that some articulation errors are developmentally normal and many times will self-correct as the child matures. Voice and fluency problems may also be included in this area. Voice and fluency are less common categories of speech disorders. It must be noted that many preschool children experience a short period of normal nonfluency, which usually disappears within a few months.

Language problems can be in the areas of receptive language, which is the understanding of language and/or expressive language, which is speaking. Semantics and pragmatics are included in a child's language development. Semantics is the meaning of language, while pragmatics is the social or functional use of language.

A child who has difficulties with speech and language may tend to socially isolate himself/herself due to the inability to communicate effectively with peers and adults. It is very important to make the child feel very comfortable in the classroom setting. A teacher must accept the child at his/her level. **Expansion** is a good way to give a child more information to build upon his/her own language development. **Modeling** good language is important because each child needs to know what is correct. For example, a child says "*Him gots* the ball." Your response would be "Oh, *he has* the ball." A child will try to clarify what he/she is trying to say. In order for a child to take this risk, he/she must feel safe in the classroom environment. Sometimes, even if we cannot understand what a child is trying to convey, a simple validation of understanding with a nod, smile, or hug is the only thing that is needed.

Speech-language pathologists are available for service in the preschool classroom or in individual therapy sessions. It is important for the pathologist to be in close contact with the child's family to ensure that the child is practicing good communication skills at home. Some children may require the use of technology in order to communicate. There are many communication devices available today, depending on the needs of the child. This form of communication can be facilitated by the speech-language pathologist or an assistive technology team made up of the occupational therapist and physical therapist. Also the teacher, family members, other staff, and the children will need to be instructed as to how to use the alternative communication system. The pathologist is also trained in techniques of how to help children with feeding problems, if needed.

Recommended Readings

Allen, K.E., and B. Hart. 1984. *The early years: Arrangements for learning.* Englewood Cliffs, NJ: Prentice-Hall.

Bartes, E., B. O'Connell, and C. Shore. Language and communication in infancy. In *Handbook for Infant Development.* 2d ed., edited by J.D. Osofsky. New York: Wiley.

Hart, B., and T. Risley. 1982. *How to use incidental teaching for elaborating language.* Lawrence, KS: H&H Enterprises.

Kaczmarek, L.A. 1982. Motor activities: A context for language/communication intervention. *Journal of the Division for Early Childhood* 6 (December): 21–36.

Kuczaj, S.A., II, 1982. On the nature of syntactic development. In *Language development*: Vol. I, Syntax and Semantics, edited by S.A. Duczaj II. Hillsdale, NJ: Erlbaum.

McCormick, L., and R.L. Schiefelbusch. 1984. *Early language development.* Columbus, OH: Charles E. Merrill Publishing Co.

Ricke, J.A., L.L. Lynch, and S.L. Soltman. 1977. *Teaching Strategies for language development.* New York: Grune and Stratton.

Snow, C.E., and C.A. Ferguson, eds. 1977. *Talking to children.* Cambridge, England: Cambridge University Press.

Language and Speech Stimulation

Suggestions to Remember

1. Repeat your statements and ideas if you think that will aid your child in understanding. This includes self-talk and parallel-talk.
2. Be a good speech model yourself.
3. Encourage your child a lot in everything he does—take notice of a job well done, small though it may be.
4. Continue to praise and reward his speech efforts.
5. Talk with your child (not at him) as much as possible, for practice.
6. Continue to extend his language world and his conversation.

Specific Activities

A. Sounds:
1. Listen for all types of sounds.
   a. Around the house (TV, radio, appliances, kitchen noises, etc.)
   b. Outside
   c. Transportation vehicles
   d. Animal sounds
2. Playtime with sounds (approximately 5 minutes daily). Give names to various speech sounds and play "Copy Cat." Say the sound, its name, give the child time to respond. *But* if he/she is not accurate in **response**, do not dwell on the mistake. Instead, praise the effort made.

   Examples: s snake sound
   b buzzing sound (bee)
   g frog sound
   k coughing sound
   f "mad" kitty sound
   p "putt-putt" sound as in a train

       b boat engine sound
       r fire engine sound
       m "good taste" sound
       n singing sound

B. Language Concepts:

Demonstrate through your own actions and words—don't demand the same from him/her. The child may understand but not be able to state what he knows. Understanding always precedes observable behavior.

1. Colors, numbers, shapes: Work on one at a time, perhaps pick up one to work on each day. Sofa pillows, food (such as fruit and vegetables), and other household items (e.g., furniture) are good items to use in demonstrating such ideas. Always remember to make these activities a fun time with a game-type atmosphere. Drawing and tracing, puzzles, and pasting various colors and shapes of paper or material to paper are other sources of entertainment. Toys such as blocks are also good "learning" materials.

2. When doing work on colors and shapes, concepts of "same-different" and **classifications** can also be emphasized. "Which are the same or alike?" "Which are different?" "What things belong with others?" Use blocks, color squares, food, animals, even articles of laundry you may sort to teach those concepts. Remember to demonstrate these yourself first, then make a game out of it which includes your child.

3. Directions and spatial relationships: up down, around, under, above, below, beside, behind, between, over, inside, outside. Games such as "I Spy" and "Copy Cat" where directions are used are good not only for those relationships but also for learning how to follow directions—a skill very important to adjustment to school. "Follow the leader" is also a fun way to promote understanding of ideas.

4. Feelings and emotions such as happy, sad, angry, can be explored using pictures of facial expressions, books, stories, even TV programs.

5. Play with other children, especially those your child's own age, is a wonderful source of stimulation and fun for him/her.

Other Fun Activities That Can Teach

1. Telling stories.
2. Reading to your child, letting him/her "read" to you.
3. Painting.
4. Pasting.
5. Making jewelry such as macaroni chain necklaces or bracelets (with string chains) or paper clip/paper chain necklaces.
6. Use sewing cards.
7. Shadow pictures.
8. Sticker books.
9. Coloring books.
10. Magazine cuttings.
11. Building with blocks.

12. Dress-up.
13. Coordination games such as ring toss, bean bag throwing, dropping clothespins.
14. Playing "I Spy" for items, animals, etc., on outings in the car or walks.
15. Making your own puzzles with magazine pictures, paste, and cardboard.
16. Dramatic play.

Reprinted from: Speech Pathology Department, Gillette Children's Hospital, 200 East University Avenue, Saint Paul, Minnesota 55101.

Speech and Language Stimulation for Infants

- Talk to your child as if he/she understands everything you say. Tell him/her about the world around him/her.
- Call your child's name as you are walking toward him/her to alert him/her that you are coming. Tell your child what you are going to do.
- Hold your child so that he/she can see your face. Encourage him/her to touch your eyes, mouth, and nose while speaking. Make funny faces to get your child's attention and entertain him/her.
- Make varied sounds by knocking on different materials (wood, tin, plastic) or use different noise-making toys. Help your child identify where the sound came from.
- Listen for your child's vocalizations. Talk to him/her in response, even if these sounds seem random.
- Encourage all vocalizations, **imitate** them, and expand on them.
- Spend time just having fun. The time does not have to be lengthy, just repeated several times a day. Your child will let you know how much is enough by withdrawing, looking away, or falling asleep.
- Play vocal games with your child, such as cooing, smiling, talking, or singing. Remember to pause and let your child respond.
- Play games such as peek-a-boo or patacake.
- Encourage your child to initiate you. Playfully repeat the sounds you have heard him/her make.
- Quick responses to your child's vocalizations will encourage him/her to repeat those sounds. Your child will learn that speech is useful.
- Remember! Language activities should be fun for both the parent and child.

Information gathered from *Hawaii Early Learning Profile Activity Guide.*

Speech and Language

18 Months   **25% Intelligibility**
                           Vocabulary, 5–10 words

	Understands simple questions
	Uses jargon speech
24 Months	**50% Intelligibility**
	Vocabulary, 20 words or more
	Follows simple commands
	Combines 2 or more words
30 Months	**60% Intelligibility**
	Vocabulary, 50 words or more
	Follows 2-part commands
	Understands many action verbs
36 Months	**75% Intelligibility**
	Vocabulary, 300–1,000 words
	Asks questions—what, where, when
	Combines 3 or more words
48 Months	**100% Intelligibility** (this does not necessarily mean perfect articulation)
	Vocabulary, 1,500 words
	Speaks in complete sentences
	Can answer simple questions such as :."What do you do when you are sleepy?"

Data collected from the following:
Weiss Comprehensive Articulation Test
Communicative Evaluation Chart from Infancy to Five Years
Birth to Three Developmental Scale
Hawaii Early Learning Profile

Learning Disabled or Developmentally Delayed Children

It is very difficult to identify a learning disabled child between three and six years of age. Children may demonstrate problems in language development, motor development, cognition, perception, and social development. In the preschool setting, children with learning disabilities are found in any classroom. They have no discernible handicapping condition but are having problems in two or more of the skill areas. Environmental factors are prevalent in "at risk" children.

It is important to offer these children many different experiences. It is necessary to give concrete and simple directions. **Manipulatives** help the child to remember things more easily. These children must be given praise for trying and doing their best. **Positive reinforcement** should be incorporated into the classroom environment. Many times these children are not risk takers, so they must be given special attention to help them become participants in the activities. It is very important to incorporate activities that help build **self esteem**. They must feel secure in the classroom environment.

It is very important that the teacher be concerned not with the final product but rather with the process. This is true for all children in your classroom, but the child with developmental delays needs the teacher to help him/her feel good about himself/herself. One strategy may not work, so an **alternative strategy** may need to be developed to maximize learning. Instructional aids like special scissors, pencil grips, and large crayons can help the child do some activities independently. Sorting and matching activities are good activities for these children to work on for concept development. Also, a variety of perceptual activities like mazes, bead stringing, pattern blocks, and pegboards give them practice in the perceptual area.

The child with developmental delays needs to be exposed to a variety of books. It is important to read to him/her. Language experience activities may include interaction at the water table. Entering into the child's play during free choice will allow you to enter into the child's area of interest. Be careful not to talk too much for the child. Let the child begin the interaction with you.

The child with developmental delays may have difficulty entering into an activity with the group. Assure the child that you only want him/her to try. If the child refuses, you may want to invite the child to just watch. But let the child know that when he/she feels comfortable, he/she is more than welcome to try or enter into the activity.

Recommended Readings

Bailey, D.B., and M. Wolery. 1984. *Teaching infants and preschoolers with handicaps.* Columbus, OH: Charles E. Merrill Publishing Co.

Bredekamp, S., ed. 1986. *Developmentally appropriate practice in early childhood programs serving children from birth through age 8.* Washington, DC: National Association for the Education of Young Children.

Flavell, J.H. 1985. *Cognitive Development.* 2d ed. Englewood Cliffs, NJ: Prentice Hall.

Greenberg, P. 1990. Why not academic preschools? *Young Children* 45(2): 70–80.

Schickedanz, J., S. Chay, P. Gopin, L. Sheng, S. Song, and N. Wild. 1990. Preschoolers and academics: Some thoughts. *Young Children* 46(1): 4–13.

Thurman, S.K., and A.H. Widerstrom. 1990. *Infants and young children with special needs.* Baltimore: Paul H. Brookes Publishing Co.

Mentally Handicapped, Including Down Syndrome

Children who are mildly mentally handicapped have below average intelligence. On a standardized intelligence test they generally score at 70 or below. They also demonstrate delays in their adaptive behaviors. Their adaptive behaviors include self-help skills like feeding, dressing, and toileting. Further these children have limited social skills. Mildly mentally handicapped children many times are not identified until they reach preschool or kindergarten age.

Mildly mentally handicapped children do well in mainstream programming. With modifications and adaptations of the curriculum these children do meet with success academically. Further the mainstream impacts social development in a positive way. They successfully take cues from classmates in social situations. Mainstream classrooms offer good role models of speech and language for mildly mentally handicapped children. Programming should focus on making the children feel good about themselves and to feel part of the mainstreamed classroom.

Children identified as having **Down syndrome** have forty-seven chromosomes instead of the usual forty-six. This condition can be diagnosed shortly before and/or after birth by administering a test. Down syndrome is associated with mental retardation, which may vary from very mild to profound.

Children with Down syndrome benefit greatly from early intervention programs. In the educational setting it is important to have a program that is kinesthetic and positively reinforces the child.

Children with Down syndrome may have poor muscle tone, visual problems, heart defects, and be at higher risk for infections. Programming for these children in the educational setting may include occupational therapy, physical therapy, speech and language therapy, and vision services.

Children with Down syndrome tend to learn skills in isolation. They have difficulty with transfer of the skills they have learned in isolation.

It is important to keep in mind the developmental stages that children go through to achieve self-help skills. Children who are mentally handicapped need much **reinforcement** in achieving these skills.

1. *Two–Three Years of Age*
   - Dressing—can take clothes off easily; interested in learning how to put clothing on but gives up easily if too hard.
   - Feeding—can drink from a glass; prefers to use a spoon or fingers.
   - Toileting and washing—begins to verbalize if he/she needs to go to the bathroom; good idea to have a potty chair in the bathroom.
2. *Three–Four Years of Age*
   - Dressing—can do some unbuttoning and zipping; can generally dress self; if asked, can put clothing away in drawers.
   - Feeding—can eat with a fork, spread with a knife, and pour from a small pitcher; can be very slow at eating.
   - Toileting and washing—very few toileting accidents in the day, but night may still be a time of accidents. A night light may help the child to get up in the middle of the night. Washing skills are beginning, but child needs help in completing the task.
3. *Four–Five Years of Age*
   - Dressing—can dress and undress independently, if the clothing is set out; may want to learn to tie shoes.
   - Feeding—uses utensils appropriately; may want to help make meals.
   - Toileting and washing—can take a bath, wash, and dry almost independently. Toileting and hand washing is almost totally independent.

Adapted from *The Exceptional Child* by K. Eileen Allen.

Recommended Readings

Allen, K. Eileen. 1992. *The Exceptional Child: Mainstreaming in Early Childhood Education*. Albany, NY: Delmar Publishers Inc.

Bailey, D.B., and M. Wolery. 1984. *Teaching infants and preschoolers with handicaps*. Columbus, OH: Charles E. Merrill Publishing Co.

Bredekamp, S., ed. 1986. *Developmentally appropriate practice in early childhood programs serving children from birth through age 8*. Washington DC: National Association for the Education of Young Children.

Cicchetti, D., and M. Beeghly. 1990. *Children with Down syndrome: A developmental perspective*. Cambridge, NY: Cambridge University Press.

Cook, R.E., A. Tessier, and V.B. Armbruster. 1987. *Adapting early childhood curricula for children with special needs*. Columbus, OH: Merrill Publishing Company.

Van Dyke, D. 1989. Medical problems in infants and young children with Down syndrome: Implications for early services. *Infants and Young Children*. 1(3):39–49.

General Resources for Children with Special Needs

Association for the Care of Children's Health
7910 Woodmont Avenue, Suite 300
Bethesda, MD 20814

Federation for Children with Special Needs
95 Berkeley Street
Boston, MA 02116–3104

MedicAlert Foundation International
Turlock, CA 95381-1009

National Center for Youth with Disabilities
Adolescent Health Program
University of Minnesota
Box 721—UMHC
Harvard Street at East River Road
Minneapolis, MN 55455

National Down Syndrome Society
666 Broadway
New York, NY 10012

National Rehabilitation Information Center
8455 Colesville Road
Suite 935
Silver Spring, MD 20910

National Information Center for Children and Youth with Disabilities
P.O. Box 1492
Washington, DC 20013

Multiple Disabilities

Some children will enter the school setting with more than one disability. The child may have limited motor ability, communication problems, and cognitive problems, along with medical implications. Children with multiple handicaps have several handicapping conditions occurring together, affecting several growth areas. A child with cerebral palsy may have a mentally handicapping condition, as well as language problems. On the other end of the spectrum, there are children with cerebral palsy who have average or above average intelligence, but are impacted by their motorical involvement.

It is important to determine the needs of the child before the child enters the school setting to ensure that the child is successful in the school environment.

Technology is an option for helping the child communicate with the others in the classroom. **Communication devices** assist in better communication. The physical environment of the room must be considered so that the child can move about freely. Curriculum and equipment may need to be adapted for the child with multiple disabilities. Diet and medication must be considered.

Integration is very important for these children in their social development. The educational classroom offers these children a sense of belonging. It is a learning experience for all.

Recommended Readings

Mather, J., and E. Wewinstein. 1988. Teachers and therapists: Evolution of a partnership in early intervention. *Topics in Early Childhood Special Education* 7(4):1–9.

Schleichkorn, J. 1983. *Coping with cerebral palsy.* Texas: PRO-ED.

Sirvis, B. 1988. Students with special health care needs. *Teaching Exceptional Children* 20(4):40–46.

Emotional Disturbances

This disability is a low-incidence disability in the preschool setting. Caution is advised to preschool teachers in using this label when working in the preschool setting.

Children may demonstrate the frustration of their social and emotional needs because they lack language expression. It is by **nonverbal** cues and indirect actions that children let us know what is bothering them. It is not because these children are emotionally disturbed, but rather they have needs that we must address. Children may also display acting out behaviors because they have a hearing loss or medical problems.

It is important for the teacher to plan ahead and to anticipate problems in an effort to prevent them. Preventive guidance by the teacher would include observation to alleviate the problem in future settings, giving the children advance warning that an activity is going to end, reducing the number of verbal directions so the child is not on overload, making sure directions are clear and in simple terms, consistent and firm discipline, and offering the child choices. Choices help a child feel more independent. Make sure the choices are reasonable and are choices that the child will be allowed to do. If a problem occurs, the teacher can help the child by talking through a problem and considering choices of proper behavior in case it should happen again. Be consistent with the child when using positive reinforcement. The goal is to decrease behaviors we do not want and replace them with more appropriate behaviors through reinforcement.

The teacher should observe the child who is displaying emotional outbursts. By noting *observable behaviors*, a *strategy* can be developed to help the child and teacher avoid situations and/or stimulus that may trigger these outbursts in the classroom environment. It is important to avoid power struggles. Tasks for the child should not be made too difficult. Through observations the teacher can determine the child's personal style and his/her social and emotional needs.

Exceptions in the preschool program would be **autism** and schizophrenia. Schizophrenia may be characterized by tantrums, bizarre behavior, unpredictable mood swings, and isolation.

Autism is a neurological disorder that affects communication, behavior, and the child's social interaction with adults and other children. It is a severe form of a pervasive developmental disorder. Autism has been a perplexing disability because its **etiology** is unknown. This disability impacts the total child.

In the educational setting, children with autism need ways to effectively communicate. Some may not speak and will require alternative communication. These children have found success facilitated by communication keyboards. It is also important for the environment in the classroom to be consistent. Behavior modification may be necessary. Open communication is necessary to give the child consistency.

One technique to use with the children with autism is to gently guide them to the activity that you may want them to do. It is important to give the children choices and to let them make some decisions.

Recommended Readings

Bee, H. 1989. *The developing child.* New York: Harper and Row.

Coleman, M. 1989. Young children with autism or autistic-like behavior. *Infants and Young Children* 1(4):22–31.

Haring, N.G., and L. McCormick. 1990. *Exceptional children and youth.* Columbus, OH: Charles E. Merrill Publishing Co.

Peterson, N.L. 1987. *Early intervention for handicapped and at-risk children.* Denver: Love Publishing Co.

Rutter, M. 1986. Infantile autism: Assessment, differential diagnosis and treatment. In A *Clinical Guide to Child Psychiatry*, edited by D. Shaffer, A. Erhardt, and L. Greenhill. New York: Free Press.

Schor, D.P. 1983. Autism. In *Medical aspects of development disabilities in children birth to three*, edited by J.A. Blackman. Iowa City: University of Iowa.

Worthington, B.S., P.L. Pipes, and C.M. Trahms. 1978. The pediatric nutritionist. In *Early Intervention: A Team Approach*, edited by K.E. Allen, V.A. Holm, and R.OL. Schiefelbusch. Baltimore: University Park Press.

Hearing Losses and Hearing Impairments

Deafness is a hearing loss that does not allow a person to process language. They may use sign language, read lips, or utilize an interpreter.

A child with a hearing impairment might use a hearing aid. Or an auditory trainer may be used by a child in the classroom. The trainer amplifies the teacher's voice directly to the child. By doing this, the trainer eliminates surrounding distractions in the classroom.

Speech therapy is necessary for language stimulation and articulation. The therapist can also work on lip reading, finger spelling, and sign language. Computer technology is also available to facilitate communication.

It is important to make the child feel secure in the classroom environment. A schedule is reassuring to the child with a hearing impairment. Things to remember in the classroom are:

- Try to sign things like what is for snack; sign the animal when singing songs or doing fingerplays.
- Let the child feel the vibrations of instruments.
- Be at the child's eye level, getting his/her attention and making sure that he/she sees your face.
- Gently touch to get the child's attention.
- Books should be brightly colored.
- Seat the child across from you during presentations.
- Try to compensate through touch and vision.

Recommended Readings

Gregory, H. 1976. *The deaf child and his family*. London: Allen and Unwin.

Horton, K.B. 1976. Early intervention for hearing impaired infants and young children. In *Intervention Strategies for High Risk Infants and Young Children*, edited by T.D. Tjossem. Baltimore: University Park Press.

McCormick, L., and R.L. Schiefelbusch. *Early language intervention*. Columbus, OH: Charles E. Merrill Publishing Co.

Health Impairments

Health impairments include chronic and acute health problems. Some health impairments are **congenital**, while others have an onset during childhood. Some health impairments that may be encountered in mainstream classroom are:

1. Juvenile diabetes mellitus—This is the most-found type of diabetes in young children. Diabetes is genetic and is caused by the inability of the pancreas to produce insulin. Insulin metabolizes the glucose in the body.
2. Seizure disorders—This impairment can cause total or partial loss of consciousness. The seizures may be psychomotor, petit mal, or tonic/clonic. With psychomotor seizures the child may exhibit a temper tantrum or some unusual behavior. A petit mal seizure can be observed as daydreaming or a brief loss of consciousness. A tonic/clonic seizure may include loss of consciousness, muscle jerking, and even cessation of breathing.
3. Leukemia—This impairment is a form of cancer. The body produces too many white blood cells, and the bone marrow is destroyed. Many times, pain is associated with this disease.
4. Cystic fibrosis—With this impairment the lungs have an excess amount of mucus, and it causes progressive lung damage. Children with this impairment are ill frequently and have difficulty gaining weight. It is important for those children to be active when they are feeling pretty well.
5. Cardiac disorders—A child may be born with heart disease. With today's technology, many of these disorders can be corrected through surgery.
6. Asthma—Asthma is a lung condition that causes tightness in the chest and difficulty breathing. Asthma attacks may be caused by allergies, stress, or by too much exercise. These children may start wheezing; they may be on medication; or they may be on inhalers. It is important to consider the needs of the asthmatic child when arranging field trips to outdoor activities or when bringing animals into the classroom.
7. Spina bifida—This is a condition of the spine, where there is not complete closure of the spinal column. These children often require many operations. There may be problems with their bowel and bladder functions. Occupational and physical therapy will probably be necessary to promote independence.

There may be other health impairments that will require special consideration when programming.

It is important to utilize the team approach with the child with health impairments. The occupational and physical therapist can assist the others on the team in understanding motor concerns, positioning for maximum learning, and feeding concerns. Adaptive equipment will be necessary for some of the children. It is important to have the classroom environment barrier free. It is important for staff to be aware of medical concerns when working with a child with a health impairment. Emergency procedures are necessary for all to know, as well as CPR (cardiopulmonary resuscitation). Lap boards allow children in wheelchairs to participate in daily activities. Large crayons and markers help the child to have better fine-motor control. Suction cups on the bottom of plates used when feeding help the child concentrate better on the control of the spoon. On their clothing, velcro is better than zippers and buttons.

Recommended Readings

Bobath, K., and B. Bobath. 1975. Cerebral Palsy. In *Physical Therapy Services in Developmental Disabilities*, edited by P. Pearson and C.E. Williams. Springfield, IL: Charles C. Thomas.

Cook, R.R., A. Tessier, and V.B. Armbruster. 1987. *Adapting early childhood programs to children with special needs.* Columbus, OH: Merrill Publishing Co.

Katz, H. P. 1975. Important endocrine disorders of childhood. In *Medical Problems in the Classroom*, edited by R. Haslam and P. Valletutti. Baltimore: University Park Press.

Myers, B.R. 1975. The child with chronic illness. In *Medical Problems in the Classroom*, edited by R. Haslam and P. Valletutti. Baltimore: University Park Press.

Sirvis, B. 1988. Students with special health care needs. *Teaching Exceptional Children* 20(4):40–44.

Tyler, N.B., and L.S. Chandller. 1978. The developmental therapist: The occupational therapist and the physical therapist. In *Early Intervention—A Team Approach*, edited by K.E. Allen, V.A. Holm, and R. L. Schiefelbusch. Baltimore: University Park Press.

Blindness and Vision Impairments

Children who have impairments in the **visual** area are classified as blind or partially sighted. According to the American Foundation for the Blind, the child affected by blindness cannot read print and needs materials in the sensory areas of touch and sound to be successful. The partially sighted child has partial vision and may need larger print and visual materials in the educational setting.

Educational interventions in the learning environment for the partially sighted child might include:

- good classroom lighting
- positioning of the child where there are no shadows or flickering light
- hand held or illuminated magnifiers
- high-quality lamp in the play area

For the child who is blind, the learning environment should include:

- beginning system of Braille, a system of raised dots of the alphabet to help the child read
- highly specialized staff in the area of blindness
- having the parent or a trained assistant with the child to ensure safety and maximum programming
- emphasis on tasting, touching, and smelling sensory activities

Children who are blind or partially sighted generally lack the ability to interact with others and their environment. Because they may have no visual sense of what is going on, they miss opportunities for interaction with their peers and other adults. Also, early in life the child had to rely on the sense of touch or smell to identify objects. Thus language development may have fallen behind. A language-rich environment helps the child become more active in communication. It is important to talk a child through an activity.

Further it is important for the child to participate in motor activities. Because of the vision loss, **developmental milestones** of crawling and walking are also delayed. The classroom should be kept safe for the visually impaired child. It is important for the child to be able to explore the environment safely, while incorporating activities that will stimulate their **gross motor development**.

Recommended Readings

Fewell, R.R. 1983. Working with sensorily impaired children. In *Educating Young Handicapped Children*, edited by S.G. Garwood. Rockville, MD: Aspen.

Fewell, R.R., and R. Kaminski. 1988. Play skills development and instruction for young children with handicaps. In *Early intervention for infants and children with handicaps*, edited by L.L. Odom and M.B. Karnes. Baltimore: Paul H. Brooks.

Rogers, S.J., and C.B. Puchalski. 1983. Social characteristics of visually impaired infants' play. *Topics in Early Childhood Special Education* 3(4): 54–56.

Themes

Our curriculum revolves around using a book in each of the lessons. We used the book as the theme, and our activities revolve around ideas in the book. Also, for our sensory units we use a subject theme. By this we mean that we choose a subject and then create a theme using sensory experiences.

Themes can be monthly, quarterly, or even weekly. When using the curriculum, you can create themes for your **learning centers** by using a weekly theme or a unit-of-study theme, as outlined in the Table of Contents.

By having a theme, the teacher is allowed to observe a child developmentally, socially, and behaviorally while the child is engaged in an activity. Teachers can interact with the child at a learning center. The importance of this is that the teacher enters into play with the child at the child's level of interest.

Our curriculum is designed as a framework for learning. The activities can be teacher directed, as outlined in the book, or a teacher can use the book as a guide to some activities to include in the lessons. It is most important to have learning centers in the room for children to expand on their learning experiences. The centers should focus on the same theme, e.g., listening, but the activities should change for each lesson or unit. A teacher may choose to use the ideas in the curriculum for the learning stations and have the room designed to work on learning stations rather than formalized instruction.

It is also important to keep a record of each child. Observation is a very powerful tool. Keeping a record through observation shows the growth of the child.

ENJOY!!

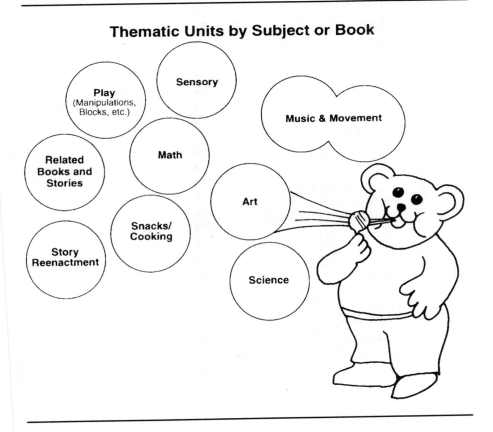

Thematic Units by Subject or Book

Play (Manipulations, Blocks, etc.)

Sensory

Music & Movement

Related Books and Stories

Math

Art

Snacks/Cooking

Story Reenactment

Science

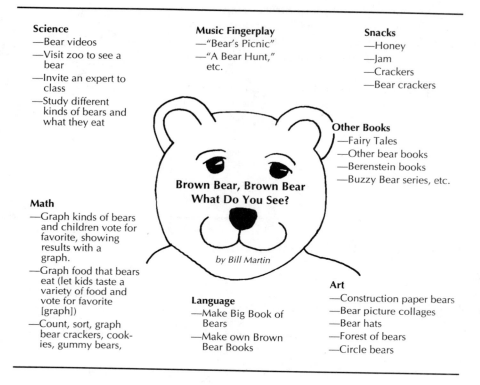

Science
—Bear videos
—Visit zoo to see a bear
—Invite an expert to class
—Study different kinds of bears and what they eat

Music Fingerplay
—"Bear's Picnic"
—"A Bear Hunt," etc.

Snacks
—Honey
—Jam
—Crackers
—Bear crackers

Other Books
—Fairy Tales
—Other bear books
—Berenstein books
—Buzzy Bear series, etc.

Brown Bear, Brown Bear What Do You See?

by Bill Martin

Math
—Graph kinds of bears and children vote for favorite, showing results with a graph.
—Graph food that bears eat (let kids taste a variety of food and vote for favorite [graph])
—Count, sort, graph bear crackers, cookies, gummy bears,

Language
—Make Big Book of Bears
—Make own Brown Bear Books

Art
—Construction paper bears
—Bear picture collages
—Bear hats
—Forest of bears
—Circle bears

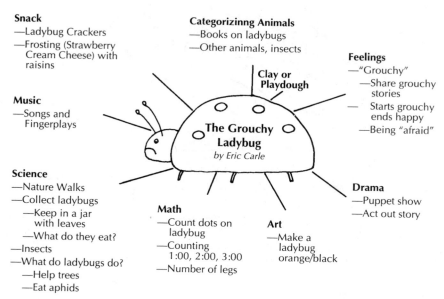

Snack
—Ladybug Crackers
—Frosting (Strawberry Cream Cheese) with raisins

Music
—Songs and Fingerplays

Science
—Nature Walks
—Collect ladybugs
  —Keep in a jar with leaves
  —What do they eat?
—Insects
—What do ladybugs do?
  —Help trees
  —Eat aphids

Categorizinng Animals
—Books on ladybugs
—Other animals, insects

Clay or Playdough

The Grouchy Ladybug
by Eric Carle

Feelings
—"Grouchy"
  —Share grouchy stories
  — Starts grouchy ends happy
—Being "afraid"

Drama
—Puppet show
—Act out story

Math
—Count dots on ladybug
—Counting 1:00, 2:00, 3:00
—Number of legs

Art
—Make a ladybug orange/black

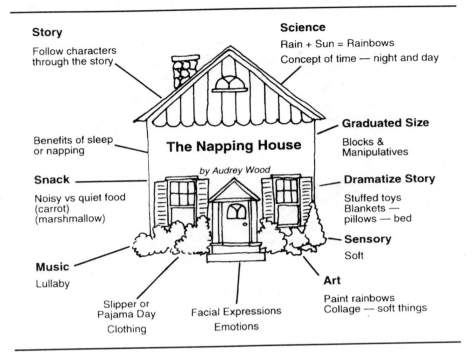

Story

Follow characters
through the story

Science

Rain + Sun = Rainbows
Concept of time — night and day

Graduated Size

Blocks &
Manipulatives

The Napping House

by Audrey Wood

Benefits of sleep
or napping

Snack

Noisy vs quiet food
(carrot)
(marshmallow)

Dramatize Story

Stuffed toys
Blankets —
pillows — bed

Sensory

Soft

Music

Lullaby

Art

Paint rainbows
Collage — soft things

Slipper or
Pajama Day
Clothing

Facial Expressions
Emotions

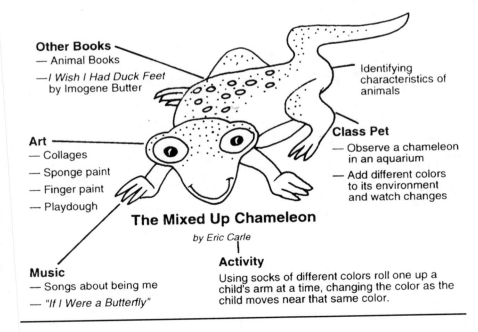

Other Books

— Animal Books

— *I Wish I Had Duck Feet*
by Imogene Butter

Identifying
characteristics of
animals

Class Pet

— Observe a chameleon
in an aquarium

— Add different colors
to its environment
and watch changes

Art

— Collages

— Sponge paint

— Finger paint

— Playdough

The Mixed Up Chameleon

by Eric Carle

Activity

Using socks of different colors roll one up a
child's arm at a time, changing the color as the
child moves near that same color.

Music

— Songs about being me

— *"If I Were a Butterfly"*

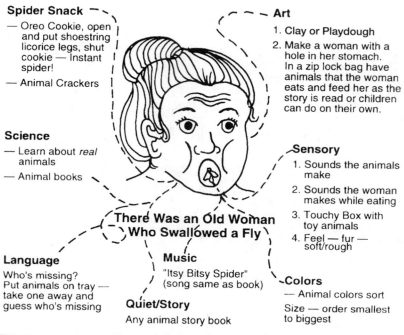

Spider Snack
— Oreo Cookie, open and put shoestring licorice legs, shut cookie — Instant spider!
— Animal Crackers

Art
1. Clay or Playdough
2. Make a woman with a hole in her stomach. In a zip lock bag have animals that the woman eats and feed her as the story is read or children can do on their own.

Science
— Learn about *real* animals
— Animal books

Sensory
1. Sounds the animals make
2. Sounds the woman makes while eating
3. Touchy Box with toy animals
4. Feel — fur — soft/rough

There Was an Old Woman Who Swallowed a Fly

Language
Who's missing? Put animals on tray — take one away and guess who's missing

Music
"Itsy Bitsy Spider" (song same as book)

Quiet/Story
Any animal story book

Colors
— Animal colors sort

Size — order smallest to biggest

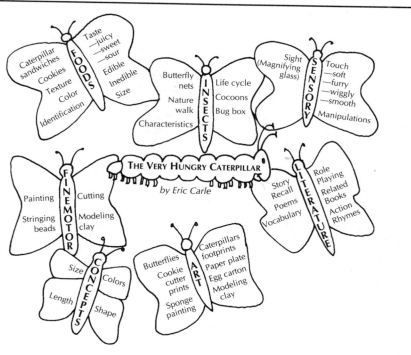

FOODS
Caterpillar sandwiches
Cookies
Texture
Color
Identification
Taste —juicy —sweet —sour
Edible
Inedible
Size

INSECTS
Butterfly nets
Nature walk
Characteristics
Life cycle
Cocoons
Bug box

SENSORY
Sight (Magnifying glass)
Touch —soft —furry —wiggly —smooth
Manipulations

FINE MOTOR
Painting
Stringing beads
Cutting
Modeling clay

THE VERY HUNGRY CATERPILLAR
by Eric Carle

LITERATURE
Story Recall
Poems
Vocabulary
Role Playing
Related Books
Action Rhymes

CONCEPTS
Size
Length
Colors
Shape

ART
Butterflies
Cookie cutter prints
Sponge painting
Caterpillars footprints
Paper plate
Egg carton
Modeling clay

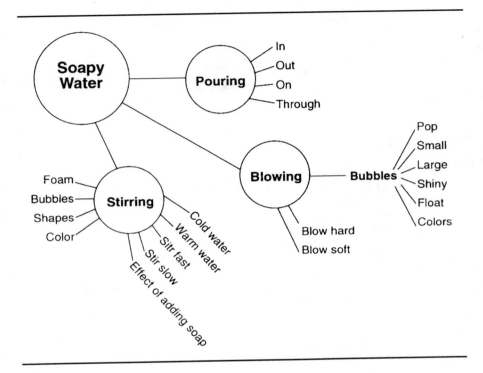

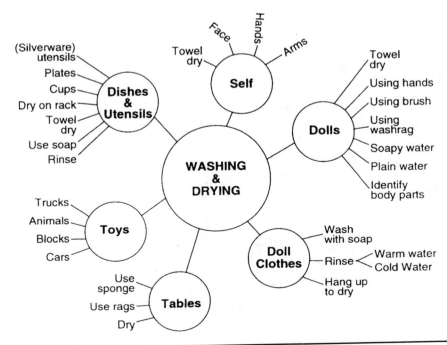

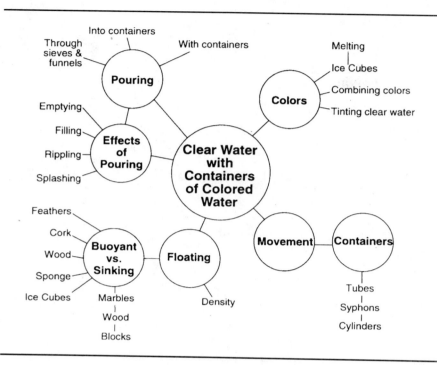

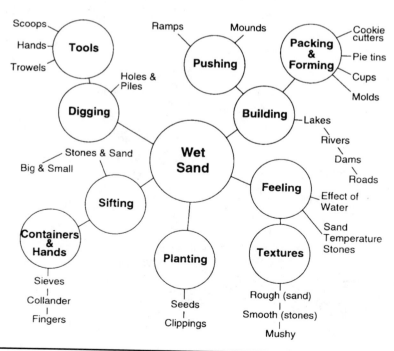

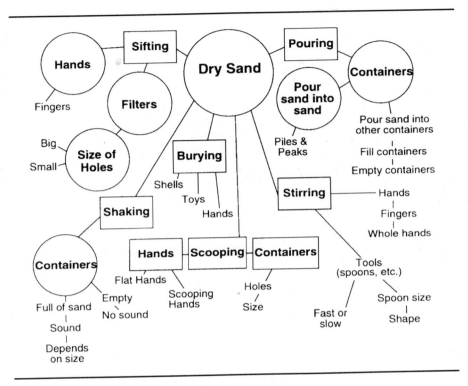

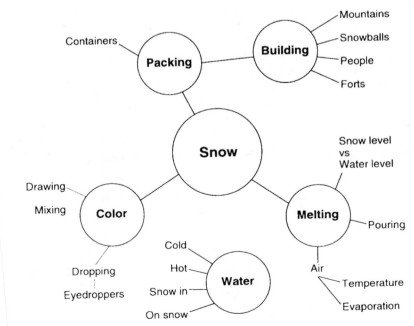

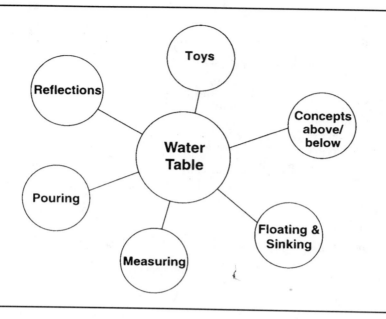

Developmental Charts

The developmental chart in Table I is included for reference. Please refer to them often to focus on normal development when working with your students. It is important for all personnel working with preschoolers to be aware of their development, because there are so many changes. Because changes occur very rapidly in the preschool years, it is important to be aware of the sequence of the development rather than the age at which it occurs. It is important too for the parents of the preschooler with disabilities to be able to understand their handicapped preschooler and his/her development.

Guidelines for Developmentally Appropriate Curriculum

NAEYC and the National Association of Early Childhood Specialists in State Departments of Education jointly developed guidelines to ensure developmentally appropriate curriculum. Each guideline is in the form of a question to which teachers developing curriculum for young children should be able to answer "yes."

1. Does it promote interactive learning and encourage the child's construction of knowledge?
2. Does it help achieve social, emotional, physical, and cognitive goals?
3. Does it encourage development of positive feelings and dispositions toward learning while leading to acquisition of knowledge and skills?

4. Is it meaningful for these children? Is it relevant to the children's lives? Can it be made more relevant by relating it to a personal experience children have had, or can they easily gain direct experience with it?
5. Are the expectations realistic and attainable at this time, or could the children more easily and efficiently acquire the knowledge or skills later on?
6. Is it of interest to children and to the teacher?
7. Is it sensitive to and respectful of cultural and linguistic diversity? Does it expect, allow, and appreciate individual differences? Does it promote positive relationships with families?
8. Does it build on and elaborate children's current knowledge and abilities?
9. Does it lead to conceptual understanding by helping children construct their own understanding in meaningful contexts?
10. Does it facilitate integration of content across traditional subject matter areas?
11. Is the information presented accurate and credible according to the recognized standards of the relevant discipline?
12. Is this content worth knowing? Can it be learned by these children efficiently and effectively now?
13. Does it encourage active learning and allow children to make meaningful choices?
14. Does it foster children's exploration and inquiry, rather than focusing on "right" answers or "right" ways to complete a task?
15. Does it promote the development of higher-order abilities such as thinking, reasoning, problem solving, and decision making?
16. Does it promote and encourage social interaction among children and adults?
17. Does it respect children's physiological needs for activity, sensory stimulation, fresh air, rest, and nourishment/elimination?
18. Does it promote feelings of psychological safety, security, and belonging?
19. Does it provide experiences that promote feelings of success, competence, and enjoyment of learning?
20. Does it permit flexibility for children and teachers?

Adapted from *Guidelines for Appropriate Curriculum Content and Assessment in Programs Serving Children Ages 3 Through 8*. A position statement of the National Association for the Education of Young Children and the National Association of Early Childhood Specialists in State Departments of Education. *Young Children*, March 1991, pp. 21–38.

Table 1. Developmental Characteristics

Birth–12 Months

GROSS MOTOR

- 3 mos. —head control
- 6 mos. —rolls over to abdomen
- 9 mos. —sits; stands by furniture
- 10 mos. —crawls
- 12 mos. —walks around furniture

FINE MOTOR

- 3 mos. —holds toy in hand
- 5 mos. —transfers object hand to hand
- 6 mos. —reaches; picks up toy using all fingers
- 8–10 mos. —picks up objects and puts in box; throws things on floor; imitates gestures and facial expressions
- 12 mos. —perceives roundness; takes off socks; chews food; holds crayon in palm of hand

SPEECH/LANGUAGE

- Birth–5 weeks —reflexive vocalizing
- 6 wks.–6 mos. —babbles at random; laughs aloud; turns head to voice; understands voice tones
- 7–10 mos. —imitates sounds (such as da, ba, ka); waves bye-bye, plays patacake, peekaboo; listens to own sounds; understands "no", responds to name
- 10–12 mos. —echoes speech; combines sounds; responds to simple commands (e.g. "Open your mouth" or "Give me the ———"); provides an action response to a question (e.g., "Where is your shoe?)

SOCIAL

- 2 mos. —attends to voice
- 4 mos. —smiles at people
- 6 mos. —knows family from strangers; smiles and talks to self in mirror
- 8 mos. —seeks attention beyond physical care
- 10 mos. —enjoys patacake, peekaboo
- 12 mos. —plays with toys; holds out toy to you but won't let go

Adapted from The Early Childhood Years by Theresa and Frank Caplan (Perigee Book 1983).

12–24 months

GROSS MOTOR	FINE MOTOR	SPEECH/LANGUAGE	SOCIAL
14 mos. —stands alone 15 mos. —walks alone (12–18 months) 20 mos. —climbs stairs holding rail; begins to run and jump; climbs, cruises; empties shelves	13–18 mos.—eyes and hands work together; reaches and grasps; builds 2- to 3-block tower; scribbles (spontaneous); eats with spoon, drinks with cup; rolls ball (two hands); throws ball overhand; attempts to catch; pounds indiscriminately with toy hammer 19–24 mos.—builds 6-block tower; copies lines; looks for missing toys; catches ball (two hands); develops space perception	12–18 mos. —demonstrates true speech; uses words intentionally; first words are really sentences; has a vocabulary of 3–50 words; uses consonant plus vowel; points to objects and body parts 18–24 mos. —responds to two simple directions; can point to two-three body parts; names objects and pictures; uses what?; has a vocabulary of 15–75 words	12–15 mos. —engages in imitative play; hugs doll, toys; enjoys bath; relates to wider world but prefers caregiver; is active in games; plays near but not with other children; watches others play 18–24 mos. —maintains verbal contact when physically apart; shows need to do things for self; develops sense of ownership (recognizes possessions); calls self by own name; frequent "no" causes temper tantrums

2–3 years

	GROSS MOTOR	FINE MOTOR	SPEECH/LANGUAGE	SOCIAL
2 yrs.	— walks stairs; kicks large ball; turns room upside down if left alone	— completes three-hole puzzle; builds five- to six-block tower; throws ball; looks for missing toys; turns book pages singly; listens to stories	— uses egocentric speech; has vocabulary of 12–200 words (average 250–300); two- to three-word sentences; refers to self by name; identifies pictures and objects; asks simple questions (Where ball?)	— likes to be independent; engages in parallel play; is curious and busy; is self-centered; throws temper tantrums (when hears "no" or doesn't get way); shows affection; doesn't share and may grab others' toys; may pout if scolded; may cling to mom; hard to be with both parents and share attention
2 1/2 yrs.	— jumps with both feet; walks on tiptoes; runs well; loves rough play and action; pushes chair and climbs to get object out of reach	— holds crayon in fingers; holds milk glass in one hand; matches objects by color, size, shape	— talks to self; uses repetitious speech; uses "I," "me"; recognizes action in pictures; recognizes objects by their use; has a vocabulary of 250–500 words; obeys commands with prepositions in them; names one color	

3–4 years

GROSS MOTOR	FINE MOTOR	SPEECH/LANGUAGE	SOCIAL
Walks stairs with alternating feet; turns in circles by self; increased arm strength; bounces ball with two hands; rides tricycle; sits for longer periods of time at play	Enjoys crayons, paints, uses modeling clay—(creative attempts don't often resemble what child says they are); builds nine- to ten-block tower; matches simple forms (circle, square, triangle); beginning to establish handedness; copies forms of circle and cross	Remembers simple songs and nursery rhymes; names two colors; has a vocabulary of 800–1200 words; makes three- to four-word sentences; displays fair speech intelligibility; is at the "why" stage; relates experiences; uses plurals; follows two directions; holds up fingers to signify age; easy repetitions and initial sound blocking may seem like beginning stuttering	May have imaginary playmates; displays emotional outbursts; doesn't want to take turns but will share unwanted toys; labels some emotions; is aware of family and work roles; imitates adult and peer behavior; is aware of sex-typed behavior; is aware of racial differences; will tease older sibling; enjoys adult company; prefers child of opposite sex; may have fears, outgrows one and moves on to a new one (dark, dogs); begins cooperative play; alternates between pestering siblings and getting along

4–5 years

GROSS MOTOR	FINE MOTOR	SPEECH/LANGUAGE	SOCIAL
Balances on one foot; has stronger grip; catches ball (two hands); hops; plays circle games; enjoys sandbox, swing, jungle gym, climbing apparatus	Buttons clothes and laces shoes; draws with pencil or crayon; two drawing of man has head, two arms, and two eyes; copies an "X" and square; colors without staying in lines; shows preference for dominant hand; completes eight-piece puzzles	Speech is less egocentric, more social; has a vocabulary of about 1500 words; uses how and why frequently; can count to four (three objects); tells age and sex; uses six- to eight-word sentences that are compound and complex (rapid advance); names primary colors; completes three-level commands; continuously asks questions, talks a lot, and tells tales; reads aloud using pictures	Fearful but may hide fears; may have imaginary playmate; imitates adults and peers; has special friends and prefers company of children to adults; cooperates, shares, takes turns, helps peers; bosses, quarrels, tattles, boasts, rebels; annoys older siblings, bullies younger ones; is at peak age for crying and whining if bored, hurt, or wanting attention; may behave badly to provoke reaction; is self-reliant; plays cooperatively, little solitary play and prefers two–three playmates; wants to please

5–6 years

GROSS MOTOR	FINE MOTOR	SPEECH/LANGUAGE	SOCIAL
Is agile and controlled; has good sense of balance, skips and jumps; rides bicycle; kicks ball distances and with accuracy; throws with one hand; catches ball in midair; bounces ball one handed; is adept on jungle gym; plays competitive games; uses sled and wagon; jumps rope	Handedness established; dresses self; drawing of man is recognizable, torso appears; includes details on drawings; handles crayons well; prints first name; completes ten-piece puzzle; copies triangle; cuts with scissors; colors trying to stay within lines; handles simple tools	Counts to ten; uses reasonably accurate grammar and sentence structure; has a vocabulary of 2000–2500 words; uses intelligible speech; uses socialized conversation, speaks of self; primitive argument emerges; great gains in sentence making; symbolic language emerging	Fears night noises; nightmares common; is dependable and obedient at home; internalizes parents' attitudes and behaviors; boasts about parents; plays cooperatively for a while, then quarrels; comforts others; prefers same-sex playmate; enjoys communication; avoids unliked peers; interested in helping with chores; enjoys talking on phone; plays well in twos but not in threes

Schedules

We have compiled a daily schedule that you may want to use in your classroom. It is not intended to be strictly adhered to, but rather is just a guide for your use. If children are really engaged in an activity, continue on with their activity rather than following this schedule.

Daily Schedule

- Thirty minutes of interactive play or **Activity Time**
  This time is designed to allow the children to explore their class environment. This time should be at the beginning of the school day. It is a time that you should be readily available to interact with the children and their choice in play. Make sure that all toys or materials that you do not want the children to play with are put away.

After this interactive play time, it is usually appropriate to have a potty and drink break.

- Forty-five minutes of the activity of the day
  This time is designed to introduce the activity that the curriculum guide has planned for the day. This is a **large group time**. This is also a time to work with some of the children who may need reinforcement in some other areas. This is a good time to schedule in specialists like speech, occupational therapy, and physical therapy to work individually with some children who have special needs. These specialists can help with adaptations and modifications to activities. The curriculum guide offers you a framework of activities for each unit. A more-structured teacher may want to follow the guide as it walks through a lesson. Learning centers around the room should revolve around the theme of the lesson. Children can engage in activities after the lesson is presented. Another teacher may not want to use the curriculum guide as the framework, but would rather use it as a reference for ideas and concepts for the learning stations. The curriculum is designed to offer flexibility to the teacher.
- Thirty minutes of snack time and potty break
  This is the time that the children can help prepare the snack, or they may just sit down to enjoy the planned snack of the day. This is a wonderful time for **socialization** and to help the children with their table manners. Interaction with each other and their interaction to the teacher is enjoyable to observe in this relaxed situation. After snack, it is probably a good idea to go for a potty break and to clean up.
- Thirty minutes for motor activities, music time, or dramatic play
  This time can be rotated from day to day depending upon what activity you may want to cover. Some groups of children may need more motor activity; others may want more music or dramatic play. It is a time for the children to experience other play experiences.
- Fifteen minutes for getting ready to go home

Materials

The following pages of the manual are designed to assist you in setting up your classroom and ordering materials. There are many quality materials on the market for the preschool classroom. However, when ordering, it is important that you keep in mind durability and safety.

Records and Tapes

Raffi
"Baby Beluga"
"More Singable Songs"
"The Corner Grocery Store"
"One Light, One Sun"
"Rise and Shine"
"Everything Grows"
Hap Palmer
"Babysong"
"Animal Antics"
"Learning Basic Skills through Music"
"Witches Brew"
"Pretend"
"Getting to Know Myself"
Lois and Bram Sharon
"Elephant Show"
"Stay Tuned"
"Smorgasbord"
"One Elephant, Deux Elephants"

Books for the Children's Library

Eric Hill
Where's Spot?
Spot's First Walk
Spot's Birthday Party
Spot Goes to School
Spot Goes to the Beach
Spot Goes to the Farm
Spot Sleeps Over
Spot Goes to the Park
Tana Hoban
Red, Blue, Yellow Shoe
Panda, Panda
What Is It?
1–2–3
Exactly the Opposite
Of Colors and Things

Look! Look! Look!
One Little Kitten
Shadows and Reflections
Shapes, Shapes, Shapes
Count and See
Where Is It?
26 Letters and 99 Cats
Big Ones, Little Ones
Dots, Spots, Speckles and Stripes
Push-Pull, Empty-Full
Eric Carle
The Very Busy Spider
Do You Want to be My Friend?
The Grouchy Ladybug
The Secret Birthday Message
1, 2, 3, to the Zoo
The Very Hungry Caterpillar
Audrey Wood
Heckedy Peg
King Bidgood Takes a Bath
Little Penguin's Tale
The Napping House
L. Ehlert
Eating the Alphabet
Fish Eyes
Mercer Mayer
Little Critter Series
Dr. Seuss
Beginner Book Series (i.e., *Cat in the Hat, I Can Read with My Eyes Shut,*
Green Eggs and Ham, I Am Not Going to Get up Today, etc.)

Books for the Teacher Library

Child Development
1. *Think of Something Quiet.* Clare Cherry. (Lake Publishers, 1981). Belmont, CA.
2. *Total Learning: Development Curriculum for the Young Child.* Joanne Hendrick. (Merrill, 1986). Columbus, OH.
3. *Ages and Stages.* Karen Miller. (TelShare, 1985). Marshfield, MA.

Art
1. *Don't Move the Muffin Tins: A Hands Off Guide for the Young Child.* Bev Bos. (Turn The Pages Press, 1982). Roseville, CA.
2. *1–2–3 Art.* Jean Warren. (Warren Publishing, 1985). Everett, WA.

Fingerplays and Rhymes

1. *Finger Frolics*. Liz Cromwell, Dixie Hibner, and John Faitel. (Partner Press, 1983). Livonia, MI.
2. *Let's Do Fingerplays*. Marion Grayson. (Luce, 1962). Bridgeport, CT.
3. *Rhymes for Learning Times*. Louise Binder Scott. (Dennison, 1984). Minneapolis, MN.
4. *Rhymes for Fingers and Flannelboards*. Louise Binder Scott and J.J. Thompson. (Dennison, 1987). Minneapolis, MN.

Music

1. *Music Activities for Retarded Children*. David R. Ginglend and Winifred Stiles. (Abingdon Press, 1985). Nashville, TN.
2. *Songs for the Nursery School*. Laura Pendleton MacCarteney. (Willis Music Company, 1938). Florence, KY.
3. *Piggyback Songs*. Jean Warren. (Warren Publishing House, 1983). Everett, WA.
4. *More Piggyback Songs*. Jean Warren. (Warren Publishing House, 1984). Everett, WA.
5. *Musical Games, Fingerplays and Rhythmic Activities for Early Childhood*. Marian Wirth et al. (Parker Publications, 1983). West Nyack, NY.
6. Creative Movement for the Developing Child: A Nursery School Handbook for Nonmusicians. Clare Cherry. (D. S. Lake, 1971). Belmont, CA.

Science

1. *Hug a Tree and Other Things to Do Outdoors with Young Children*. R.E. Rockwell, E.A. Sherwood, and Robert A. Williams. (Gryphon House, 1983). Mt. Ranier, MD.
2. *Mudpies to Magnets: A Preschool Science Curriculum*. Robert A. Williams, Robert E. Rockwell, and Elizabeth Sherwood. (Gryphon House, 1987). Mt. Ranier, MD.

Musical Instruments

Sand blocks
Bells
Maracas
Tom-tom
Triangle
Rhythm sticks
Tambourine
Handle castanets
Cymbals
Xylophone
Bongo drums

Manipulatives

Bristle blocks
Magnet blocks
Pound-a-ball
Wooden blocks
Stringing beads
Pegboards
Duplos
Busy gears
Magna shapes
Lacing cards
Bead maze
Assorted wooden puzzles
Hammer and nail design kit
Super bricks

Visual and Auditory Perception

Geometric design cubes
Large colored beads with patterns
Teddy bear or clown counters
Touch board
Shape sorting box
Geometrical pegboard
Magnetic mosaics
Playshapes
Geometric dominoes
Magnetic mazes
Shells for sorting
Simon Says
Remember Where game set

Language Development and Cognition

Puppet stage
Puppets
Colorforms
Flannel board
Flannel board story pieces
Fisher-Price playsets
Play telephones
Sequencing cards
Flip and Learn Alphabet
Memory Match
Alphabet puzzles
Speech mirrors

Individual chalk lapboards
Color Bear Bingo
Picture card library
The Mystery Box
Magnetic letters and numbers
Stamp sets for storytelling

Math

Manipulatives
Cubes
Counters
Links
Beads
Peg number boards
Tabletop counting frame
Teddy Bear Number Bingo
Student clock
Balance buckets or scales
Measuring set
Play money
Locking numbers
Hi Ho Cherry O game
Measure Me Ruler on the wall
Monthly Calendar Activity

Science

Giant magnifiers
Small magnifying glasses
Kaleidoscope
Plastic dinosaurs
Magnets
Stethoscope
Plastic insects
Globe

Sand and Water Toys

Sand and water table
Water pumps
Sand buckets
Sand shovels
Sifters
Scoops
Basters
Squirt bottles

Pretend and Dramatic Play

Cooking sets
Carpentry tools
Food sets
Dishes and tableware
Plastic fruit assortment
Plastic vegetable assortment
Play toaster
Housekeeping set (broom, mop, etc.)
Mini grocery set
Cash register
Dress-up clothes
Medical kit
Dollhouse
Plastic animals
Cars and trucks
Traffic signs
Drive Around Town Carpet
Train set
Dolls (male and female)
Play vacuum
Iron
Ironing board
Shopping cart

Large Equipment

Table and chairs
Highchair for dolls
Play microwave
Play sink and shelf unit
Play stove
Cradle
Play washer and dryer
Teepee or playhouse
Three-way shatterproof mirror

Furniture

Beanbag chairs
Tables
Small chairs
Storage shelves
Bookshelf center
Utility cart
Mats

Active Play Toys

Wagon
Play tunnel
Activity hoops
No Topple Teeter Tot
Barrel of Fun
Giant tumble balls
Balance beam
Scooter boards
Rocking boat
Playground balls
Parachute
Beanbags
Streamers
Ring Toss
Batting set
Play slide
Velcro mitts and balls

Arts and Crafts

Crayons
Play-Doh
Cookie cutters
Clay hammer
Watercolor paints
Tempera paints (assorted colors)
Finger paints (assorted colors)
Paintbrushes
Easel
Yarn
Popsicle sticks
Glue
Glue sticks
Felt
Wiggly Eyes
Construction paper (assorted colors)
Tissue paper (assorted colors)
Paper rolls (assorted colors)
Markers
Pencils
Clothespins
Scissor rack
Scissors
Chain strips
White drawing paper

Newsprint
Finger paint paper
Painting aprons or shirts
Drying rack
No-spill paint storage containers
Sponges
Stencils
Chalk
Pom-poms

Teacher Aids

Stapler
Tape dispenser
Scotch tape
Masking tape
Paper punch
Pencil sharpener
Permanent markers
Paper clips
Paper fasteners
Thumbtacks
Pencil grips
Stickers
Beginners scissors
First aid kit
Lesson plan book
Calendar kits
Tote organizers
Cassette player
Headphones
Record player
Bulletin board trimmers
Rulers
Corkboard
Storage bins
Crates
Crown for birthdays
Birthday badges and/or certificates
Awards
Charts
Name tags
Stars
Timer
Double-handed training scissors
Stamp pads
Post-It Notes

Section II

LESSONS

part one
The Basics

Speech/Language, Developmentally Delayed and Mentally Handicapped

- Model good language expansion in learning stations or group instruction.
- Stimulate language through use of "I wonder" questions.
- Request clarification from the child when you do not understand what was said.
- Reinforce concepts at the various learning centers and during free play time.
- Build in success for the child.
- Keep directions simple.
- Assist the child with fine motor activities.

Multihandicapped and Orthopedically Impaired

- Make sure someone will be able to push the child in the wheelchair, whether another child or adult.
- Position the child with motor involvement so that he/she can participate fully in the flannel board activities.

Emotionally Disturbed

- When fishing, carefully watch that the child does not poke or hurt another child with the fishing pole.
- Allowing a choice of the various centers may cause some agitation in this child. Plan ahead and direct him/her to a less stimulating activity. **Planning time** is essential for the staff to meet the needs of all children.

Other Health Impaired

- When doing sensory activities, make sure smelling activities won't trigger an asthma attack.
- Some of the children may be **tactilely defensive**, so use good judgment regarding their participation in some of the activities. For example, the activity with the powder and paintbrushes on the feet may not be for all children.
- Exercise caution regarding food activities for the diabetic child and the child with allergies.

Deaf and Hearing Impaired

- Help the child follow the activities in the fingerplays and chants.
- Let the child feel the vibrations of the musical instruments in sensory activities.

Blind and Vision Impaired

- Let the child feel the objects in the classroom and outside on the play-ground.
- Help give direction to the child during the hunt.
- Make sure to let the child feel the difference between the big and little fish. For reinforcement you can let them feel the difference between the big and little ball or the big and little bear.

#1   Let's Begin

Objective

By working with teddy bears and other favored toys, the children will experience learning through their senses and will develop their fine-motor capabilities.

Day 1: Getting Acquainted

Materials

- Construction paper and lengths of yarn
- Camera that develops pictures instantly
- Variety of dolls, stuffed animals, toys, and kitchen items

Preparation

Before the first day of school, write the parents a letter in which you ask them to bring to school on the first day a photograph of their child and a photograph of their family. Be sure to ask parents to write their family name on the backs of the pictures to ensure their safe return. Further explain in your letter that the children should bring a favorite teddy bear, stuffed animal, doll, or other toy.

Make each child a name tag by cutting out a construction-paper bear, printing the child's name on it, and attaching it to a length of yarn to make a necklace.

Establish a play area in the classroom and place all the toys, kitchen items, dolls, and stuffed animals you have collected there.

Learning Activities

1. As the children arrive put a name-tag necklace around each child's neck, Figure 1-1. If some children fear the tag, simply encourage them to hold it. Collect the children's pictures from home. If some children have no pictures, use a camera that develops pictures instantly to take the children's pictures for use later in this first class.

Figure 1.1

Music Note: Sing "I Am Special" from *Piggyback Songs.*

2. Show each child the play area and invite the children to play in it.
3. After free play, gather the children around you for a group activity and encourage them to hold their favorite toy. One by one, show the pictures of the children and invite the children to identify themselves and to name their family members and their teddy bear, doll, or stuffed animal. Do not demand sharing, but encourage the children to share as they feel comfortable doing so. While you and the children are looking at the pictures, be aware of the children's age and verbal abilities. If some of the children have limited speech and language, invite these children to point to their photograph while you say their name. If some of the children want to move from the group back to the play area, permit them to go but continue to encourage them to participate.
4. Tell the children that they get to go for a walk around the room and the building with their favorite toy. With the help of your assistants, tour the room, pointing out all the interesting things you have collected for the children to use throughout the year. Say something about the things the children see. For instance, you might say, "That is a dolly with black hair" or "With those blocks you can build things" or "You can cook on that play stove"—and so on. Then tour the building. If possible, go outside and walk around the building.

> *Note:* Establishing a routine on this day is important, but be very patient about this because the children need to adjust to their new environment. Remember that on this first day of school you want the children to be comfortable.

Having wedges, bolsters, standers, corner chairs, and assistants to help the more-involved children is essential for maximum learning. Keep the name-tag necklaces and put them on the children each day of the first week to help both you and your aides identify the children and help them feel part of the group.

Keep the photographs for use in an art activity on Day 3.

If possible, for the first week or so keep the favored teddy bears, dolls, stuffed animals, and toys that the children brought to class. This may help the child that may be having **separation anxiety**.

Music note: "Getting to Know Myself" from Hap Palmer.

Day 2: Feeling at Home

Materials

- Storybook *Goldilocks and the Three Bears*
- Variety of stuffed animals, dolls, teddy bears, toys, and a playhouse
- Rice table equipped with rice, scoops, containers, shells, small cars, and so on
- Plastic shower curtain liner, blanket or other cover, and teddy-bear counters
- Flannel board with the characters from the storybook

Preparation

Prepare the rice table by putting a sheet of plastic beneath it for easier cleanup. Then put the equipment on the table and hide some teddy-bear counters in the rice. Cover the table and keep it covered until you are ready to use it after the snack.

Find a copy of *Goldilocks and the Three Bears*. (See the bibliography in Section III.) Prepare to read the story out loud with expression. Then prepare a flannel board and flannel figures representing the characters from the story.

Learning Activities

1. Begin the day by inviting the children to go to the play area and play with the other children and with the toys they will find in this area.
2. Gather the children around you and read *Goldilocks and the Three Bears*. Afterward invite the children's comments and questions. Then talk about the size of the three bears. If possible, use teddy bears that the children have brought to school or ones from your own classroom collection and demonstrate different sizes. Stress the words *big* and *little*. You may want to show the children examples of big and little like big ball and little ball.
3. Take the children for a short walk and talk about the things they see along the way. Help the children recall what they saw and heard on their walk on Day 1. You may want to have strollers and wagons available for those children who may have difficulty walking or those who may tire easily. Let the other children help push or pull those in wheelchairs, wagons, or strollers. Even though the walk you take today is a repeat of the walk of Day 1, the children will not be bored with this. Remember that recall is an important language-development activity. This walk is repeated because this is a time for the children to become acquainted with their new school environment.
4. Provide a snack. A snack with a bear shape would be good.
5. Show the children a teddy-bear counter, tell them that you have hidden many of these in the rice at the rice table, and invite the children to find these counters. As the children play in the rice, talk about colors, the concepts of same and different, the texture of rice, and where the counters are hiding.
    CAUTION: Some of the children may try to put the counters into their mouths.
6. If some children lose interest in the rice table, invite them to go to the flannel board and use the characters there to retell the story of *Goldilocks and the Three Bears*.

    Fingerplay Fun: "The Family" from *Let's Do Fingerplays*.
    Note: Keep the rice table set up for use during the rest of this unit. Note that you will often use the rice table in this year-long program as an activity that promotes sensory experiences, Figure 1-2. To reuse the rice, keep the bin of rice covered when not in use.

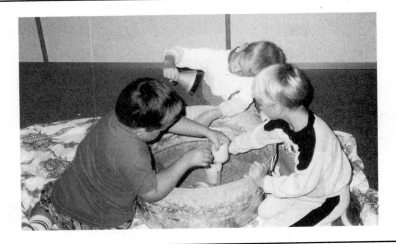

Figure 1-2

Day 3: Discovering Teddy Bears

Materials

- Many shapes and sizes of teddy bears
- Large sheets of paper, white construction paper, felt-tipped markers, the photographs from Day 1, and tape
- Brown construction paper, cotton balls, and paste
- Teddy-bear graham crackers

Preparation

Collect a variety of teddy bears, at least one per child, that the assistants can hide in the room during one of the art activities. Use the teddy bears the children brought to school on the first day as well as teddy bears from your own class collection, Figure 1-3.

Figure 1-3

On sheets of white construction paper prepare several outlines of teddy bears for those children who do not want to outline their own bodies in the first art activity.

On sheets of brown construction paper prepare the outline of a teddy bear for each child for the second activity. You may wish to cut out these teddy bears.

Learning Activities

1. Begin the day by inviting the children to select toys from the play area to play with for a time. Then tell the children that today they get to do two art projects.
2. Introduce the first art project by inviting the children to make outlines of their bodies and their teddy bears, dolls, or stuffed animals. Demonstrate how to do this by lying on a large sheet of paper and having an aide outline your body with a felt-tipped marker. Explain to the children that when you have finished tracing, they will be able to see how their body looks.

   Invite the children who want to participate to lie on a large sheet of paper. Then outline their bodies and the bodies of their stuffed animals, dolls, or teddy bears. Afterward print the child's name on his or her outline and the name of the stuffed animal, doll, or teddy bear on its outline. Tape the child's photograph to his or her outline. Finally, tape these outlines on the wall.

   If some children are reluctant to lie on the floor to have you trace their outline, use the teddy-bear outlines you prepared before class and tape the children's photographs to these outlines.

   Note: Children in wheelchairs can be carefully taken out of their chairs and placed on the paper. You may have to talk some of the children through the process in order for them to relax. Children with cerebral palsy may startle from the crackling of paper. Use your own judgment as to whether or not you want all children to participate.
3. Give each child a construction-paper bear and some cotton balls. Show the children how to add paste to these cotton balls and then attach them to the bears. During this activity talk about the word *soft.*
4. While the children are adding cotton balls to their paper bears, have your assistants hide teddy bears (the children's and the classroom's) throughout the classroom.

   After the children complete their second activity, explain that they get to go on a teddy bear hunt. Tell them that you have hidden their teddy bears and other bears in the classroom. Invite them to find their bear or another bear. Participate in the hunt with the children.

   While the children hunt, talk about what you and they are doing. Say things like "John is looking under the chair" or "I'm going to look up on the shelf for my bear."

   Note: Assist the children who have difficulty walking. Some children may become discouraged because they have a short attention span.

Give these children some extra clues so they will be encouraged to continue with the activity. For children in wheelchairs, make sure some of the bears are hidden at their eye level.

5. For a snack, serve teddy-bear graham crackers.

Day 4: Experiencing the Senses

Materials

- White paper, shallow pans of tempera, and liquid dishwashing soap
- Tape or record of "teddy bear" music and cassette player or phonograph

Preparation

Draw the outline of a teddy bear on a sheet of white paper. Then duplicate one copy for each child. Prepare tempera by mixing the dishwashing soap with it for easier cleanup.

Select some music that is about teddy bears or that is happy sounding.

Learning Activities

1. Invite the children to go to the play area and play with dolls, stuffed toys, or any toy of their choice.
2. Encourage the children to create teddy bears decorated with their hand- and footprints. Put the sheets of prepared paper on the floor and show the children the pans of tempera. Take off your shoes and demonstrate how to step into the pan and then leave your footprint on a paper teddy bear. Next, demonstrate how to make a handprint. Help the children take off their shoes and socks. Encourage them to make footprints and handprints on their own paper teddy bear. Play tapes or records of "teddy bear" music while the children work. After the art work dries, send each child's paper teddy bear home.

    Note: For children in wheelchairs, remove their shoes. Then paint their foot and place their imprint on the paper.
    Note: Children with a lot of spasticity in their hands need help to relax. This is a good tactile experience for the children.
    Note: In Learning Activity 2, if some children do not want to make their foot- and handprints, invite them to use the rice table or to listen to music. Instead of having the children step into a shallow pan of tempera for Learning Activity 2, you may want to paint the children's feet.

Additional Activities

1. Lacing card. Make a teddy bear outline on tagboard and invite the children to lace around the outside with yarn or shoelaces. If you use yarn,

knot one end and put masking tape on the other for easier lacing.

2. *Winnie the Pooh.* Have some *Winnie the Pooh* books available on a table for the children to look at. If possible, show a video of one of the Pooh stories.

3. I Am Special. Draw the outline of a teddy bear on a sheet of paper. Within the outline write incomplete sentences such as the following:

   "My favorite toy is _____."
   "My favorite color is _____."
   "My favorite food is _____."

   At the top of the sheet of paper print "I Am Special." Then duplicate a copy of this page for each child. Gather the children around you and complete a page for each child, or send the sheet home and ask parents to fill out the sheet with their children and return it to school. Take time to share the information on the returned sheets with all the children.
   Music Note: "I am Special" from *Piggyback Songs*

4. Discuss various types of real bears. Have photos and books available. Discuss where they live, hibernation, what they eat, etc. You may even want to go to the zoo for a field trip.

#2   Family

Objective

By listening to a storybook and role playing, the children will be introduced to the concept of gender.

Note: This week of lessons revolves around family members, Figures 2-1A and 2-1B. Note that the suggested lessons use only one storybook—*Just Like Daddy*—and provide activities that complement that book. You may choose to use other books each day of the week and adapt the activities suggested for use with *Just Like Daddy*. Some recommended titles:

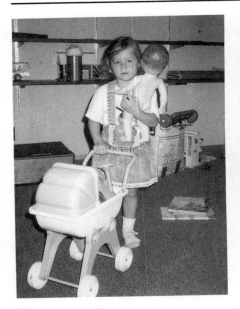 

Figures 2-1A and B

My Mom Is a Runner. Mary Gallagher Reimold. (Abingdon Press, 1987). Nashville.

Big Sister and Little Sister. Charlotte Zolotow. (Harper and Row, 1966). New York.

Big Brother. Charlotte Zolotow. (Harper and Row, 1960). New York.

Grandpa. Barbara Borack. (Harper and Row, 1967). New York.

If I Could Be My Grandmother. Steven Krott. (Pantheon Books, 1977). New York.

Grandparents. Maria Ruis and J. M. Parramon. (Barron's Educatioal Series, Inc. 1987). New York.

You may also want to use a different story book on the role of a daddy. If so, consider the following:

Daddy Is Home. Aliki. (Holt Rinehart and Winston, 1963). New York.
Come on Out, Daddy. Inger and Lasse Sandberg. (Delacorte Press, 1971).
But Not Our Daddy. Leonard Everett Fisher. (Dial Press, 1962). New York.
A Father Like That. Charlotte Zolotow. (Harper & Row, 1971). New York.

Day 1: Going Fishing

Materials

- Storybook *Just Like Daddy*
- Dowels (one per child), string, and magnets (one per child)
- Construction paper or tagboard, paper clips, tape, and a large pan or a child's plastic wading pool

Preparation

Find a copy of *Just Like Daddy*. (See the bibliography in Section III.) Prepare to read the story out loud with expression.

The children will be imitating fishing like in the storybook. Make each child a magnetic fishing pole by tying a string to a magnet and then to a dowel. Cut out a variety of construction-paper or tagboard fish of different sizes and colors. (Laminate these if you want to keep the fish for future activities.) Tape a paper clip to each fish. Put the fish in a large pan or in a child's plastic wading pool.

Learning Activities

1. Gather the children around you and read *Just Like Daddy*. Afterwards encourage the children to talk about their daddies, grandfathers, uncles or other significant males in their lives. Try not to ask questions about their daddies, but rather say things like "My daddy likes coffee" or "My daddy goes to work" or "My daddy likes to cook." Let the children talk freely. You may want to write on a chart some of the occupations that their daddies may have.

2. When you feel that the children are ready to begin another activity, invite them to go fishing just like in the story they heard. Give each child a magnetic fishing pole and show them the pool with the fish in it. Pretend that this pool is filled with water and elusive fish. As the children and you fish, talk about the size and color of the fish. Say things like "Oh, I caught a little fish" or "Help! This one is so big, I can hardly pull it in!" or "My fish is bright red."

Note: Children in wheelchairs can be positioned right next to the pool and can fish from their chairs.

Music Note: "Rocking Boat" from *Creative Movement for the Developing
   Child*
Fingerplay Fun: "Helping Dad" from *Finger Frolics*
Note: Keep the storybook for use on Day 2, or you may choose another
   one from the list.

Day 2: Role-Playing Being Daddies

Materials

- Storybook from Day 1
- Picture cards or magazine pictures
- Beauty-shop area equipped with shaving cream, combs, blow-dryers,
  shoes, polish, shampoo, towels, and other bathroom and self-care articles

Preparation

Before class prepare a set of picture cards or cut out magazine pictures
that show self-care skills or people performing self-care tasks (shaving, combing hair, blow-drying hair, polishing shoes, and so on). Set up a beauty-shop
area in the classroom and equip it with self-care paraphernalia. Do not plug
in the blow-dryers.

Learning Activities

1. When the children are assembled, gather them around you and reread the
   story from Day 1.
2. Show the children the cards or magazine pictures you have assembled.
   Talk about the self-care actions shown in the pictures. Invite the children
   to think of other things that people do when they take care of their bodies
   and their appearance.
3. Take the children to the beauty-shop area and invite them to role-play
   their mommies, daddies, or any other significant adult in their lives.

   Note: Assist the children who are not able to move their arms indepen-
      dently to comb their hair or pretend to shave.
   Music Note: "The Barber" from *Songs for the Nursery School*

Day 3: Role-Playing Being Parents

Materials

- Storybook *Goldilocks and the Three Bears*
- Kitchen area equipped with utensils, plastic foods, and other cooking and
  eating paraphernalia
- Dolls
- Newspapers and magazines

Figure 2-2

Preparation

Find a copy of *Goldilocks and the Three Bears.* (See the bibliography in Section III.) Prepare to read the story out loud with expression.

Set up a kitchen area in the classroom, Figure 2-2. Equip it with cooking paraphernalia and plastic foods.

Learning Activities

1. Gather the children around you and read *Goldilocks and the Three Bears.* Invite the children's comments on the story.
2. Direct the children to the kitchen area and encourage them to role-play being a mommy or a daddy in the kitchen. Suggest that they take care of the dolls and cook them some food. Encourage other children to read newspapers and magazines at the table while they wait for their pretend breakfast.

    Note: This is a good opportunity to learn nursery rhymes such as "Little Tommy Tucker," "Little Jack Horner," "Old Mother Hubbard," "Little Miss Muffet," etc.

Day 4: Practicing Self-Care

Materials

- Washcloth, towel, toothbrush, toothpaste, comb or brush, plastic bag (one of each item per child)
- Mirrors, small pans of water, and paper cups of water (one cup per child)

Preparation

Before class prepare a personal grooming set of items for each child. Include in the set a washcloth, towel, toothbrush, toothpaste, and comb or brush. For each child make a carrying case for the toothbrush and comb by labeling a plastic bag with the child's name.

Learning Activities

1. Gather the children around you and tell them that today they get to practice washing their faces and hands, brushing their teeth, and combing their hair. Give each child his or her personal grooming set of items. Show the children the pans of water for washing their faces, the mirrors for looking at their clean faces, and the cups of water for rinsing their teeth. Demonstrate how to wash the face and brush the teeth. Then help the children wash their faces and brush their teeth.

2. Give each child his or her labeled plastic bag and encourage the children to put their combs or brushes and their toothbrushes in the bags, Figure 2-3. Tell the children that they will use these again when they practice their self-care skills.

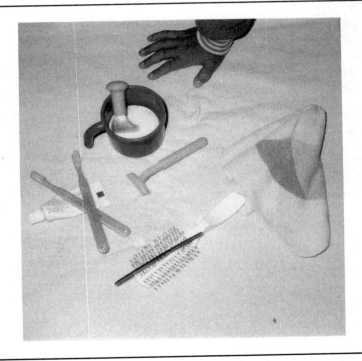

Figure 2-3

Note: Children with physical challenges will need to be assisted with their motor skills.

Additional Activities

1. Cars. Invite the children to role-play their families as they play with small cars.
2. Washing the Car. If weather permits, have the children wash their tricycles, scooters, and play cars. Have soap and water available.
3. Carpenters. Invite the children to use play tools to pretend being their parents fixing things at home.
    Fingerplay Fun: "The Carpenter" from *Finger Frolics*

3   The Senses

Objective

By visiting a series of sense stations, the children will use their five senses to become familiar with the world around them.

Day 1: Using the Senses of Sight and Sound

Materials

*   The materials listed under each sight and sound station in "Preparation"

Preparation

While you and the children walk outside, have your assistants set up the following sight and sound stations:

A. An array of professional musical instruments
B. An array of magnifying glasses and numerous objects for the children to examine through the glasses
C. A listening area equipped with cassette players, phonographs, and tapes

and records containing children's stories and music
D. An array of mirrors for children to use as they look at themselves
E. An array of children's horns, rattles, and whistles
F. An array of toys the children can pound
G. An array of food that makes noise as the children eat it—crunchy cereal, popcorn, apples, pears, celery, and so on
H. An array of flashlights

Learning Activities

1. Begin the sensory week by taking the children outside on a sight and sound walk. Invite the children to use their eyes to look around them and to see as many different things as they can. Encourage the children to listen with their ears and to hear as many different things as they can.
2. When you return from your walk, explain to the children that they will find more things to see and hear at the various sight and sound stations in the classroom. Encourage the children to visit each of the eight stations and to explore its contents.

    Fingerplay Fun: "Sight" from *Finger Frolics*
    Note: Assign an adult to each sense station to help the visually- and hearing-impaired children experience the activities. Also, try to follow each child's lead in the activity he or she has chosen and let the children initiate the interaction with the adults.
    Music Note: "Sounds I Hear" and "Listen" from *Music Activities for Retarded Children*

Day 2: Exploring with the Sense of Touch

Materials

*   Paintbrushes and baby powder
*   The materials listed for each touch station in "Preparation"

Preparation

Before class set up the following touch stations in your classroom:

A. An array of surprise bags or boxes filled with a variety of items of different sizes, shapes, and textures
B. An array of finger paints, paper, and textured items
C. An array of warm and cold things for the children to touch
D. An array of colorful construction paper, cornmeal, and glue
E. An array of finger gelatin in various shapes
F. An array of texture boards
    Music Note: "Toes are Tapping" from *Piggyback Songs*

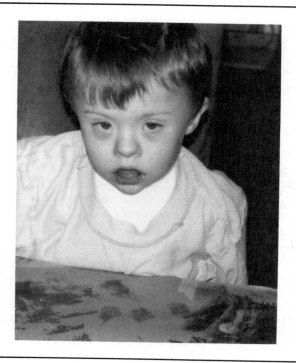

Figure 3-1

Learning Activities

1. Help the children remove their shoes and socks. Give each child a paint-brush and then sprinkle some baby powder onto the brush. Encourage the children to stroke the brush on their feet and to pull up the legs of their pants and brush their legs. Invite their comments on the experience.
   Note: You will need to help children in wheelchairs with this activity. Also be aware that some children may not want to take off their shoes. Do not insist that they participate in this activity; simply encourage them to watch or to choose a touch station to visit. Modeling this activity will help some of the children who may be fearful.
2. Encourage the children to visit the six touch stations and explore their sense of touch. At touch station A have the aide invite the children to reach inside the bags or boxes and guess what they are feeling. At touch station B have the aide invite the children to dip the textured items in the paint and use them to paint with. At touch station D have the assistant show the children how to put glue on paper and then sprinkle cornmeal on the glue to make cornmeal pictures.
   Fingerplay Fun: "Touch" from *Finger Frolics*

Day 3: Sniffing with the Sense of Smell

Materials

- Scratch-and-sniff stickers
- The materials listed for each smell station in "Preparation"
- "Smelly" jars

Preparation

Make "smelly" jars from empty liquid-dishwashing soap bottles. (Use these kinds of containers so that the children can squeeze them to release the fragrance.) Drop a cotton ball full of a fragrance into each plastic bottle.

Before class set up the following smell stations:

- Station A: an array of jars containing the following odors: lime, lemon, cinnamon, licorice, peppermint, watermelon, vinegar, garlic, orange, grapefruit, pine, onion, pickles, peanut butter
- Station B: a second array of jars with pleasant and unpleasant odors. (You may want to repeat some from Station A)
- Station C: an array of very familiar smells—lemon, vanilla, chocolate chip cookies, oranges, and so on, Figure 3-2

Figure 3-2

- Station D: a popcorn popper with popcorn popping in it; have butter, salt, and bowls
- Station E: a smelly snack, like oranges
- Station F: a book containing scratch-and-sniff stickers

Learning Activities

1. Give the children some scratch-and-sniff stickers to explore. Then explain to the children that they are going to use their noses today to discover the smells of their world.
2. Tell the children about the various smell stations and invite them to use their noses to explore the smells in these stations. In smell station *C* have an assistant blindfold the children or have the children close their eyes and invite them to guess what they are smelling.
3. Have the children gather together and explore with their noses the smelly jars you prepared before class. Gently squeeze the bottles, allowing the fragrance to emerge through the open top. Talk about the smells. Invite the children to talk about the smells they like and the ones they dislike.

> *Note:* Rather than using smelly jars in this activity, you may want to bring out smelly stickers. Let the children smell them and make their own books of smells. You may want the children to tell you if the smell is good or bad. Let the children take their books home.

Music Note: "Popcorn" from *More Piggyback Songs*
Fingerplay Fun: "Popcorn" from *Finger Frolics*

Day 4: Enjoying the Sense of Taste

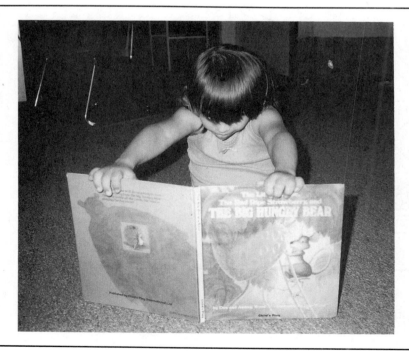

Figure 3-3

Materials

- Storybooks *The Old Lady Who Swallowed a Fly* and *The Little Mouse, the Red Ripe Strawberry, and the Big Hungry Bear*, Figure 3-3.
- The materials listed for each taste station in "Preparation"

Preparation

Find copies of the two storybooks listed under "Materials." (See the bibliography in Section III.) Prepare to read the stories out loud with expression.

Set up the following taste stations:

- Station A: peanut butter play dough. (See "Recipes" in Section III.)
- Station B: an array of sweet and sour things for the children to taste.
- Station C: an array of crunchy and soft foods for the children to taste.
- Station D: a flannel board with the characters from *The Old Lady Who Swallowed a Fly*.

Learning Activities

1. Gather the children around you and read the two storybooks. Invite the children's comments after each story.

Figure 3-4

2. Explain to the children that today they get to use their sense of taste at the various stations in the room. Encourage the children to enjoy the many different things that they will be tasting today. Ask them what some of their favorite things are to taste. You may want to write their responses on large sheets of paper or on the chalkboard so the children can see their written words.

Additional Activities

1. Storybook. Read the book *Piggies* (by Audrey Wood) to the children. After reading the book, let them look at their own fingers and toes. Let them take off their shoes and look at their toes. They may even want to look at each others fingers and toes and make some comparisons.
2. Fingerplays. Do various fingerplays with the children, Figure 3-4. For instance, you might do "Itsy Bitsy Spider," "Five Little Monkeys," and "Open, Shut Them." (See "Tapes and Records" in Section III.)
3. Water table. Fill the water table with warm water. Put ice cubes in for the children to watch and feel as the cubes melt.
4. Field trip. Take the children to visit the bakery of a local supermarket to taste and smell the many good things.

part two
The Seasons

Speech/Language, Developmentally Delayed, and the Mentally Handicapped

- When playing with the clay, it is a good time to reinforce the concepts of *in*, *out*, *on*, and *under*.
- Sorting and matching activities are good for concept development of *same* and *different* and should be reinforced in the learning station.
- Help the child with fine-motor difficulties hold onto the clothespin in the sponge painting activity.
- Discuss body parts when making the leaf person.
- Mitten matching is a good time to reinforce colors.
- Horseshoes, ring toss, and t-ball are good activities for gross-motor development. Consult with the physical and occupational therapists to maximize involvement and continued success.
- Assist the child with fine-motor difficulties in spreading peanut butter.

Multihandicapped and Orthopedically Impaired

- The child may be tactilely defensive with the shaving cream activity. Gently help the child become aware of texture by putting some on the hands and arms.
- Attach the grocery bag for collecting nature objects to the back of the wheelchair or to the child's walker.
- Positioning the child is important when using finger paint and shaving cream. If it is not possible to position the child at the table, use the lap board and invite another child to participate with the child in the wheelchair.
- Make sure to include in the role-playing area clothing that has velcro.
- Position the children in wheelchairs, walkers, and crutches for the ring toss and horseshoes so that they have good balance.

Emotionally Disturbed

- Plan ahead so that the child does not throw shaving cream at another child. This can be done by engaging the child in the process or by discussing what the child is making.

- Make sure that the child understands that marbles stay in the cereal box when marble painting.
- The wading pool may be overstimulating and the child may need an alternative activity.
- Sand play may be calming to the child.

Other Health Impaired

- Asthmatic children may have difficulty with the nature walk and also when leaves are brought into the classroom. Pollen may adversely affect children in the spring. An alternative activity should be planned.
- Check to make sure that the snacks are appropriate. If not, choose an alternative. Apple slices are not appropriate for the children with feeding problems; applesauce would be a good substitute.

Blind and Visually Impaired

- Describe items the child collects on the nature walk.
- Use styrofoam balls to help the child feel what the construction of a snowman involves.
- Have the child hold an ice cube and let it melt in his/her hand to describe melting.
- Guide the child through the spring games.

Deaf and Hearing Impaired

- Make sure the child is looking at you when you are demonstrating group activities.
- Have pictures of winter for the child to manipulate when stories are read.

#4   Autumn

Objective

By taking a walk outside and using the objects of nature, the children will deepen their appreciation of autumn, develop body awareness, and extend their language skills.

Day 1: Experiencing the Senses

Materials

- Bowls, shaving cream, oatmeal, rice, and tapioca
- Colorful large and small beads, yarn or shoelaces, and glue or tape
- Plastic sheet and rice table equipped with rice, scoops, and containers
- Commercial or homemade modeling clay/dough and cookie cutters
- Apple slices (applesauce), peanut butter, spoons, paper plates, and napkins

Preparation

For Learning Activity 1, put shaving cream into three bowls. Mix oatmeal in one bowl of shaving cream, rice in a second, and tapioca in the third.

For Learning Activity 2, prepare pieces of yarn by knotting one end and dipping the other end in glue or taping it. Or purchase shoelaces for this activity.

For Learning Activity 3, prepare a rice table by spreading a plastic sheet on the floor and then placing a table on it. On the table put rice, scoops, and containers.

For Learning Activity 4, buy modeling clay/dough or prepare your own. (See "Recipes" in Section III.)

For Learning Activity 5, peel apples and cut individual slices. Think about applesauce as a good alternative for those children who cannot eat apple slices.

Learning Activities

1. Tell the children that today they get to use their senses as they participate in five activities. Explain that during the next two weeks they will talk about picnics and that on a picnic people use all their senses—touch, smell, hearing, sight, and taste.

   Invite the children to experiment in the three bowls of shaving cream. Note that some children may not like the textured feeling and may want to play only with the shaving cream, Figure 4-1.
2. Provide the children with beads of many colors and sizes and invite them to string these on prepared yarn or shoelaces.

   Note: Some children may have difficulty with this activity so you will want to have large beads available for them. Be careful that the children do not put beads in their mouth.

Figure 4-1

3. Invite the children to explore and experiment at the rice table.
   Note: Keep the equipped rice table for use throughout this unit.
4. Invite the children to play with nontoxic modeling clay/dough.
5. Invite the children to share a treat of fall apples and peanut butter. Encourage them to dip their apple slices into peanut butter or to use a spoon and spread peanut butter onto their apple slices. Provide the children with small paper plates and napkins. Make the applesauce a special treat for those who cannot eat the apple slices.
   Music Note: "Shake the Apple Tree" from *Songs for the Nursery School*

Day 2: Taking a Nature Walk

Materials

- Grocery bags (one per child)
- Tagboard or large sheet of drawing paper and tape or glue
- Individual sheets of drawing paper (optional)

Preparation

Plan the route of the nature walk you and the children will take today.

Learning Activities

1. Before beginning the walk, give each child a grocery bag. Invite the children to put things from their walk in their bags. Stress that they should not pull any flowers from people's lawns. As you walk, talk about the wonders of nature. You might point out a squirrel's nest or a squirrel hiding food for the coming winter. Talk about the crunching of leaves beneath their feet.
    Music Note: "The Leaves are Falling Down" from *More Piggyback Songs*
2. When your return to the classroom, use the things the children found to make a collage on a large piece of tagboard. While putting the collage together, talk about the color, shape, and texture of the various items.
    Note: If some children want to take their nature items home or make their own collages, encourage them to do so. Assist the children who are unable to gather their own things for their collage because of physical challenges. Ask the children what they would like, rather than just putting things in the bag for them. You can even tape the bag to the side of their wheelchair and hand them the objects for them to put in.
    Keep the classroom collage for use in Day 3.

Day 3: Matching Colors and Shapes

Materials

*   Collage from Day 2
*   Plastic sheet, long sheet of white paper, saucers or bowls of tempera paint, liquid dishwashing soap, and brushes
*   Construction paper
*   White drawing paper (one sheet per child)

Preparation

Prepare the saucers or bowls of tempera paint (brown, yellow, red, and orange). Mix liquid dishwashing soap with the paint for easier cleanup.

Cut many leaves of various sizes and shapes from brown, yellow, red, and orange construction paper. Laminate these leaves if you want to use them in later lessons.

For each child prepare a sheet of white drawing paper on which you have drawn the outline of a tree.

Learning Activities

1. Gather the children around you and talk about their nature walk on Day 2. Use the collage they made to help them recall the walk.
2. Initiate a discussion about trees. Then bring out a sheet of white paper and place it on a sheet of plastic. Draw a big tree trunk on the paper and

tell the children that they are going to use their hands to make fall leaves for the tree. Show the children the bowls or saucers of tempera. Invite each child to choose what fall color he or she wants to use for a leaf. Show the children how to brush paint onto their hands and then put their handprints onto the paper. (You may have to help some of the children brush the paint onto their hands.)

3. Display the large tree on a wall so the children can see their work. Then give the children construction-paper leaves and invite them to match the color of the leaf to a color on the display.

4. If the children want to make their own trees to take home, provide the children with smaller sheets of paper onto which you have drawn tree trunks and invite them to use the tempera to add leaves to their tree trunk.
   Note: Keep the laminated leaves for use on Day 7. Keep the classroom collage for use on Day 8. Keep the tree displayed for use on Day 8.
   Fingerplay Fun: "Falling Leaves" from *Let's Do Fingerplays*

Day 4: Painting with Sponges

Materials

* Storybook *Goblin Walk*
* Easels, tables, and/or lap boards
* Saucers or bowls of tempera and liquid dishwashing soap, two-inch-square sponges, and spring-type clothespins
* Brown felt-tipped marker
* Variety of sorting activities

Preparation

Find a storybook about autumn and prepare to read the story out loud with expression.

Prepare the bowls or saucers of tempera paint and mix each color (orange, red, brown, and yellow) with liquid dishwashing soap for easier cleanup.

Make a paintbrush for each child by attaching a spring-type clothespin to a two-inch-square sponge, Figure 4-2.

Prepare a variety of sorting activities. Sorting activities develop one-to-one correspondence, classification skills, and ordering skills. You may put out various sizes and colors of beads and blocks. They can sort by color and size. Let them also decide how else the beads and blocks could be sorted. They can really be creative.

Learning Activities

1. Gather the children around you and read *Goblin Walk*. Invite the children's comments and questions. Remember that learning is a process. Encourage the children to share their knowledge with the group. You may even want to divide them into groups to talk about various aspects of

Figure 4-2

autumn. Assistants can help facilitate these groups.

Note: Keep the storybook for use on Day 8.

2. Tell the children that they get to make their own fall tree. Divide the class into two groups. Invite Group 2 to play with a variety of sorting activities. Tell the children in this group that in a short while they will get to paint.

3. Gather the children in Group 1 in the painting area. Give each child a sponge "paintbrush." Show the children how to dip the sponge into a bowl of tempera and press the sponge onto their paper to get a burst of colorful leaves, Figure 4-3. As the children work, name the colors they are using. After the children have finished, draw the trunk of the tree with a brown marker. The children may want to make more than one.

Note: Children who are physically challenged may need help positioning the clothespin in their hand. Visually-impaired children can be guided through this activity by guiding them through the process and talking as you do each step.

4. When the children in Group 1 complete their work, shift the two groups.

Figure 4-3

Day 5: Printing with Apples

Materials

- Lengths of yarn and red and green construction paper
- White construction paper (one sheet per child), apples, and a knife
- Plastic fruit, variety of sorting games, kitchen equipment, shelf toys
- Paper, saucers or bowls of red tempera paint, liquid dishwashing soap, knife and apples (one for every two children)
- Apples, electric frying pan, water, cinnamon, paper bowls, napkins, and spoons
- Apple juice and rice cereal (optional)

Preparation

From red or green construction paper cut out two-inch apples. Then make each child a yarn necklace and attach one paper apple to each necklace.

Prepare a free-play area in which you put the plastic fruit, sorting games, kitchen equipment, and toys.

Prepare saucers or bowls of red tempera and mix in liquid dishwashing soap for easier cleanup.

Peel and slice a number of apples to make applesauce.

Learning Activities

1. When the children arrive, greet them with their necklaces. Tell the children that today is Apple Day.
   Music Note: "Apple Song" from *More Piggyback Songs*
2. Divide the class into two groups. Explain to the children that today they get to play and to make prints using apples. Invite Group 2 to go to the free-play area for a while. Tell them that in a short while they will get to do some printing with apples. Lots of apple books should be available for the children to look at.
3. Gather Group 1 around a table. As the children watch, halve each apple. Point out the seeds and the shape of the core in an apple half. Put one half aside and ask the children if they know what will happen to the apple that sits out without being covered. Then give each child half an apple and a sheet of paper. Demonstrate how to dip the apple into tempera and print with it. Then invite the children to use their apple half to make a colorful design on their paper. Look at the apple at the end of this activity and see if the children were right in their guesses.
4. When the children in Group 1 finish their printing, have them wash their hands and go to the free-play area. Then show Group 2 how to do apple printing.
5. When all the children have printed with apples, tell the children that they are going to make their own applesauce. As the children watch, cut up peeled apples into an electric flying pan and add a little water. Let the apples cook until they become sauce. You can have the children help you cut the apples. It is a good idea to talk about safety in the kitchen at this time. You can talk with the children about sharp knives and hot pans.
6. After the applesauce has cooled, dish some up for the children to eat. Have cinnamon available so that the children can taste it on their applesauce.
   Note: Depending upon your group, you may want to cook the applesauce while the children do their painting.

For children with feeding problems who might not be able to eat applesauce, have available apple juice and thicken it with rice cereal.

Day 6: Experiencing Leaves

Materials

- Paper or plastic trash bags
- White construction paper and glue
- Plastic rakes

Preparation

Plan the route of the nature walk you will take with the children.

Learning Activities

1. Give each child a grocery bag or a plastic garbage bag. Then invite the child to walk outside with you to gather leaves, Figure 4-4.

Figure 4-4

2. When you return to the classroom, invite the children to dump their leaves onto the floor. Encourage the children to walk through the leaves and touch and explore them. Take this opportunity to talk to the children about their body parts (arms, legs, feet, toes, head) and the placement of these body parts.
   Fingerplay Fun: "Parts of the Body" and "Hands on Shoulders" from
      Rhymes for Learning Times
3. Demonstrate how to use leaves to make a "leaf person." Then give glue and a sheet of white construction paper to each child who wants to make a leaf person. If some children do not choose to make leaf people, simply encourage them to play in the leaves. Note that playing with leaves helps children become more aware of their bodies. Talk through with the children when the head, arms, legs, and body are put on their leaf person. This helps them with their own body awareness.
4. Invite the children to rake and sweep the leaves on the floor into piles. Save a grocery bag full of leaves for Day 7. Put the remaining leaves in plastic bags or a wheelbarrow and take them back outside.

Day 7: Making Leaf Rubbings

Materials

- Bag of leaves from Day 6

- Thin sheets of white paper, crayons, and tape
- Laminated leaves from Day 3
- Puzzles and commercial or homemade modeling clay/dough

Preparation

Following the directions given for the learning activities, make a few leaf rubbings ahead of time so that you become aware of any problems the children might have with this project.

Buy commercial nontoxic modeling clay/dough or prepare your own. (See "Recipes" in Section III.)

Learning Activities

1. Using the leaves from Day 6, show the children how to make a leaf rubbing. Demonstrate the process by placing a thin sheet of white paper on top of a leaf and rubbing the paper with crayon. Encourage the children to note how the shape and the veins of the leaf appear as if by magic.
2. Provide the children with crayons and thin sheets of paper and invite them to make their own leaf rubbings. To help the children succeed at this, tape each child's paper to the tabletop to secure it. Encourage the children to make as many leaf rubbings as they wish.
3. Invite the children to use the laminated leaves from Day 3 and match them to their rubbings and to the leaves they collected. Encourage the children to match colors and shapes. While some children do this, provide puzzles and modeling clay/dough for other children to use.

Day 8: Painting with Marbles

Materials

- Toys
- Storybook from Day 4
- Collage from Day 2
- Tree from Day 3
- Empty cereal boxes (one per child), tape, and construction paper
- Marbles in a sealed box
- Spoons, saucers or bowls of tempera, and liquid dishwashing soap

Preparation

Before class, cut leaves from white construction paper (one leaf per child). Tape each leaf into the bottom of a cereal box (one leaf per box). Prepare the dishes of tempera (orange, red, brown, and yellow) by mixing liquid dishwashing soap with the paint so that the children can clean their hands more easily.

Learning Activities

1. When the children first gather, invite them to choose toys with which to play. Afterward gather the children around you, and depending on your group, you may choose to do some storytelling of the book read on Day 4. You may even choose another book to read or you may just want to reread the storybook from Day 4.

2. Point out the collage from Day 2 and the tree from Day 3 and invite the children's comments. Next show the children a cereal box and point out the leaf taped inside the bottom of the box. Invite the children to shake the box in which you have placed the marbles and to guess what is inside the box. Ask the questions as to whether it is big or little, hard or soft, and round or square.

3. Open the marble box, and using several marbles show the children how to make a marble painting by dipping the marbles in tempera, taking the marbles out of the tempera with a spoon, dropping the marbles into the cereal box, and then rolling them back and forth across the bottom of the box. Untape the leaf from the bottom of your cereal box and show the children how the marbles colored the leaf.

4. Invite the children to put marbles into tempera paint and make their own marble painting, Figure 4-5. Encourage the children to roll their cereal box back and forth so that the marbles will roll across the leaf. Talk about what the marbles are doing and the motion of going back and forth. Afterward let the marble paintings dry so that the children can take them home.

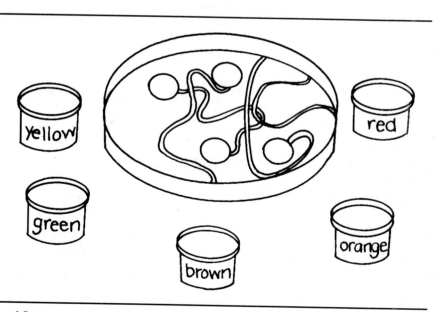

Figure 4-5

Additional Activities

1. Field trip. Take the children to an apple orchard to see apples growing on trees. If possible, invite the children to pick apples from the trees. Encourage the children to taste and enjoy the different varieties of apples.

2. Leaf pictures. Invite the children to choose some leaves to put inside black frames that you have made. Laminate the pictures so the children can take them home. On each individual picture, print the child's name and the date.

3. Scavenger hunt. Tell the children that they are going to find some things outside. Show the children an example of each thing you would like them to find (for instance: an acorn, rock, twig, pine cone, flower, leaf). If you do not have the actual items to show, use colored pictures. Be careful to make the hunt relatively easy for the children by choosing items that they will be able to locate. Give each child a paper bag in which to put their scavenger treasures.

#5 Winter

Objective

By making many types of snow people, playing with snow and ice, and talking about birds, the children will explore cold, develop their fine-motor coordination, become more aware of their bodies, and begin to explore their responsibility to care for all creation.

Day 1: Experiencing the Senses

Materials

- Large containers, textured materials, such as rice, sand, oatmeal, shaving cream, and cotton, and towels
- Tape or record and cassette player or phonograph
- Finger paints, easels, and paper
- Winter clothes, such as mittens, caps, coats, sweaters, neck scarves, boots, snowsuits, and so on.
- Water table equipped with snow or ice, scoops, and spoons

Preparation

Prepare texture bins for Learning Activity 1 by obtaining containers that are large enough for one child to stand in. Into each container put a textured material like oatmeal, cotton, or sand.

Decide what music you will use for Learning Activity 2 and set up easels and paper in one section of your classroom.

For Learning Activity 4 bring snow from outside or use ice at the water table.

Learning Activities

1. Gather the children around you and tell them that today they get to do many activities that invite them to use their senses to enjoy their world. Help the children take off their shoes and socks. Then invite the children to explore textures with their bare feet in the texture bins you prepared before class. Have towels handy for the children to wipe off their feet after they have explored the texture bins.
2. Invite the children to listen to music and to fingerpaint what they feel when they hear the music.
3. Invite the children to dress up in the winter clothes you have provided. Encourage them to role-play in their winter clothes. In their role-playing, they could dress for skating, going to school, going to Grandma's, etc.
   Note: Be ready to help physically challenged children dress up.
   Fingerplay Fun: "Make a Snowman" from *Finger Frolics*
4. Encourage the children to play with snow or ice at the water table and to watch the snow or ice melt in the water. Encourage them to use the utensils you have supplied to play with the water and snow.

Day 2: Playing with "Frosty"

Materials

- Storybook *Frosty the Snowman*
- Video of storybook (optional)
- Tape or record of "Frosty the Snowman" and phonograph or cassette player

- White paper
- Tape, paste, or glue; felt-tipped markers; crayons; and scraps of colored construction paper

Preparation

Find a copy of *Frosty the Snowman*. (See the bibliography in Section III.) Prepare to read the story out loud with expression.

Cut three large circles (one for Frosty's head, one for his chest, and one for his bottom) that can be made into a snowman for the classroom.

For each child, cut three circles from white paper. Make each circle a little bigger to represent Frosty's snowball head, chest, and bottom. This is a good science and math activity. The children are experiencing the concept *big, bigger,* and *biggest.* Explain that Frosty is a big snowman. To make him, they will need the biggest circle for the bottom. Ask them what they think will come next in the middle.

Learning Activities

1. Gather the children around you and read the story or show the video or have the children tell the story. Afterward invite the children's comments and questions.
2. Show the children the three large circles you cut out. Put these circles on the floor and help the children tape or paste the circles together to make a snowman like Frosty. Provide decorating materials so that the children can add facial features, a hat, arms, buttons, and so on, to the snowman. When the children have completed Frosty, display him somewhere in the classroom.
Music Note: "I Can Make a Snowman" from *Piggyback Songs*
3. Give each child three white circles. Invite the children to make their own snow person to take home. While they are working, play the recording of the storybook.
Note: You may want to use this lesson to talk about body parts.

Day 3: Making Paper Mittens

Materials

- Storybook *The Mitten Story*
- Mittens (one pair per child) and large bag
- Colored construction paper, blunt-edged scissors, felt-tipped markers or crayons, hole punch, and yarn

Preparation

Find a copy of *The Mitten Story*. (See the bibliography in Section III.)

Prepare to read the story out loud with expression.

Put all the mittens in a large bag and mix them around.

Decide if the children have the ability to make paper mittens. (See Learning Activity 3.)

Fingerplay Fun: "Mittens" from *Let's Do Fingerplays*

Learning Activities

1. Gather the children around you and read the story. Invite the children's comments and questions.
2. Keep the children in a circle and put your bag of mittens in the middle of the circle. Invite the children, one by one, to reach into the bag and pull out two mittens. Encourage the children to try to match the mittens. As the children match the mittens, say something like "John has two red mittens" or "Sue has two that look the same" or "Jami has a green mitten and a white mitten."
3. If the children are able to trace around their hands, give each child two sheets of the same-colored construction paper. Invite the children to trace around their closed fingers to make mittens. Provide materials so that the children can decorate their paper mittens. Afterward help the children cut out their mittens, punch a hole in the corner of them, and tie them together, Figure 5-1. Encourage the children to take home their paper mittens.

Figure 5-1

Fingerplay Fun: "The Mitten Song" from *Let's Do Fingerplays*
Note: If some children are unable to cut, simply punch a hole in the corners of the sheets of construction paper on which the children have traced their hands and tie the two sheets together.

Day 4: Dressing for Winter

Materials

- Winter clothes such as coats, boots, scarves, mittens, caps, snowsuits, and so on.
- Flannel board and characters dressed for rainy, snowy, and sunny days
- Colored construction paper (four sheets per child) felt-tipped markers and crayons, and blunt-edged scissors
- Hole punch and prepared yarn (two lengths per child) or shoelaces (one pair per child)

Preparation

Provide a variety of winter clothes (Figure 5-2) by asking parents to supply clean, old clothes or by going to a used-clothes store and purchasing some. (Remember: You do not need a coat or a cap for each child. You simply need a few of each kind of winter apparel.) It is important that the clothing be clean for sanitary reasons.

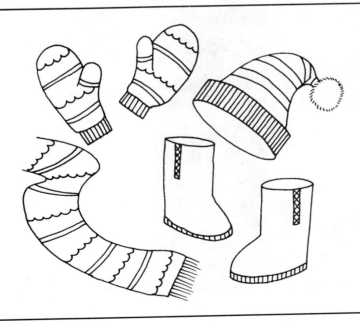

Figure 5-2

Following the directions for Learning Activities 3 and 4, make your own set of mittens. If you are using yarn instead of shoelaces for the lacing activity, prepare the yarn by knotting one end and taping or gluing the other end.

Learning Activities

1. Recall the story from Day 3. Discuss the story with the children. Then show the children the clothes you have collected and invite them to dress for winter. Encourage role-playing. Encourage them to dress like Mommy or Daddy.
2. Use the flannel board to show the children how to dress for rainy, snowy, and sunny days.
3. Invite the children to make their own paper mittens that they can wear, Figure 5-3. Show the children the mittens you made.

    Give each child four pieces of colored construction paper. Help the children trace around their hands and make four mitten shapes. Invite the children to use felt-tipped markers or crayons to decorate their mittens.
4. Help the children cut out their paper mittens. Punch holes around the edge of the mittens for lacing and give each child two shoelaces or two

Figure 5-3

pieces of yarn with which to lace. Help the children lace their mittens together and print their names on their mittens. Afterward tie each set of mittens together and hang them in the room.

Note: Learning Activities 3 and 4 are good for **fine-motor development**. Modify the activity for each child's individual needs.

Note: If you do not live in a climate that gets cold enough for winter clothes, provide rainy-weather clothing for the children to use as they dress up and pretend. Or provide dolls and winter doll clothes and invite the children to dress the dolls and to pretend that it is a snowy winter day outside.

Day 5: Investigating Ice Cubes

Materials

- Large supply of ice cubes and paper cups (one per child)
- Warm water
- Mittens (one pair per child)
- Plate and salt
- Ice, ice crusher or blender, holders for ice cones, and colored liquid flavoring
- Paper cups and drink mix or juice (optional)

Preparation

To prepare yourself to answer the children's questions, put salt on ice and watch what happens.

Learning Activities

1. Gather the children around you and give each a paper cup with ice in it. Invite the children to swirl the ice in the cup, to listen to the ice, to lick it, to touch it, and to smell it. Invite the children's comments.
2. Put some warm water in the children's cups and say things like "See how the ice cubes are getting smaller" or "I think my ice cubes are going away."
3. Give the children mittens to wear and invite them to hold an ice cube. If some children do not want to hold an ice cube, invite them to watch it melt on the floor or table.
4. Put a plate of salt on a table and put ice cubes on the salt. Encourage the children to watch what happens on the plate. Talk about the concept of melting.
5. Use the ice crusher or blender to make crushed ice for snow cones. Help the children make their cones and pour a liquid flavoring over the ice. If you do not have the equipment to make ice cones, prepare a premixed drink or provide juice in which the children can put an ice cube.

Day 6: Feeding the Birds

Materials

- Pictures of birds
- Pine cones (one per child), peanut butter, yarn, and bird seed
- Plastic bags

Preparation

Following the directions for Learning Activity 2, prepare a bird feeder from a pine cone, peanut butter, and birdseed, Figure 5-4.

Figure 5-4

Learning Activities

1. Gather the children around you and talk about birds and how people need to help them eat when cold weather comes. Show the children pictures of birds and discuss what they eat and how they survive in the winter.
2. Show the children the bird feeder you made. Provide each child with a pine cone. Invite the children to explore the pine cone and discover its secrets. Next help each child make a bird feeder by attaching a length of yarn to the pine cone, spreading peanut butter onto the cone, and rolling the cone in the birdseed.
3. Put each bird feeder in a small plastic bag to take home. Tell the children

that they should ask their parents to help them put their feeder outside their house.

Day 7: Playing with Snow

Materials

- Book of winter poems or the story *Snowy Day*
- White construction or typing paper and cotton balls
- Blue construction (one sheet per child), brushes, saucers or bowls of white tempera, and liquid dishwashing soap
- Cotton balls, large sheet of paper, glue, and felt-tipped markers or crayons
- Large sheet of paper (optional)

Preparation

Find a copy of the storybook *Snowy Day* or a book of winter poems. Prepare to read the story or poems out loud with expression.

From white construction paper or typing paper, cut out a large variety of paper snowflakes of many different sizes. Display some of these paper snowflakes in the classroom by taping them to the bulletin boards and hanging them from the ceiling.

Put white tempera in bowls and saucers and mix it with the dishwashing soap for easier cleanup.

For Learning Activity 4 draw the outline of a large snow person on a sheet of white paper.

Learning Activities

1. Gather the children around you and read some winter poems or the story *Snowy Day*. Invite the children's comments on the poems or story and on the snowflakes you have displayed in the classroom.
   Music Note: "Snow Flakes" from *Piggyback Songs*
2. Give the children paper snowflakes or cotton and invite them to pretend that snow is falling in their classroom. Encourage the children to be creative in their snow play.
3. Invite the children to do a winter wash. Provide the children with blue construction paper, brushes, and the tempera mixture, Figure 5-5. Show the children how to brush the paint mixture across the paper to make a snowy day. Make sure the brush is very wet when it goes into the tempera. This makes for a good consistency for the wash.
4. Gather the children around a table on which you have placed the outline of a snow person. Show the children how to put glue on the snow person and then cover it with cotton balls. Encourage the children to use felt-tipped markers to add facial features to the snow person.

Figure 5-5

Note: If time permits you may want to provide a large sheet of paper and invite the children to make a winter classroom mural, using their white tempera.

Day 8: Eating Snow People

Materials

- Large marshmallows (three per child), raisins, stick pretzels, slivers of red licorice
- Cooking pan, margarine or butter, and Rice Krispies

Preparation

Follow the directions in Learning Activity 2 to make a marshmallow snow person.

Learning Activities

1. Gather the children around you and show them the marshmallow snow person you made before class.
2. Invite the children to make their own snow people. Give each child three marshmallows. Show the children how to hold the three together with

one or two stick pretzels, how to decorate the snow person's face with raisins and red licorice, and how to add pretzel arms.

3. Heat a pan containing margarine or butter. Then invite the children to watch the process of making the snow people. Tell them that when spring comes, the snow melts and all the snow people go away, just as Frosty did. Help the children remove the raisins, pretzels, and licorice from their snow people. Invite them to add marshmallows to the pan. They may keep their own snow people pieces to eat while the marshmallows are melting. When the marshmallows have melted, add Rice Krispies and make bars.

4. Invite the children to eat their marshmallow bars and to enjoy!

Additional Activities

1. Outside play. If you have snow and ice in your area, take the children outside to make their own snow people and to crawl or walk on ice.

2. Penguins. Read the children a story about penguins and then provide materials so that the children can make and color penguins. Emphasize that these animals live where it is cold. Two books you might consider reading are *Funny Feet* by Leatie Weiss (Franklin Watts Publishers, 1978) and *Penguins, of All People* by Don Freeman (The Viking Press, 1971).

3. Snowflakes. Provide materials so that the children can make their own paper snowflakes with tissue or white typing paper.

4. Snow people. Show the children how to use a paper plate to make the head of Frosty. Provide materials, such as scraps of construction paper, felt-tipped markers or crayons, glue or paste. Invite the children to add facial features to Frosty, e.g., a hat, eyes, nose, mouth, and a warm scarf.

#6   Spring

Objective

By participating in sensory activities and flying kites, the children will experience lifetime activities and develop their gross-motor skills.

Day 1: Flying Kites

Materials

- Storybook *Curious George Flies a Kite*
- Kites or materials for making kites

Preparation

Find a copy of *Curious George Flies a Kite*. (See the bibliography in Section III.) Prepare to read the story out loud with expression.

If the children in your class are young, buy a kite for each child. If the children are older, assemble materials for making and decorating kites and plan time for this activity. (Making kites is usually a two-day project.)

Learning activities

1. Gather the children around you and read *Curious George Flies a Kite*. Invite the children's comments about the story and their own experiences. *Music Note:* "My Kite" from *Piggyback Songs*
2. Give each child a kite, and if the day is windy, go outside and fly kites. Or give the children materials and help them make kites. Then invite them to fly their kites.
    Note: Children in wheelchairs can be given their kites, once someone gets it in the air for them. For visually-impaired children, hold their hand and run with them.

Day 2: Playing Games

Materials

- Equipment for games, such as horseshoes, ring toss, and a sponge bat and balls
- Ingredients and kitchen utensils for making "bird nest clusters." (See "Recipes" in Section III.)

Preparation

Make "bird nests" for snack before beginning the activities outside. Set up an area outside for play.

Learning Activities

1. Take the children outside and invite them to play horseshoes, ring toss, or

baseball. Encourage the children to try all three games and to play with the other children. Children in wheelchairs can participate in all the games from their chairs, Figure 6-1.

Figure 6-1

2. Take the children on a nature walk. Look for birds and their nests. Also look for other signs of spring. Talk about sounds and smells.
   Fingerplay Fun: "Sounds of Nature" from *Finger Frolics*
3. After returning to the classroom, invite the children to eat the snacks.

Day 3: Painting Spring

Materials

* Washable paints and brushes
* Colored chalk
* Large therapy balls

Preparation

Pick out a place on the playground or school sidewalk that the children can paint.

Learning Activities

1. Take the children outside by a sidewalk. Provide them with washable paints and brushes. Invite them to paint the sidewalk with large stokes of their brushes. Encourage them to be creative.
2. When children lose interest in painting with brushes, provide them with colored chalk and invite them to draw on the sidewalk.
   Note: Be prepared to hose or wash away the children's sidewalk art work at the end of the day.
3. Invite the children to roll on the therapy balls in the grass. Help children in wheelchairs get on the balls and lie in the grass The children need to be carefully supervised during this activity.

Day 4: Enjoying Spring!

Materials

- Sand table equipped with rice, scoops, containers, and shells
- Water table equipped with water, scoops, floating toys, turkey baster, and eggbeater
- Buckets and bubble solution
- Potting soil, flowers for potting, trowels, clay pots or other containers, small sprinkling cans, and water
- Child's plastic wading pool and water (optional)

Preparation

Set up a sand table and a water table outside.

Prepare large buckets of water and put bubble solution in them. Buy a commercial solution or make your own. (See "Recipes" in Section III.)

Music Note: "Blowing Bubbles" from *Piggyback Songs*

Learning Activities

1. Take the children outside and invite them to play at the sand table and the water table. Put out your buckets of bubble solution and invite the children to blow bubbles. Encourage the children to play at all three activities.
2. Invite the children to help you plant some flowers. Show them your soil, plants, trowels, and containers. Demonstrate how to plant a small flower and then invite the children to follow your example. Afterward encourage the children to use the sprinkling cans to give the plants a drink.
   Fingerplay Fun: "My Garden" from *Finger Frolics*
3. If the day is especially warm, fill a wading pool with water and invite the children to take off their shoes and socks and wade. Be sure that an adult constantly supervises this activity.

Figure 6-2

Note: While you and the children are outside, some of them will move to different areas while others will stay in only one area. Do not force the children to move around.

Note: This is a nice time to position children with physical challenges, so they can put their feet in the pool.

Figure 6-3

Additional Activities

1. Caterpillars. Invite the children to make caterpillars from egg cartons. Show the children how to paint the cartons green and how to add pipe-cleaner antennae. Or make caterpillars from pom-poms. Glue brightly colored pom-poms together and then add a magnetic strip to the back.
    Fingerplay Fun: "Roly-Poly Caterpillar" from *Finger Frolics*
2. Flowers. Cut large flower shapes from colorful construction paper. Give each child a flower shape, a cupcake paper, a cotton ball, a tongue depressor for a stem, and a paper leaf. Help the children glue the cupcake paper to the center of the flower shape. Then glue the cotton ball inside the cupcake paper. Help the children glue stems and leaves to their flower. Display the children's work in your classroom.
    Fingerplay Fun: "Yellow Daffodil" from *Rhymes for Fingers and Flannel-boards.*

#7   Summer

Objective

By pretending to camp, hike, and fish, the children will meet situations requiring problem solving and will enjoy tactile experiences.

Day 1: Making Tents

Materials

- Storybooks *You're the Scaredy Cat* by Mercer Maye. 1974. *Parents Magazine Press, New York,* or *Camping Out—A Book of Action Words* by Betsy & Guilio Maestro. 1985. Crown Publishers, New York.
- Blankets, chairs, and tables

Preparation

Find a copy of *You're the Scaredy Cat* or *Camping Out*. (See the bibliography in Section III.) Prepare to read the story out loud with expression.

Select an area of the room where the children can erect blanket tents that can remain up all week.

Learning Activities

1. Gather the children around you and read one of the stories. Encourage the children to read along with you during repetitive phrases because this will help them feel that they are reading too. Afterward invite their comments.
2. Take the children to the area of the room you have set aside for tent building. Bring out some blankets and invite the children to use them along with chairs and tables to make tents. Let the children do much of the work and let them problem solve how to make the tents. As they work, talk about what they are doing. Try, however, to stay away from the how, what, and why questions.
   Note: Put children in wheelchairs on the floor so they can help by crawling. If children in wheelchairs cannot crawl, put them on the floor and encourage them to enjoy the feel of the blankets.

Day 2: Pretending to Camp

Materials

- Camping equipment, such as canteens, binoculars, backpacks, fishing poles, firewood, and sticks
- Clean grill and plastic hot dogs, hamburgers, and buns
- Marshmallows, graham crackers, chocolate bars, and microwave
- Sand table equipped with a plastic sheet, containers, scoops, and shells of various sizes
- Water

Preparation

Prepare the sand table by putting a large sheet of plastic under it to make clean up easier.

Learning Activities

1. Gather the children around you and show them the camping equipment you have collected. Invite them to pretend to camp.
   Note: Keep the camping equipment you have collected as you will need it again on Day 4.
2. After a few minutes, bring in some logs and some long sticks and invite the children to pretend to make a fire and cook something like marshmallows.
3. Show the children a clean grill and invite them to cook plastic hamburgers and hot dogs.
4. Help the children make S'Mores by melting the marshmallows in a microwave and putting them on graham crackers with a piece of chocolate.
   Note: If some children have allergies and cannot eat chocolate S'Mores, invite them to put only their melted marshmallows on graham crackers.
5. After the children have eaten and completed their play with the camping equipment, invite them to play at the sand table. Help them to take off their shoes so that they can feel the sand on the floor when it falls from the table.
6. Pretend that you and the children are at a warm beach, Figure 7-1. Encourage them to feel the dry sand. Then add a little water to the sand so that the children can experience damp sand. Talk to the children about what they are doing at the sand table.

Figure 7-1

Note: If you have some children in wheelchairs, put sand into a plastic bin for them to touch. Take off the children's shoes and socks and let them feel the texture on their feet.

Music Note: "To the Beach" from *Piggyback Songs*

Day 3: Taking a Hike

Materials

- Grocery sacks (one per child)
- Felt-tipped markers and crayons
- Stapler, staples, and construction paper
- Bread (two slices per child), peanut butter, jelly, fruit, cookies, small containers of juice or a jug or thermos of juice, paper cups, and small plastic bags
- Maps, blankets, binoculars, and cleanup paraphernalia

Preparation

Following the directions for Learning Activities 3 and 4, make your own paper backpack.

Cut two-inch-wide strips of construction paper that are long enough to make arm loops for the children.

For your picnic, select a place within easy walking distance.

Learning Activities

1. Gather the children around you and tell them that today they get to pack their own lunch, carry a backpack, use maps, and hike like campers.
2. Show the children the paper backpack you made before class. Demonstrate how to wear it. Tell the children that each of them needs a backpack for their picnic lunch. Today they will make their own paper backpacks.
3 Give each child a large grocery bag. Invite the children to use felt-tipped markers or crayons to decorate the bags.
4. Help the children make backpacks out of their grocery bags. First, fold down the top of the grocery bag. To make loops on the backpacks for the children's arms, staple a wide vertical band of construction paper to the top and bottom of the bag on one side. Staple a second band on the other side. Help the children print their names on their backpacks.

   Note: Before stapling the arm straps to the backpacks, check to see if the bands are too tight for the children. You will need to help children in wheelchairs attach their backpacks to the back of their wheelchairs.

You may want to keep the backpacks for use in the unit entitled "Antless Picnic." However, if the children want to take them home, the "Antless Picnic" unit provides instruction and time for making backpacks a second time.

5. Provide ingredients so that the children can make peanut butter and jelly sandwiches. Help them put their sandwiches into small plastic bags. Also have some fruit for the children to put in their backpacks. Invite the children to put some cookies into small plastic bags. Lastly, give each child an individual juice container or carry a jug and pour each child a glass of juice when you get to your "campsite." Help the children put all their food into their backpacks.

   Note: If some children have feeding problems, provide small containers of applesauce for them.

6. Take out the maps and pretend with the children to read them and to find a place to go for a picnic, Figure 7-2. Help the children put on their backpacks. Prepare to leave the classroom and take with you blankets, binoculars, and clean-up paraphernalia.

7. Take a map with you on the walk and pretend to read it as you search for the perfect location for your picnic. After a short walk tell the children that you have found the perfect place for a picnic. Help them take off

Figure 7-2

their backpacks and invite them to help you collect twigs for a pretend campfire.
8. Spread the blankets on the ground and encourage the children to eat their lunch from their backpacks. After eating, invite the children to help you clean up. Help the children put on their backpacks and head back to school after looking at the map.

Day 4: Going Fishing

Materials

- Camping equipment from Day 2
- Magnets and dowels (one each per child), yarn or sting, construction paper, paper clips, and child's plastic wading pool
- Flying pan and firewood
- Water table or sand table
- Small goldfish crackers

Preparation

Prepare magnetic fishing poles by attaching a small magnet to a length of yarn and then attaching this to a dowel. Make a fishing pole for each child. From colored construction paper cut a variety of fish of different sizes and shapes. Tape a paper clip to each fish. Put the fish in a child's wading pool.

Learning Activities

1. Bring out the camping equipment and invite the children to recall the hike from Day 3 and to share their memories. Explain that today they are going fishing.
2. Bring out the magnetic poles and the pool of fish and invite the children to fish. As the children catch the fish, you may want to mention the color of fish they caught by saying, "Jacob caught a red fish" or "Oh look, Amy, you have a blue fish on your pole." You may also wish to count out loud the number of fish that each child catches.
   Music Note: "I'm a Fish" from *Piggyback Songs*
3. Invite the children to put their paper fish into a large frying pan. Then bring out firewood and invite the children to make a pretend fire over which they can cook their fish.
4. Encourage the children to play at the sand table or water table while the fish cook.
5. As the children's attention is diverted by play, place some little goldfish crackers into the flying pan and remove the paper fish. After the children are finished playing at the sand table or water table, have them come to the snack area. Bring over the pan and invite them to eat their "cooked" fish!

Additional Activities

1. Real camp. Invite the children to help you pack lunch to cook outside. Provide hamburgers and hot dogs to cook. Also provide ketchup, mustard, potato chips, cookies, fruit, a drink, napkins, paper cups and plates, and clean-up material. Go to a park and make an actual wood fire or take along a grill and charcoal. (Encourage the children to gather the wood for the fire.)

   Note: Children with asthma may have problems breathing by a wood fire. Be sure to check with their parents.

2. Sleeping out. Set up a tent in the classroom and have the children pretend that they are going to sleep out. Let them use their own sleeping bags from home or invite them to bring blankets and pillows to class. Encourage them to get ready for bed by washing their faces and hands and brushing their teeth.

part three
Sounds

Speech/Language, Developmentally Delayed, and Mentally Handicapped

- Offer a variety of sounds for the children to identify. This is good language stimulation and expansion.
- Giving children directions provides a good direction-following activity. Keep the directions simple!

Multihandicapped and Orthopedically Impaired

- Have the other children in the class push the child in the wheelchair.
- Dress-up clothing must include some items with velcro.
- Lap boards would be good when the child is making his/her own instrument.

Emotionally Disturbed

- Plan ahead so the child using an instrument will not begin pounding or making excess noise. You can assign the child a special part when playing.

Blind and Visually Impaired

- Give the child plastic animals to feel when reading the book *Too Much Noise.*
- Let the child feel the rhythm instruments.

Deaf and Hearing Impaired

- Let the child feel the vibration of things like the telephone or various rhythm instruments.
- Make sure the child can see others in the marching parade.

#8 What's That Noise?

Objective

By playing with plastic animals and rhythm instruments, listening to sounds and music, and making instruments, the children will use their listening skills to identify the sources of various sounds and their creativity to make music.

Day 1: Discovering Animal Sounds

Materials

- Storybook *Too Much Noise*
- Plastic cows, donkeys, sheep, hens, dogs, and cats or pictures of these animals (one animal per child)
- Play barn (optional)

Preparation

Find a copy of *Too Much Noise*. (See the bibliography in Section III.) Prepare to read the story out loud with expression, Figure 8-1. Practice making the sounds for the various animals mentioned in the story.

Learning Activities

1. Gather the children around you and read *Too Much Noise*. Invite the children's comments.
2. Show the children the plastic animals you have brought to class or display

Figure 8-1

pictures of these animals. Make the sound each animal makes and invite the children to repeat the sound, Figure 8-2. Invite the children to talk to one another with animal sounds. Arrange the children to allow for maximum interaction.

MOOO

HEE HAW

BAAA

CLUCK CLUCK

Figure 8-2

3. Invite the children to role-play the animals in the story.
4. Encourage the children to play with the plastic animals or pictures. If you have a play barn, invite the children to use the barn and animals to pretend to be farmers.

Music Note: Sing songs like "Old MacDonald," "Farmer in the Dell," and "Mary Had a Little Lamb"

Day 2: Discovering Everyday Sounds

Materials

- Storybook about everyday sounds
- Tapes or records of everyday sounds and a cassette player or phonograph
- Objects that make noises children hear every day (play telephones, cash registers, music boxes, cars, and so on)
- Crunchy food such as popcorn, apple slices, or celery

Preparation

Select a favorite storybook that contains pictures of things that make sounds the children can imitate, Figure 8-3. Prepare to read the story out loud.

Figure 8-3

Purchase a tape or record of sounds or make your own. Try to find everyday sounds, such as a baby crying, a door closing, thunder, an airplane, a train, a car horn, a motor running, and so on.

Set up a play area in which you put objects that make sounds that the children hear everyday.

Learning Activities

1. Gather the children around you and read them a story about sounds. Invite their comments and questions.
2. Play the records or tapes for the children and invite them to imitate each sound or guess what is making each sound.
3. Invite the children to use the objects in the play areas to make everyday sounds.
4. Provide a crunchy snack that makes noise when the children bite into it. Depending on the age of the children, you might want to serve popcorn. Or serve apples or celery.

Day 3: Making Music

Materials

- Storybook illustrating a song
- Record or tape of the song (optional)
- Rhythm band instruments, such as bells, tambourines, triangles, rhythm sticks, cymbals, and wood blocks (one instrument per child)
- Tape or record of marching music and of lullaby music and a cassette player or phonograph

Preparation

Select a story book that illustrates a song the children may know. Prepare to read the story out loud with expression.

Select marching music that the children can accompany with their rhythm instruments.

Learning Activities

1. Using rhythm instruments. Announce with a flourish that the children get to make music today, using rhythm instruments. Then gather the children around you and read them the story illustrating a song. If you have a record or tape of the song, play it for the children. Sing the song for and with the children.
2. Show the children the rhythm instruments you have collected. Invite the children to select instruments and to experiment creatively with them. If necessary, demonstrate techniques for each instrument. As the children

experiment with their musical instruments, you may want to talk to them about how to best request that a peer exchange an instrument with them. Also, involve yourself with the children today as they make music.

3. After the children have made their own music, invite everyone to get in line for a parade. Play the marching music you selected and invite the children to accompany the music with their rhythm instruments.

4. After the parade, play some quiet music like a lullaby for the children and invite them to pretend to sleep.

Day 4: Making Maracas

Materials

- Tape or record of marching music and cassette player or phonograph
- Paper cups (two per child), rice, crepe-paper streamers, and glue or tape

Preparation

Following the directions for Learning Activity 2, make two or three maracas (shakers).

Learning Activities

1. Show the children the musical instruments you have made. Invite them to play with the instruments and to pass them around to one another.

2. Tell the children that today they get to make their own maracas (shakers) to use as musical instruments. First, demonstrate how to make maracas. Put rice into one paper cup and then tape the edge of that cup to an inverted cup and glue or tape crepe-paper streamers to each end, Figure 8-4. Afterward help the children make their own maracas.

Figure 8-4

3. Play some marching music and invite the children to parade around the room, keeping time to the music with their maracas.

   Note: You may also want to send a letter home and ask parents to give the children old kettle covers for cymbals and old pieces of wood for blocks. In class, show the children how to sand the blocks to make them smooth. Or wrap sandpaper around block and fasten securely. Then invite the children to rub the blocks together to make music.

   Note: Some of the children may startle from the loud noises. Be aware of these children and choose alternative activities.

Additional Activities

1. Pounding. Provide the children with commercial pounding benches or a little carpenter table with a variety of tools. Invite the children to make noise by using play tools, such as hammers, drills, etc., Figure 8-5.

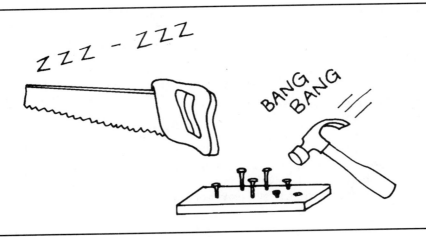

Figure 8-5

2. Sounds. Go outside and invite the children to make a variety of noises with their mouths. Lead the children in making loud noises, soft noises, long noises, short noises, and so on.
3. Listening. Set up a variety of listening centers in the classroom. If possible, include the following: animal sounds, musical instruments, sounds at home, and a story center. Provide tapes and cassette players so that the children can listen independently.

#9   Strike Up the Band!

Objective

By making and playing musical instruments, the children will become more aware of their sense of hearing and the joy of making music.

Day 1: Making Drums

Materials:

- Storybook *The Snow Parade*
- Empty coffee cans, oatmeal boxes, white construction paper, felt-tipped markers or crayons, and short sticks or dowels.
- Tape or record of marching music and cassette player or phonograph

Preparation

Find a copy of *The Snow Parade*. (See the bibliography in Section III.) Prepare to read the story out loud with expression.

Following the directions for Learning Activity 3, make one or two drums, Figure 9-1.

Learning Activities

1. Gather the children around you and read *The Snow Parade*. Afterward invite the children's comments and questions.
   Note: Keep the storybook for use on Day 2.
2. Show the children the drums you made before class. Pass them around

Figure 9-1

and encourage the children to hold them and play a few notes on them.

3. Tell the children that today they get to make drums. Demonstrate how to cover the outside of a container such as a coffee can or oatmeal box with paper. Then give each child a sheet of paper. Encourage the children to use felt-tipped markers or crayons to decorate their papers before taping them to their containers.

4. Give the children sticks or dowels with which to play their drums, or invite them to play their drum with their hands. Put on some marching music. Invite the children to make music with the instruments they made today. Keep the instruments the children made for use on Day 4.

Day 2: Enjoying a Musical Parade

Materials

- Storybook from Day 1
- Rhythm instruments, such as spoons, triangles, tambourines, drums, rattles, maracas, whistles, and so on
- Dress-up clothes
- Tape or record of marching music and cassette player or phonograph

Preparation

Select marching music that the children can easily accompany with their rhythm instruments.

Learning Activities

1. Gather the children around you and read them the story from Day 1. Invite the children to read along with you, Figure 9-2.

Figure 9-2

2. Show the children your collection of musical instruments. Invite each child to choose an instrument to play. Encourage the children to parade around the room and practice playing their instruments.
3. Show the children your collection of dress-up clothes. Invite them to choose some clothes to wear in a musical parade.
   Note: Whenever the children dress in play clothes, try to let the children put on as many things as they can by themselves.
4. When the children are ready, play some marching music and let the children practice marching to the music and playing their instruments.
5. After the children have practiced playing and marching, invite them to parade out into the hallway or into other rooms, Figure 9-3.

   Note: Loud noises sometimes startle children, especially those with cerebral palsy. So prepare them for the "noise" of this lesson. Or remove the children to another classroom where they can enjoy something else while the sounds of this lesson are occurring in your classroom.

Figure 9-3

Note: Keep the drums handy for use on Day 3 and Day 4.

Day 3: Celebrating Animals

Materials

- Storybook *The Boy with a Drum*
- White construction paper (one sheet per child) and felt-tipped markers or crayons
- Construction paper (one sheet per child), hole punch, and lengths of yarn
- Drums from Day 2 (one per child)
- Tape or record of marching music and cassette player or phonograph
- Rubberized animal noses or masks or materials to make masks (optional)

Preparation

Find a copy of *The Boy with a Drum*. (See the bibliography in Section III.) Prepare to read the story out loud with expression.

On each sheet of white construction paper, draw one of the following animals: cat, frog, dog, cow, mouse, horse, duck, chicken, pig, goose, goat, and rooster.

Learning Activities

1. Gather the children around you and read *The Boy with a Drum*. Afterward invite the children's comments and questions. Then tell the children that they are going to have their own parade of animals, just like in the book.
2. Show the children the sheets of white construction paper you prepared before class. Invite the children to choose which animal they want to be. Provide materials so that the children can color their chosen animals.
3. Help each child make a placard to wear by placing the child's sheet of construction paper (on which you have drawn an animal) next to a blank sheet of the same size. Then punch holes at the top right and left sides. Tie yarn through both pieces to make straps that can go across the children's shoulders. Help the children slip their placards on for the parade. Encourage the children to make the sound their animal makes as they wait to join in the parade.
4. Give the children musical instruments to play as they parade. Choose a child to be the boy with the drum in the story or have an assistant take this part. Then read the story a second time as the children parade.
5. Play a cassette or tape of marching music and invite the children to use their instruments to accompany this music as they march again. Encourage the children to develop their own ideas as to how the animals in the parade should line up and march to the music.

> *Note:* The activities of Day 3 help children learn the names of animals. Instead of making animal placards, you may want to buy rubberized animal noses or animal masks. Or you may want to make farm-animal masks. Be sure the eye openings are big enough.

Day 4: Making Tambourines

Materials

- Paper plates (two per child), crayons and felt-tipped markers, beans, crepe-paper streamers, and tape or stapler and staples
- Tape or record of marching music and cassette player or phonograph
- Drums made on Day 1
- Professional rhythm instruments from Day 2
- Xylophone and autoharp (optional)
- Long shoelaces or lengths of yarn (optional)

Preparation

Following the directions for Learning Activity 2, make your own tambourine. Decide whether you will have the children staple, tape, or lace the tambourine parts together. If you want the children to lace them together with yarn, knot one end of each yarn length and tape or glue the other end for easier lacing.

Learning Activities

1. Gather the children around you and show them the tambourine you made. Pass it around so that the children can feel and play it. Tell the children that today they get to make musical instruments like this.
   Fingerplay Fun: "I'm a Fine Musician" from *Let's Do Fingerplays*
2. By following the directions given here, demonstrate how to make a tambourine. Then give each child two paper plates to decorate and some decorating materials, Figure 9-4. When the children have completed their decorating, help each child assemble a tambourine by placing the edges of the two plates together so that the bottom of each plate is facing outward. Staple the edges, leaving a small place through which the children can push some beans. After the children have added the beans to their instrument, finish stapling. Invite the children to staple or tape crepe-paper streamers to their musical instrument.

Figure 9-4

> *Note:* If your class is good at fine-motor activities, you may want to punch holes around the rim of the paper plates instead of stapling them. Then invite the children to string yarn or shoelaces through the holes to hold the tambourines together. Be sure to prepare the yarn by knotting one end of each piece and taping or gluing the other end for easier lacing.

3. Put on some marching music. Invite the children to make music with the tambourines they made today, with the drums they made on Day 1, and with the professional instruments from Day 2.

4. Encourage the children to take home the drums they made on Day 1 and the tambourines they made today.

> *Note:* If you have a xylophone and an autoharp, use this opportunity to play these for the children. Invite the children to try to make some sounds on these instruments as well.

Additional Activities

1. Band. If you are in a school that has band instruction, try to arrange for the children to go and watch a practice.

2. Visitors. Invite the children's parents, grandparents, or siblings who play an instrument to come to class and entertain the children. Or invite a music teacher in your building to play a musical instrument for the children.

part four
Animals

Speech/Language, Developmentally Delayed, and Mentally Handicapped

- Have reinforcement activities at the various centers in animal identification in books or sounds on cassettes.
- Continue matching activities of baby and mother animals.
- Talk about the concepts of *smooth, around, up, down,* and *under* when finger painting.
- Role-playing characters in *The Grouchy Ladybug* can help the children with sequence.
- Use of glue sticks rather than paste can help the child with fine-motor difficulties.
- Reinforce the concepts of color and size in the fishing activity.
- Reinforce the characteristics of fruit.
- Assist the child with fine-motor difficulties spread peanut butter, tuna salad, and egg salad when making the caterpillar.
- Work on the pincer grasp when picking up the marigold seeds.
- When searching for bananas in the hunt, make sure some are hidden at wheelchair level.

Emotionally Disturbed

- Make sure children are well supervised in the egg hatching area.
- The pool of balls may be overstimulating, so the child may need to have a time limit set.

Other Health Impaired

- Caution must be exercised for some children around hay, animals, and food.
- Tactilely defensive children will probably not want to do the footprinting.
- Because of snacks that are sweets, check on special diets for some children.

Blind and Visually Impaired

- Assist the child through action rhymes.
- Try to have small animal models available for the child to hold while stories are being read.

- Have the child describe how his/her face looks when he/she is mad, sad, happy, etc.
- Describe how various fruits look and try to have plastic fruit for the child to hold and explore.
- Assist the child in the banana hunt by giving oral directions to help find the bananas.

Deaf and Hearing Impaired

- Sign the animal name when reading or singing.
- Hearing-impaired children can watch the teacher's lips to make the correct sound.
- Let the child feel the pages of *The Very Busy Spider* for better attention.

#10 Farm Animals

Objective

By taking a field trip, listening to animal sounds, and examining pictures, the children will learn the names of farm animals, recall their sounds, and match the baby animal to its mother.

Day 1: Introducing the Animals

Materials

- Storybook about farm animals

- Plastic farm animals, farm equipment, and barn
- Tape or record of farm animal sounds and cassette player or phonograph
- Toys that makes farm animal sounds (optional)
- Animal crackers

Preparation

Find a storybook that introduces the farm and farm animals. Prepare to read the story out loud with expression.

Find a tape or record of farm animal sounds or a toy that produces these sounds.

Learning Activities

1. Gather the children around you and read the story you have selected. Be sure the children can see the pictures as you read. Afterward invite the children's comments and interact with them.
2. Show the children the plastic farm animals and other farm objects you have collected. Invite the children to play with these and to pretend to be farmers, Figure 10-1.

Figure 10-1

3. Encourage the children to listen to the tape or record of animal sounds and to imitate these sounds.
   Music Note: Songs for Nursery School and More Piggyback Songs
4. Sing and play "Farmer in the Dell" with the children. Provide assistance as necessary and decrease the number of characters in the song if the children's attention waivers.
5. For a snack serve animal crackers.

   Note: Keep all the materials you assembled for this class, with the exception of the animal crackers, for use on Day 3.

Day 2: Visiting Animals

Materials

- Eggs and incubating light

Preparation

Get an incubating light and start incubating a few eggs. Be sure to make plans for where you will take the chickens after they hatch.

Arrange to visit a petting farm or a baby-animal farm. Schedule buses and vans for this trip. Be sure to find plenty of adults to go on the trip with you and the children.

Learning Activities

1. Point out the eggs you have started incubating and explain what will happen to the eggs in twenty-one days. Talk about how the chicks will emerge from the eggs. Invite the children's comments and questions.
   Fingerplay Fun: "When a Little Chicken Drinks" from Let's Do Fingerplays
2. Take the children to a petting farm or a baby-animal farm.
   Note: If you are unable to take the children to a petting farm or a baby-animal farm, invite a guest to bring some baby farm animals to class. Note that baby animals can sometimes be pretty frisky and that the children may be afraid. Also watch carefully when the children hold or pet the animals. Explain how humans must be gentle and caring when they hold and pet animals.

   Note: Children with asthma and allergies need to be given special consideration when taking them to a farm.

Day 3: Playing Farmer

Materials

- Tape or record of farm music and cassette player or phonograph (optional)
- Storybook about a farm and farm animals

- Pictures of farm animals and their babies
- Tape or record of farm animal sounds and cassette player or phonograph
- Toys that makes farm animal sounds (optional)
- Plastic farm animals, equipment, and barn
- Handful of hay or straw
- Blocks (optional)

Preparation

If you do not know any farm songs, practice the three songs listed for Learning Activity 1. Or find a tape or record with farm music on it.

Learning Activities

1. Gather the children around you and sing some farm songs like "Old MacDonald Had a Farm," (on tape or record) and "In the Barnyard."
2. Read the story you selected.
3. Show the children some pictures of farm animals and their babies. Let the children take the lead as to whether they will make animal sounds, match mothers and their babies, or just look at the pictures.
4. Play a tape or record of animal sounds and invite the children to match the sounds to the pictures you showed them in Learning Activity 3.
5. Encourage the children to play in the play area with the farm equipment, animals, and barn, Figure 10-2. If you have a handful of straw or hay, show it to the children and invite them to touch and smell it. Invite the children to pretend to be farm animals.

Figure 10-2

Note: If you do not have a play barn, invite the children to make one with blocks. Before playing with hay or straw in this activity, be sure to ascertain if any children have an allergy to these plants.

Day 4: Imitating Farm Animals

Materials

• Sheets of paper, finger paints, easels, and smocks or old shirts

Preparation

Practice the two action rhymes listed in Learning Activity 2 and Learning Activity 3. Be prepared to demonstrate the actions and the sounds for the rhymes.

Prepare the art area with easels and paints. On sheets of white drawing paper, draw large outlines of farm animals (one animal per child).

Learning Activities

1. Gather the children around you, sing some farm animal songs, and play and sing the "Farmer in the Dell."
2. Invite the children to imitate the actions given in the action rhyme "Act Like an Animal." (See "Action Rhymes" in Section III.) Do this action rhyme several times.
   Note: While doing this action rhyme, encourage the children with physical challenges to participate as much as possible. For instance, encourage them to move their feet for a hop or a jump. You can also move their arms for swimming and flying.
3. Invite the children to make the sounds given in the action rhyme "Sound Like an Animal." (See "Action Rhymes" in Section III.) Do this action rhyme several times.
   Note: Children with physical challenges will enjoy making these animal sounds. Decide whether you want the children to stay in their wheelchairs for this activity or whether you want to position them on the floor.
4. Gather the children in the art area and help each child put on a smock or old shirt for painting. Invite the children to use finger paints to complete the pictures you prepared for them.

Additional Activities

1. Books. Prepare a book of farm-animal pictures. Then invite the children to tell you the sound each animal makes. Write down what the children tell you. When the parents visit the classroom, invite them to look at the book and to share your delight at the sounds their children think an animal

makes. Or make a cassette recording of the sounds the children think the animals make and play this cassette for visiting parents.

2. Puppets. Provide puppets of farm animals for the children to play with.
3. Flannel board. Cut felt farm animals for the children to use on a flannel board. Make sure to include a barn.

#11   Insects and Fish

Objective

While learning about insects and fish, the children will experience sensory and tactile play, identify feelings and concepts, and follow simple directions.

Day 1: Experiencing Sensory Activities

Materials

- Modeling clay/dough, animal cookie cutters, and rolling pins
- Rice or bean table equipped with plastic sheet, rice or beans, scoops, shells, and other containers
- Variety of building blocks
- Large shallow pan, cornstarch, water, and tempera

Preparation

For Learning Activity 1 buy or make some modeling clay/dough. (See "Recipes" in Section III.)

For Learning Activity 2 prepare the rice or bean table and put a plastic sheet on the floor beneath the table for easier cleanup.

Learning Activities

1. Gather the children around a table and invite them to play with modeling clay/dough, cookie cutters, and rolling pins, Figure 11-1. Invite their comments about the texture of the dough.

Figure 11-1

2. Invite the children to play at a rice or a bean table and to feel the texture of the rice or beans.
3. Encourage the children to build with blocks.
4. Gather the children around a pan of cornstarch and help them add water to the pan. Invite them to use their hands to make a paste. Add some tempera paint for color. Talk about the different motions the children are using as they work with the cornstarch (going *up and down*, going *round and round*).

Day 2: Discovering Insects

Materials

- Storybook *The Grouchy Ladybug*
- Paper storybook characters, tongue depressors, and paste or tape
- Large mirror
- Old shirts or painting smocks, sheets of painting paper, easels, and finger paints or tempera and brushes
- Books on insects
- Magnifying glasses

Preparation

Find a copy of *The Grouchy Ladybug.* (See the bibliography in Section III.) Prepare to read the story out loud with expression.

After preparing to read the story, make paper puppets to represent the various characters in the story. Draw and cut out each character and then tape or paste each character to a tongue depressor.

For each child, draw the outline of a ladybug on a sheet of painting paper.

Learning Activities

1. Gather the children around you and read *The Grouchy Ladybug.* Invite the children's comments.
2. Give the children the puppets and invite the children to use the puppets to retell the story you read. Or reread the story yourself and invite the children to hold up their puppets whenever the story mentions that particular character.

   Note: Keep the storybook for use on Days 4, 5, 6, and 8: keep the storybook puppets for use on Day 5.

   Fingerplay Fun: "The Ladybugs" from *Rhymes for Learning Times*
3. Talk to the children about how people look when they are grouchy and when they are happy. Hold up a mirror and invite each child to make a funny face and a grouchy face in front of the mirror, Figure 11-2.

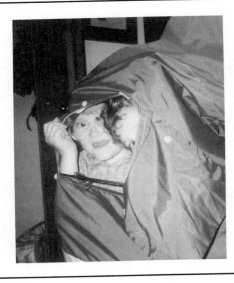

Figure 11-2

4. Direct the children to the easels in the art area. Help the children put on smocks or old shirts. Provide painting materials and invite the children to paint the ladybug pictures that you have prepared.
5. During free play, invite the children to look at your collection of insect books.
6. Demonstrate how to use a magnifying glass. Invite the children to discover any bugs in the room and to look at them through their magnifying glasses.

Day 3: Painting Whales

Materials

- Two eight-foot-long sheets of painting paper, tape, painting smocks or old shirts, blue tempera, and liquid dishwashing soap
- A variety of painting tools, such as brushes, sponges, and rags.
- Magnets and dowels (one each per child), yarn or string, construction paper, paper clips, tape, and a child's plastic wading pool

Preparation

Using your two sheets of paper, make two outlines of a large whale. Mix the blue tempera with a little dishwashing soap for easier cleanup.

Prepare magnetic fishing poles by attaching a small magnet to a length of yarn and then attaching this to a dowel. Make a fishing pole for each child. From construction paper, cut out a variety of fish of varied shapes, sizes, and colors.

Tape a paper clip to each fish. Put the paper fish in a plastic wading pool.

Learning Activities

1. Invite the children to make whales. Tape the two sheets of paper you prepared on the floor. (Because of the art activity for Day 4, be sure that the right side of one whale is facing up and the left side of the other whale is facing up.) Help the children put on smocks or old shirts. Then invite the children to use the painting materials to paint the outlined whales blue.
2. Give each child a fishing pole and invite the children to fish in the plastic wading pool, Figure 11-3.

    Note: Keep the painted whales, the magnetic fishing poles, the paper fish, and the wading pool for use on Days 4 and 7.

Day 4: Stuffing a Whale

Materials

- Storybook from Day 2
- Painted whales from Day 3, stapler, and staples

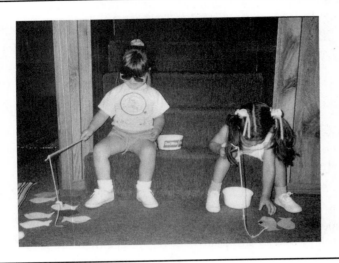

Figure 11-3

- Newspaper or other paper for crumpling
- Scraps of construction paper
- Magnetic fishing poles, paper fish, and plastic pool from Day 3
- Giant magnifying glass

Preparation

Cut out the two whales from Day 3 and staple around the body. Leave the mouth unstapled. Make a ladybug from scraps of construction paper.

Learning Activities

1. Gather the children around you and read *The Grouchy Ladybug.* Then encourage them to participate in a "wanna fight" role-playing exercise.
   Note: Keep the storybook for use on Day 5.
2. Show the children the whale you stapled together. Demonstrate how to crumple paper. Invite the children to crumple paper and stuff the whale through its mouth. As the children work, stress the concept *in* by saying things like "I'm putting the paper *in* the whale" or "Sally is putting the paper *in* the whale."
   After the whale is stuffed, staple shut its mouth and attach to it the ladybug you made. Invite the children to help you hang the whale in the classroom.
3. Divide the class into two groups. Invite Group 1 to fish at the plastic pool or to look. Invite Group 2 to look at insects under the giant magnifying glass. After a short while have the groups shift activities.

Note: Keep the magnetic fishing poles and child's wading pool for use on Days 5 and 7. Keep the prepared fish for use on Day 7.

Day 5: Fishing for Whales

Materials

- Storybook from Days 2 and 4
- Story puppets from Day 2
- Large whale made on Day 4
- Magnetic fishing poles and child's plastic pool from Days 3 and 4
- Construction paper, paper clips, and tape

Preparation

From construction paper, cut out a variety of whales of different sizes, shapes, and colors. On each whale write a set of three directions. For instance, you might print the following: "1. Turn a circle; 2. Touch the floor with your hand; 3. Go get a book." After writing a set of directions on each whale, tape a paper clip to each whale so that the children can fish. Consider whether you want to laminate the whales for future use. Put the whales in the plastic wading pool.

Learning Activities

1. Gather the children around you and give them the puppets representing the characters in the story from Day 2. Then reread the story and invite the children to manipulate the puppets as you read.
   Note: Keep the storybook for use on Day 6.
2. Draw the children's attention to the large whale they made and displayed on Day 4. Tell the children that today they get to fish for whales. Show the children the plastic wading pool in which you have put the paper whales you prepared with directions.
3. Give each child a magnetic fishing pole and invite the children, one by one, to fish for whales. As each child catches a whale, read the directions to the child and invite him or her to perform the directions for the class.
   Note: Keep the directions short and repeat, if necessary, so all children are successful.

   Note: Keep the magnetic fishing poles and the wading pools for use on Day 7.

Day 6: Role Playing

Materials

- Storybook from Day 2

- Mirrors
- Dress-up clothes

Preparation

Consider whether you want to find mirrors made from plastic so that you do not have to worry about the children breaking them and cutting themselves.

Learning Activities

1. Gather the children around you and reread the story.
   Note: Keep the storybook for use on Day 8.
2. Invite the children to role-play the story. One child is the ladybug, and the other children pretend to be the other animals. Continue role-playing as often as a different child wants to be the ladybug.
3. Using mirrors, talk about feelings with the children. Name a feeling, such as grouchy, happy, sad, and mad; invite the children to make the face representing the feeling in front of the mirror.
4. Invite the children to put on some dress-up clothes and pretend, Figure 11-4.

Figure 11-4

Day 7: Matching

Materials

- Magnetic fishing poles, construction-paper fish, and child's plastic wading pool from Day 3
- Construction paper
- Matching activities

Preparation

For Learning Activity 2, using colored construction paper, cut several sets of the characters who appear in the storybook *The Grouchy Ladybug*, Figure 11-5. Be sure to cut out two of each character so that the children can match them. Keep the shapes and sizes of the various characters quite different.

Figure 11-5

Create a number of other matching activities.

Game Idea: Game of Ladybugs—commercially made game, where children collect ladybugs while matching dots on dice.

Learning Activities

1. Gather the children around the wading pool, point out all the fish in the pool, give each child a magnetic fishing pole, and fish with the children. As you and the children fish, emphasize the concepts *big* and *little* by saying things like "Oh, I caught a big fish" or "Mary, you have a little fish on your pole!"
2. Gather the children around you. Show the children the cutouts you made of the storybook characters. Invite the children to match the cutouts. Encourage the children to continue looking until they have matched all the characters.
3. Show the children the other matching activities you have prepared and invite them to match the items.

Note: In a matching activity, always respond positively to a child's efforts, even if the child fails to make a match. Do this by saying something like "Both of your characters are brown!" or "They both have four legs!"

Figure 11-6

Day 8: Making Ladybugs

Materials

- Storybook from Day 2
- Modeling clay/dough, red coloring, black pipe cleaners (one per child), black construction paper, and plastic bags (one per child)

Preparation

Buy or make some red modeling clay/dough. (See "Recipes" in Section III.) Cut each black pipe cleaner in half and cut small dots from black construction paper. Prepare one set of these materials for each child.

Learning Activities

1. Gather the children around you and reread the story.
2. Invite the children to make their own ladybugs to take home. Gather them in the art area. Demonstrate how to make a ladybug by modeling the body out of clay (Figure 11-6), sticking the pipe cleaners into the clay for antennae, and pressing on a number of black dots.
3. Provide each child with modeling clay/dough, pipe cleaners, and black dots. Help the children make their ladybugs. Help the children put their ladybugs in plastic bags for carrying home.
   Fingerplay Fun: "The Ladybugs" from *Rhymes for Learning Times*

Additional Activities

1. Insect hunt. Try to find some ladybugs and let the children look at them under the giant magnifier.

2. Faces. Ask the children to make faces that show how they feel when they are mad, sad, happy, and grouchy. Draw their faces on white drawing paper and invite the children to color their faces.
3. Obstacle course. Set up an obstacle course with a tunnel, barrel, and small bridge, Figure 11-7. At each point along the course have some children portray characters from *The Grouchy Ladybug*. Then invite the other children to pretend to be a ladybug. Encourage them to go through the obstacle course and to visit the characters along the way. Note that the children can become very excited during this activity.

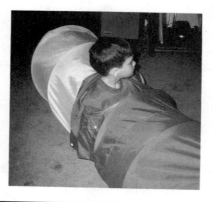

Figure 11-7

Note: To help settle the children, you may want to dim the lights. You may also begin to sing one of their favorite songs and then slowly sit down with them. Lastly, an idea would be to take out a storybook and begin reading.

#12   Caterpillars and Butterflies

Objective

While learning about insects, the children will experience sensory and tactile play, recall events of a story, explore foods of different textures, further develop the concepts *sweet* and *sour*, review the concept *round*, and experience the life cycle of a caterpillar.

Day 1: Experiencing Sensory Activities

Materials

- The materials listed under each of the five sensory stations in "Preparation"

Preparation

Before class prepare the following sensory stations:
- Station A: Touch—a child's swimming pool filled with plastic balls.
- Station B: Touch—cooked spaghetti, tempera paint, white paper, paint shirts.
- Station C: Touch—modeling dough, rolling pins, and cookie cutters.
- Station D: Sight—an array of objects (leaves, buttons, thread spools, feathers, pebbles, blocks, etc.) and magnifying glasses.
- Station E: Touch—a water table with water toys and plastic fruit. Put a plastic sheet on the floor beneath the water table.

Learning Activities

1. Gather the children around you and point out the five sensory stations. Walk with the children from one station to the next and explain what they might do at each station.

   For instance, at Station A invite the children to roll around among the plastic balls in the pool. (Encourage the children to keep all the balls in the pool.)

   At Station B invite the children to swirl the paint on the paper with the spaghetti or to dip the spaghetti into the paint and leave it on the paper to make a design. (Encourage the children to be very creative in this activity.)

   At Station C invite the children to explore the texture of the modeling clay or dough and to use the rolling pins and cookie cutters as they play, Figure 12-1.

   At Station D invite the children to use the magnifying glasses to explore the objects.

   At Station E invite the children to enjoy the water and to play in it with the toys and plastic fruit, Figure 12-2.

2. As the children roam freely from station to station, go around the room and enjoy their delight in these sensory experiences.

Figure 12-1

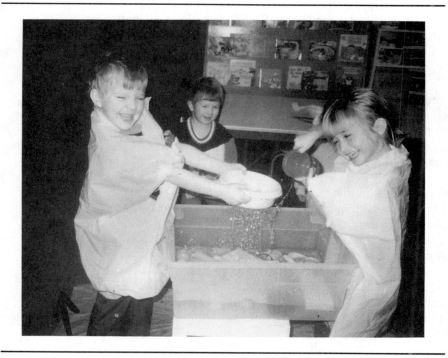

Figure 12-2

Note: Assign an adult to each station to help the visually-hearing impaired children experience all the activities. Have wedges, standers, corner chairs, and assistants at each station to help the children who are physically challenged. Also try to follow each child's lead in the activity that each may choose and let the child initiate the interaction.

Day 2: Making a Caterpillar

Music Note: For a variety of rhymes and singing games relating to caterpillars and butterflies, use *Creative Movement for the Developing Child.*

Materials

- Storybook *The Very Hungry Caterpillar*
- Plastic fruit to represent the fruit in the story
- Old shirts or painting smocks, paper plates, green tempera, and sponge pieces
- Staples and stapler and two pipe cleaners
- Egg carton (optional)
- Three-inch circles cut from colored construction paper, glue or paste, and two pipe cleaners per child (optional)

Preparation

Find a copy of *The Very Hungry Caterpillar.* Prepare to read the story out loud.

After preparing to read the story, use several colors of construction paper to make three-inch circles. Glue these together in a row to make a caterpillar body, Figure 12-3. Then add pipe cleaners for antennae.

Figure 12-3

If you wish to have the children make individual caterpillars, prepare several three-inch circles for each child.

Learning Activities

1. Gather the children around you and read *The Very Hungry Caterpillar*. Invite the children's comments. Inquire as to what they like to eat. What are yummy foods and what are yucky foods?
   Note: Keep the storybook for use on Days 3, 4, 5, 6, and 8.
2. Show the children the plastic fruit you have collected and reread the story. As the caterpillar in the story eats each piece of fruit, hold up the plastic piece. Invite the children to touch the plastic pieces and the book. They might even pretend to feed one another.
3. Tell the children that today they are going to make their own very hungry caterpillar. Take the children to the art area and point out the material there. Show the children the caterpillar you made before class, Figure 12-4.

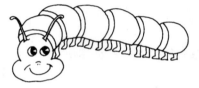

Figure 12-4

4. Help the children put on smocks or old shirts. Demonstrate how to dip a piece of sponge into the green tempera and dab it onto a paper plate. Then give each child a paper plate and invite the children to paint it.
5. While the plates are drying, invite the children to retell the story of *The Very Hungry Caterpillar*. Make sure the plastic fruit is out.
6. When the plates are dry, staple them together in a row to make a caterpillar. For the head of the caterpillar, overlap the staple of two of the plates, so that a mouth is formed by the curvature of the two plates overlapping. Use two pipe cleaners to make antennae. Mount the caterpillar between two pieces of an egg carton or simply mount it on the chalkboard.
   Note: Keep the caterpillar for use on Days 3, 6, and 7.
7. If time permits, invite the children to make their own caterpillars to take home. Provide three-inch circles cut from colored construction paper, paste, and pipe cleaners. If some children do not want to make caterpillars, invite them to play with the plastic fruit and to retell the story.

Day 3: Feeding a Caterpillar

Materials

- Storybook from Day 2

- Class caterpillar from Day 2
- Basket containing small miscellaneous items (edible and inedible), such as banana, apple, leaf, orange, comb, brush, paper cup, rock, and so on

Preparation

Practice the voice you will use for the caterpillar as it "eats" the miscellaneous items.

Learning Activities

1. Gather the children around you and reread *The Very Hungry Caterpillar*. Invite the children's comments.
2. Get the class caterpillar that the children made on Day 2 and bring out a basket filled with the edible and inedible items you collected. Tell the children that today they get to feed the very hungry caterpillar.
   Note: Make sure to move the caterpillar around, so all children are able to feed it, especially those children in wheelchairs.
3. Have the children, one by one, feed the caterpillar by taking items from the basket. As the children do feed it a correct item, you will want to give positive feedback like, "Megan fed the caterpillar a juicy, red apple. The caterpillar really likes it!" Or for some of the younger children you might just say "The caterpillar likes red apples." If a child tries to feed the caterpillar an inedible object, like a comb, shake the caterpillar's head and say something like "Caterpillars don't like combs!" Do not tell them that the caterpillar doesn't eat combs but reinforce by saying "Please give me a banana or a juicy red apple." The children will be delighted that the caterpillar is talking to them and will be reinforced as to what is healthy to feed the caterpillar.

Day 4: Eating Caterpillar Food

Materials

- Storybook *The Very Hungry Caterpillar*
- Different fruits from the story
- Strainer to wash the fruit before eating
- Knife for cutting

Preparation

You can wash the fruit before or let the children help with the task when the lesson begins.

Learning Activities

1. Begin by having the children recall the things that the caterpillar ate in the story. While the children are doing this, write down their responses for all

to see. You can then show them a picture of the fruit or the plastic fruit.

2. When the children feel that they have all the fruit from the story, have one of the children open the book and name the fruit the caterpillar has eaten. Check off on the list all the fruit they were able to recall.

3. Place the fruit on the table and allow the children to name the ones that they know. Let them hold it carefully. You may want to discuss how it feels, if it is soft or hard, what a peeling is, is it fuzzy, etc.

4. Have the children decide which fruits will need to be washed. Let the children help wash the fruit.

5. Begin tasting the fruit in the order they are in the book. Cut the fruit into pieces for the children to taste.

6. Discuss if the fruit is juicy, how it tastes, if it has a peeling, if it has seeds, etc.

7. Make sure you leave time for the children to talk about what their favorite fruit was and maybe even the one that they liked the least.

> *Note*: Children with feeding problems will have to have the fruit substituted with things that they can tolerate. For instance, applesauce for the apples, strawberry juice for strawberries, etc. The juice may need to be weighted with rice cereal for them.

Day 5: Eating a Caterpillar

Materials

- Storybook from Day 2
- Bread (one slice for each child)
- Knife or children's scissors
- Two licorice sticks
- Tuna salad, egg salad, or peanut butter and jelly to spread on the bread
- Plates and napkins

Preparation

Practice cutting a piece of bread into a circle. Set up the food and eating items on a long table. Decide which spread you will use on the bread—tuna salad, egg salad, or peanut butter—and prepare it.

Practice saying the action rhyme "The Roly-Poly Caterpillar." (See "Action Rhymes" in Section III.)

Learning Activities

1. Gather the children around you and reread the storybook from Day 2. Invite comments. Today the children may want to help read it as the story is very familiar to them now.

2. Tell the children that today they are going to make a caterpillar out of bread. Gather the children around the snack table. Give each child a slice

of bread and allow the children to help you cut each slice into a circle. You may also want to use a round cookie cutter to cut the bread.

3. Arrange the circles of bread into the body and head of the caterpillar. Use two licorice sticks or two sticks of celery or carrot for the antennae. If the children are adept at spreading food on bread, invite them to help you spread the tuna salad, egg salad, or peanut butter and jelly on the caterpillar's bread body.

   Note: Lap boards are good for the children in wheelchairs. Children with visual impairments should be talked through this process.

4. Finally, invite the children to eat their bread caterpillar for snack.

Day 6: Making a Cocoon

Materials

- Storybook from Day 2, or choose another one about caterpillars or butterflies
- Class caterpillar from Day 2
- Small edible and inedible items from Day 3
- Large piece of paper or a blanket
- Several rolls of tape
- Giant magnifying glass

Preparation

Plan where you want to take the children on a caterpillar hunt.

Learning Activities

1. Gather the children around you and have one of the children read *The Very Hungry Caterpillar* or another book on caterpillars or butterflies.
2. Feed the caterpillar again like you did on Day 3.
3. Explain to the children that the caterpillar takes long naps in cocoons. Then invite the children to wrap their large class caterpillar into a cocoon. Help them wrap the caterpillar in a large sheet of paper or a blanket. Provide tape so that the children can tape the cocoon around the caterpillar. Then put the cocoon away and tell the children that they can check on it tomorrow.

   Music Note: "Spinning My Cocoon" from *Creative Movement for the Developing Child*
4. Take the children outside on a nature walk. Look for caterpillars and cocoons. Invite the children to use small magnifying glasses as they explore. They may find some things that they want to look at under the giant magnifying glass.

   Idea: Butterfly garden kits are available in many catalogs. They come with a feeding kit and a coupon for larvae.

Day 7: Making Butterflies

Materials

- Cocoon and class caterpillar from Day 6
- Various colors of tempera in large shallow containers, sheet of plastic, white paper, soapy water, towels
- Staple and stapler, pipe cleaners, yarn or thread
- Tissue paper and pipe cleaners
- Beads and strings
- Nontoxic modeling dough or clay and a butterfly cookie cutter

Preparation

Following the instructions in Learning Activity 3, make your own footprint butterfly to show the children. Make a butterfly from tissue paper and pipe cleaners. Make a caterpillar out of beads and string. Make a butterfly out of modeling clay.

Learning Activities

1. Gather the children around the cocoon they made on Day 6. Invite them to investigate the cocoon to see if the caterpillar is still sleeping.
2. Gather the children in the art area. Have them take off their shoes. Take off your shoes and show them how to step into the shallow trays of tempera and make colorful footprints on the white paper. Invite each child to make two sets of footprints. Afterward help the children wash the tempera from their feet.

   Note: Children who are tactilely defensive may not want to participate in this activity. Children in wheelchairs will need to have you bring the paint to them and then put their prints on the paper.
3. Show the children the footprint butterfly you made before class, Figure 12-5. Then demonstrate how to make a footprint butterfly. Cut out your own footprints, stapling together the outer edges of the footprints so that the small toes come together. Attach pipe cleaners for antennae. Attach yarn or string to the butterfly and hang them from the ceiling.

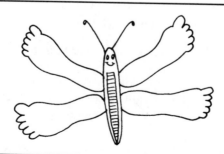

Figure 12-5

4. Help each child cut out his or her two sets of footprints and make two butterflies, one to hang in the classroom and one to take home.
5. As the children wait their turns for cutting, invite them to do one of the following activities: use tissue paper and pipe cleaners to make butterflies; use beads and string to make a caterpillar; cut butterflies from modeling clay.
   Note: Bead stringing is a good fine-motor activity.
6. Encourage the children to take home the second footprint butterfly that they made.

Day 8: A Butterfly Appears

Materials

- A large colorful butterfly
- White cakes
- Frosting
- Licorice
- Storybook *The Very Hungry Caterpillar*

Preparation

Make sure the butterfly is made out of large paper. It should be colorful, like in the story. Put the cocoon wrapping on the floor and remove the caterpillar to another area, out of sight of the children. You may want to have the children help you mix the cakes if you have an oven available to you. If you do not, bake the cakes the night before and then just let the children help you decorate.

Learning Activities

1. Ask the children to recall what happens to the caterpillar at the end of the story. Then show them the book. Invite them over to see the class caterpillar. Show them that the outer covering of the caterpillar is on the floor. Ask them if they see the caterpillar and pretend to look around. Do so until one of the children sees the butterfly.
2. Do "The Roly-Poly Caterpillar" again and have the children fly over to the snack table.
3. Have the children help stir the cake mix. Read the directions as you go along. Let each child help mix it. Pour it into greased pans and put it in the oven. Have other activities planned while the cake is baking. If the cakes are baked the previous night, the children can help decorate the cakes.
4. Cut the cakes into butterfly wings and a long narrow piece for the body in the middle. Then have the children help frost the cake. The frosting can

be commercially made, or you may want to have the children help you make it. When the cake is completely frosted, have the children help decorate with colored sugar or sprinkles to make it more colorful. Put two pieces of licorice for antennae or you may want to use pipe cleaners.

5. Eat and enjoy!

Additional Activities

1. Egg carton caterpillars. You will need half of a row of an egg carton. The children can paint the carton and then add pipe cleaners for the antennae and feet.
2. Pom-pom caterpillars. The children can glue various colored pom-poms onto paper in a row to make a caterpillar. You can then have them draw the antennae on with a black marker. This is a nice texture for them to experience.
3. Bug catchers. Using small milk cartons, cut away two sides. Then use masking tape to secure fine mesh screen over the openings. Close up the top of the milk carton and staple. Then it is happy bug hunting or caterpillar hunting.
4. Caterpillar matching. This is a good time to check on the children's ability to match colors. Have various caterpillars made and then make sure that there are two of each kind that match. Then have the children select the two that do match. If you prefer, you can match butterflies.

13   Spiders

Objective

By participating in sensory and interactive play, the children will become more aware of the wonder of the world around them.

Day 1: Experiencing Sensory Play

Materials

- Small containers, potting soil, scoops for digging, water, sprinkling can, plastic sheet, and marigold seeds
- Child's plastic wading pool and plastic balls of varied sizes
- Bubble solution and bubble blower
- Modeling clay/dough, rolling pins, and animal cookie cutters
- Rice table equipped with plastic sheet, bins of rice and scoops, shells, other containers, small farm animals, and small plastic bugs

Preparation

Set up all the sense stations before class begins. Be sure to have an adequate number of aides to help the children as they work separately at the various stations.

- At Station 1 put a plastic sheet under a table for easier cleanup. Then put all the equipment for planting marigolds on the table.
- At Station 2 put the plastic balls in the wading pool.
- At Station 3 have a commercial or homemade bubble solution. (See "Recipes" in Section III.) Also, have bubble blowers available.
- At Station 4 have commercial or homemade modeling clay/dough. (See "Recipes" in Section III.)
- At Station 5 prepare a rice table by placing a sheet of plastic under the table for easier cleanup and by having rice and other items for play, Figure 13-1.

Figure 13-1

Learning Activities

1. Begin the sensory time by gathering the children around you. Explain each of the five stations you have set up. Then invite the children to participate in as many of the activities as they like. Allow the children to move freely about the room.

   At Station 1 demonstrate how to plant marigold seeds by putting dirt in a container and then planting some seeds. Cover the seeds with dirt and add water. After your demonstration, invite the children to plant their own seeds. When the children finish their planting, direct them to put their plants by a window for light.

   Note: As the children pick up the small marigold seeds in their hands, note their fine-motor development.

      Keep the plants in the classroom until they bloom. Invite the children to use a small sprinkling can to water the plants each day. Assign one student per week to be the watering person. Note that watering need not be messy if you put the children's containers in a shallow pan that will hold the excess water. If you have a very young group, you may want to assume the responsibility for watering the plants each day.

      For this activity, lap boards are good for children in wheelchairs.

2. At Station 2 invite the children to roll around in the pool and feel the plastic balls touch their bodies. Caution the children to watch out for other children and to keep the balls in the pool.

3. At Station 3 invite the children to use the bubble solution to blow bubbles. Or blow bubbles for them and invite them to break the bubbles.

   Note: You will want to be aware that some children are unable to blow bubbles. Nevertheless these children may enjoy the bubbles falling gently on them. Use caution with the children who cannot tolerate too much touch because the bubbles may not be a pleasant experience for them.

4. At Station 4 encourage the children to experiment with the materials you have provided for playing with modeling clay/dough.

5. At Station 5 invite the children to experiment at the rice table.

Day 2: Discovering Spiders and Other Animals

Materials

- Storybook *The Very Busy Spider*
- Play barn and plastic farm animals
- Toys that makes farm animal sounds or a tape or record of farm animal sounds and a cassette player or phonograph

Preparation

Find a copy of *The Very Busy Spider*. (See the bibliography in Section III.) Prepare to read the story out loud with expression.

If purchasing a toy that makes farm animal sounds is not possible, find a record or tape of farm animal sounds and set up a cassette player or phonograph in the play area.

Learning Activities

1. Gather the children around you and read *The Very Busy Spider.* Invite the children's comments and encourage them to feel the book as you read it. Invite the children to imitate the sounds the animals in the story make.
   Note: Keep the storybook for use on Days 3, 4, 5, and 7.
2. Gather the children in the play area and show them the farm toys you have collected. Invite them to play with the toys and to pretend to be farmers and animals.
   Note: Keep the plastic farm animals for use on Days 3, 4, and 5.
3. Gather the children around the cassette player or phonograph and invite them to stretch out on the floor. Encourage the children to listen to the sounds that farm animals make.
   Note: You will want to position children in wheelchairs on a mat with a wedge or a bolster.

Day 3: Visiting Farm Animals

Materials

- Storybook from Day 2
- A tape or record of the song "In the Barnyard" by Raffi and a cassette player or phonograph
- Pictures of farm animals and plastic farm animals
- Play barn
- Modeling clay/dough, rolling pins, and animal cookie cutters
- Plastic zoo animals
- Storybooks about farm animals
- Tapes or records of farm animal songs and a cassette player or phonograph

Preparation

Buy commercial modeling clay/dough or make some. (See "Recipes" in Section III.)

Set up a listening center where the children can listen to tapes or records of farm animal songs. Have an aide stationed at this center to help the children use the cassette player or phonograph.

Learning Activities

1. Gather the children around you and reread the story from Day 2. Invite the children's comments. Encourage the children to talk about farms they have visited.

2. Listen to the song "In the Barnyard."
3. Show the children pictures of farm animals and plastic farm animals. Encourage the children to identify the animals and to make the sound each animal makes. Describe the animals so the visually-impaired children are receiving input.
4. Give each child one of the plastic animals or animal pictures. Then direct the children to the play area and invite them to play with the play barn and the animals.
5. Point out the table on which you have put the modeling clay/dough, rolling pins, and cookie cutters. Encourage the children to experiment with these things. Use lap boards for children in wheelchairs.
6. If the children are old enough to know where animals live, give them some plastic zoo animals and some plastic farm animals or pictures of these animals, Figure 13-2. Invite the children to decide which animals belong on the farm and which in the zoo.

Figure 13-2

7. Invite the children to look through the storybooks to find stories about farm animals.
8. Encourage the children to go to the listening center and listen to farm animal songs.

> *Note:* Keep the storybook, the plastic farm animals, and the animal pictures for use on Day 4.
> *Game Idea:* Puzzles of farm animals

Day 4: Role-Playing

Materials

• Plastic animals or animal pictures and the storybook from Day 2
• Painting shirts or smocks, easel boards, black and white crayons (one of each for each child), white painting paper (one sheet per child), brushes, and watercolor wash

- Paper (one sheet per child), watercolors, and brushes
- Farm animal templates (optional)

Preparation

Find plastic animals or animal pictures that represent characters in the story.

Prepare a watercolor wash for the children to use as they do their magic pictures in Learning Activity 3.

On sheets of white construction paper prepare the outline of a farm animal for each child. If some children in your classroom are old enough and skilled enough to trace, make or buy farm animal templates for them to use during this class.

Learning Activities

1. Give each child a plastic animal or a picture of one of the animals in the story. As you reread the story, invite the children to role-play it. After reading, allow the children to interact on their own with the farm animals and the spider.
2. Direct the children to the easel boards in the art area. Help the children put on their painting shirts or smocks. Then demonstrate how to do a magic picture: Use a black crayon to draw a spider on a sheet of drawing paper; use a white crayon to draw a spider web on the paper; use the watercolor wash to cover the web and spider. With the children, exclaim over how the web appeared as if by magic.
3. Give each child a sheet of white paper and a black crayon. Encourage the children to use the crayon to draw a black spider on their paper. Give each child a white crayon and invite the children to use it to draw a spider web over their picture. Then invite the children to use the watercolor wash and paintbrushes to make the spider's web appear as if by magic.
4. Give each child a sheet of paper on which you have drawn a farm animal. Invite the children to use watercolors and brushes to paint their animals.

> *Note:* For the activities in the art area, seat children who cannot stand at tables or give them lap boards. For Learning Activity 4, if some children want to draw their own animals, provide them with crayons and paper. For older children who can trace, provide templates of farm animals.

> *Note:* Keep the storybook, the plastic animals, and the animal pictures for use on Day 5.

Day 5: Finding Spiders

Materials

- Storybook from Day 2

- Plastic farm animals or pictures of them
- Plastic, rubber, or paper spiders
- Tape or record of the song "There's a Spider on Your Head" by Raffi and cassette player or phonograph
- Paper bag, basket, or large jar
- Jar with lid

Preparation

Purchase a large quantity of plastic or rubber spiders or make spiders from construction paper. Laminate or put clear plastic on these homemade spiders.

Prepare your assistants for their task of hiding the spiders after Learning Activity 3 once you and the children are out of the room.

Put air holes in the lid of a jar.

Learning Activities

1. Give the children the plastic farm animals or pictures of the animals in the story from Day 2. Then reread the story and invite the children to manipulate the animals as you read.
2. Give the children the rubber, plastic, or paper spiders and invite them to pretend with them.
3. Play the song "There's a Spider on Your Head" and invite the children to manipulate their spiders as they listen to the song. Afterward collect the spiders and give them to your aides.
4. Take the children out of the classroom so that your aides can hide the spiders in the classroom and halls.
5. When you return to the classroom, explain to the children that today they get to hunt for spiders. As the children search, comment that they are looking *over, under, on,* and *by.* As the children find the spiders, put them in a paper bag, a jar, or a basket.
6. Take the children into the hall to look for spiders and bugs that are alive. Place any you find in a jar with air holes in the lid. When you return to the room, put the spiders and bugs in a safe place.

   Note: Keep the jar of bugs and the tape or record of "There's a Spider on Your Head" for use on Day 6. Keep the storybook for use on Day 7.

Day 6: Exploring Spiders

Materials

- Tape or record of "There's a Spider on Your Head" by Raffi from Day 5
- Magnifying glasses, the jar of live insects from Day 5, and a giant magnifier

- Tree branches, black construction paper, and yarn
- Itsy-Bitsy Spider Game (commercially made and an optional activity)

Preparation

Look at Learning Activity 3. If your group has the fine-motor development to make spider webs, check to be sure that they will be able to find fallen tree branches by your school. If branches are not available by the school grounds, bring a small branch to school for each child. Cut out a spider for each child from black construction paper. Cut a length of yarn for each child to use to make a spider web.

Learning Activities

1. Play the tape or record of "There's a Spider on Your Head." Invite the children to sing and hum along.
2. Give the children small magnifying glasses and a giant magnifier and invite them to look at the live insects they found on Day 5. Talk to the children about the number of legs on their insects, the colors, and the difference in sizes. Use the words *big* and *small*.
3. Tell the children that today they get to make spider webs. Take the children outside so that each can find a small branch. Or, give each child a branch. Demonstrate how to wrap yarn around a branch to create a web.
4. Invite the children to use yarn and their branches to make spider webs. Then give each child a paper spider to put in the webs.

Day 7: Being a Spider

Materials

- Storybook from Day 2
- Hula hoops (one per child)
- Oven or microwave, aprons or smocks, cake mix and required ingredients, measuring cups, mixing bowl, spoon, and two eight-inch cake pans or cupcake papers

Preparation

Read through Learning Activity 3. Then consider what directions you can give to the children as they pretend to be spiders in their hula-hoop webs.

Purchase a cake mix for making cupcakes or two eight-inch cakes. Prepare to bake the cake or cupcakes in the classroom. If you will be using a microwave, be sure to purchase a mix that can be baked in a microwave. However, if baking at school is not feasible, be ready to bake the mix at home.

Learning Activities

1. Gather the children around you and reread the story from Day 2.

2. Give each child a hula hoop and explain that this hoop is their very own spider web. Invite them to be spiders, to put their hoops on the floor, and to get inside their web. Invite the children to play at being spiders for a short while.

3. After the children are comfortable with their webs (hula hoops), tell them that you are going to give them some directions to follow. Depending on your group, give one-, two-, or three-step directions. For example, for a one-step direction you might say, "Jump out of your web!" For a two-step direction you might say, "Jump out of your web and then jump back into your web!" For a three-step direction you might say, "Clap your hands, blink your eyes, and twitch your nose inside your web!"

   Note: Give some directions that children in wheelchairs can follow, like "Blink your eyes in your web!" and "Clap your hands inside your web!"

4. Invite the children to come up with other directions they might give for using their hula-hoop webs.

5. Invite the children to help you make two eight-inch cakes or some cupcakes from a cake mix. Gather the children in the cooking area and invite them to help you open the box, measure the ingredients, pour the mixture into the mixing bowl, and mix. If you don't have an oven or a microwave to use, tell the children that you will bake the mix at home and bring the cakes or cupcakes to class on Day 8.

Day 8: Making Edible Spider Webs

Materials

- Painting shirts or smocks
- Styrofoam balls (one per every two children), brushes, black tempera, liquid dishwashing soap, black pipe cleaners (one per child), lengths of string (one per child), and envelopes (one per child)
- Cake or cupcakes baked on Day 7, white frosting, black frosting, spatulas or plastic knives, black paper or black candy (one piece per child), paper plates, and napkins

Preparation

Cut each styrofoam ball in half. For each child, cut a pipe cleaner into six equal pieces and put this set of "spider legs" into an envelope. Then following the directions in Learning Activity 2, make a sample spider.

Mix the black tempera with liquid dishwashing soap for easier clean-up. Following the directions in Learning Activities 2 and 4, make a sample spider.

From black paper or black candy, cut a spider for each child.

Figure 13-3

Learning Activities

1. Show the children the spider you prepared before class. Invite the children to touch it and to bounce it around by jerking the attached string.
2. Gather the children in the art area. Help each child put on a painting shirt or smock. Give each child half a styrofoam ball and demonstrate how to paint it with tempera. Help the children paint their styrofoam balls.
3. While the painted styrofoam dries, invite the children to help you frost the cakes or cupcakes with white frosting. After using this frosting, drizzle a thin black frosting over the cake in circles. Then using a knife, gently spread the black frosting outward to create a webbed look. Give each child a small paper or candy spider and invite the children to place these on the cake or cupcakes. Then eat and enjoy, Figure 13-3.
4. After the children finish their snack, give each child an envelope containing a set of pipe-cleaner spider legs. Show the children how to stick the six pieces of pipe cleaner into a painted styrofoam ball to make spider legs. Help the children attach a length of string to each spider. Hang the spiders in the classroom or encourage the children to take their spiders home.

Additional Activities

1. Barn. On a large sheet of paper, draw a barn and display the drawing on a classroom wall. Provide painting materials (brushes, sponges, tempera, finger paints, and so on) and invite the children to paint the barn. Then give the children pictures of farm animals and invite them to glue these to the barn after it is dry.

2. Webs. Give each child a piece of construction paper and some glue. Show the children how to squeeze the glue onto the paper in circles so as to form webs. Then demonstrate how to sprinkle colored sand or corn-meal over the glue. Shake off the excess. When the glue has dried, put a black paper spider within the webs.

3. Farm animals. Buy commercially made cardboard farm animals that the children can paint. After the figures dry, invite the children to wear them. Encourage the children to pretend to be the animal they are wearing and to practice the animal's sounds.

4. Song. Teach the children the action rhyme "Itsy-Bitsy." (See "Action Rhymes" in Section III.)

#14 Zoo Animals

Objective

By visiting the zoo and working with play animals, the children will ex-pand their understanding of the animal world.

Day 1: Discovering Zoo Animals

Materials

- Storybook *The Wild Kingdom*
- Plastic or paper zoo animals (one per child)
- Tape or record of wild-animal sounds and cassette player or phonograph
- Materials for "Elephant Feely" box and "Seal"
- White construction paper, black felt-tipped marker, paste or glue sticks, and small pictures of zoo animals
- Animal crackers, juice, and paper cups
- (Optional) Childcraft has a "Zoo Play Set." It includes twenty-one animals and one zoo keeper

Preparation

Find a copy of *The Wild Kingdom*. (See the bibliography in Section III.) Prepare to read the story out loud with expression.

If you do not have plastic zoo animals, cut some from colored construction paper.

Make an "Elephant Feely" box and a "Seal." (See directions given under "Classroom Equipment" in Section III.)

For each child, prepare a sheet of construction paper to represent a cage by drawing spaced, vertical black lines on the paper.

Learning Activities

1. Gather the children around you and read *The Wild Kingdom*. Invite the children's comments and talk about the animals in the story.
2. Give the children the plastic or paper zoo animals and invite them to pretend with them.
   Music Note: Zoo songs from *Piggyback Songs for Infants and Toddlers*
3. Put on the tape or record of wild-animal sounds. As each sound is made on the tape or record, point out the appropriate animal on the animal pictures or point to the appropriate plastic animal a child is holding. Encourage the children to imitate the animal sounds.
4. Talk about which zoo animals are big and which are small.
5. Put out the "Elephant Feely" box and the "Seal" that you prepared before class. Invite the children to play with them.
   Note: Keep the "Elephant Feely" box for use on Day 3.
6. Have stuffed animals for the children to use in pretend play.
7. Direct the children to the art area. Give each child a sheet of prepared paper representing a cage, an animal picture, and some paste or a glue

stick. Invite the children to paste their animal in the cage. Talk about modern zoos in which animals are not in cages. Invite the children's comments on this. Encourage the children to take their work home with them.

8. For a snack, share animal crackers and juice.

Day 2: Becoming Monkeys

Materials

- Storybook *Monkey Face*
- Painting shirts or smocks, green tempera, liquid dishwashing detergent, brushes, and large sheet of paper
- Brown construction paper and lengths of laundry rope
- Bananas, peanut butter, and spoons

Preparation

Find a copy of *Monkey Face*. (See the bibliography in Section III.) Prepare to read the story out loud with expression.

Figure 14-1

On a large sheet of paper draw a tree trunk, Figure 14-1. Mix the tempera with the detergent for easier cleanup.

Prepare your assistants to hide bananas in the classroom after you and the children leave the classroom at the end of Learning Activity 3.

For each child, cut out a pair of monkey ears and attach these to a circular strip of paper that will fit about the child's head. From laundry rope make a monkey tail for each child. Make the tail long enough to tie around the child's waist and to touch the floor.

Note: You can attach the tail to the back of a child's wheelchair.

Learning Activities

1. Gather the children around you and read *Monkey Face.* Invite the children's comments.
    Fingerplay Fun: Zoo Action Rhymes from *Rhymes for Learning Times*
2. Direct the children to the art area and help each child put on a painting shirt or smock. Show the children the large sheet of paper with the tree trunk on it. Tell the children that they are going to make a tree that a monkey could sit in. Brush tempera on one of your hands and then put a handprint on the tree to make the first leafy mass. Talk about how your handprint looks like a leaf.
3. One by one, paint the children's hands and encourage them to make handprints on the tree. After the painting dries, display it on a classroom wall.
    Note: Some of the children will not want to get their hands dirty with paint. Encourage, but do not force.
4. Take the children for a walk outside the classroom so that your aides can hide bananas around the room.
5. When you and the children return to the classroom, show them the monkey ears and tails you prepared. Put a set of monkey ears on your own head and attach a tail by tying the rope around your waist. Ask the children how a monkey would act and then pretend to be a monkey for the children.
6. Help the children put on their monkey ears and tails. Then tell them that you have hidden bananas in the classroom. Invite them to go on a banana hunt.
    Note: If some children do not want to wear the monkey ears and tails, simply encourage them to participate without these accessories.
7. After the children complete their hunt, invite them to the snack area and encourage them to eat their banana. Be sure to have some extra bananas for any child who did not find one.
8. Tell the children that monkeys like peanuts, too. Then invite the children to taste some peanut butter.

Day 3: Making Elephants

Materials

*   "Elephant Feely" box from Day 1
*   Large paper plates, gray construction paper, pink construction paper,

paste or glue sticks, unsharpened pencil, felt-tipped markers or crayons, black or brown construction paper (optional)

Preparation

Cut each child a set of elephant ears from gray construction paper. Cut two smaller pink ears and a long strip of gray paper for each child. If you want the children to add eyelashes to their elephant faces, cut a two-inch-long strip of black or brown construction paper for each child.

Following the direction in Learning Activity 2, make a sample elephant face.

Learning Activities

1. Invite the children to feel the objects in the "Elephant Feely Box."
2. Direct the children to the art area. Show the children the elephant face you made. Pass the face around and let the children examine it. Demonstrate how to make an elephant face by attaching to a paper plate two large gray circles for ears and then pasting two smaller pink ears onto the gray ones. Paste the strip of gray to the middle of the face to serve as the elephant's trunk. Roll the trunk around an unsharpened pencil so that it is flexible. Make eyes with felt-tipped markers. If you wish, make eyelashes for the elephant.

Figure 14-2

3. After your demonstration, help the children make their own elephant faces to take home, Figure 14-2.
4. Gather the children around you and teach them the action rhyme "Elephant in the Spider's Web." (See "Action Rhymes" in Section III.)

Day 4: Visiting a Zoo

Materials

- Money for entrance fee at the zoo or petting farm

Preparation

Be sure to get parents' permission for going on this field trip. Have plenty of adults to help you manage the trip.

Learning Activities

1. Take the children to a zoo in your area or to a petting farm.
2. As the children visit each animal, encourage them to "talk" to the animals by making the appropriate animal sounds.

Additional Activities

1. Mural. Draw large zoo animals on sheets of white paper and invite the children to paint them.
2. Dress-up. Provide zoo-animal masks or rubberized noses and invite the children to wear them and pretend to be in a zoo, Figure 14-3.

Figure 14-3

part five
Storybooks

Speech/Language, Developmentally Delayed, and Mentally Handicapped

- Keep the directions simple for Stone Soup, so that the child meets with success.
- Develop the concepts of *smooth, rough,* and *hard* in the learning stations.
- Write out the recipe in large print for all the children to see.
- Reinforce the colors and color words in the learning centers.
- Sewing cards are good practice before the lacing activity.
- Obstacle course is good for language expansion of the concepts *in, out, on, under,* etc., as the child moves through the course.

Multihandicapped and Orthopedically Impaired

- Allow for enough space in the role-playing area for wheelchairs.
- Make sure bears hidden in the hunt are at wheelchair level.
- You may need to position children in chairs for maximum participation when making dough. Lap boards may be used and then place the bowl on the board for the child to help mix.
- Large puppet patterns and holes for lacing may help the child who is physically challenged.

Emotionally Disturbed

- Plan ahead and make sure the child meets with success in the bear hunt. The child may become frustrated and then the activity would be lost and the child will just run around.

Other Health Impaired

- Diet is important to follow when serving Stone Soup. Also be aware of allergies.

Blind and Vision Impairments

- Let the child feel vegetables as they are described.

- Help the child follow along with the other children when doing the various rhymes in the unit.
- Assistance is needed to help guide the child through the obstacle course. Make sure to give good verbal input.

Deaf and Hearing Impairment

- Call attention to the bright pictures in *Brown Bear, Brown Bear* to keep the child's attention.

#15   Stone Soup

Objective

By responding to the storybook *Stone Soup*, the children will become more skilled at identifying vegetables, sorting, and following directions.

Day 1: Making Stone Soup

Materials

- Storybook *Stone Soup*
- Play stove or large cardboard box
- Felt-tipped markers and crayons (optional)
- Soup kettle, spoons, aprons, hot pads, vegetable brush, plastic fruit and vegetables, and stones
- Play ironing board and iron, blender, tea kettle, and other kitchen utensils and tools
- Dress-up clothes

Figure 15-1

Preparation

Find a copy of *Stone Soup*. (See the bibliography in Section III.) Prepare to read the story out loud with expression.

Prepare a kitchen area in your classroom. Put in this area all the kitchen materials listed above.

Learning Activities

1. Gather the children around you and read *Stone Soup*. Invite their comments.
   Note: Keep the storybook for use on Day 3.
2. Take the children to the prepared kitchen area. If you do not have a play stove and want the children to make one, show them the cardboard box. Invite them to use felt-tipped markers and crayons to add dials, burners, and an oven door.
3. Show the children all the materials you have gathered in the kitchen area. Help them put on aprons. Then invite them to role-play the story.
   Note: Keep the kitchen materials in the kitchen area for the entire unit of study.
4. Encourage the children to use the kitchen area for other activities that happen in the kitchen in their home.

Day 2: Following Directions

Materials

- Plastic vegetables

- Sheet of writing paper, a felt-tipped marker or pen, and envelopes (one per child)
- Paper bag and stones
- Soup kettle

Preparation

Select a stone for each child. On each stone print a different direction, such as "Touch the ground," "Clap your hands," "Turn around," and so on. Put these stones in a paper bag.

Learning Activities

1. Gather the children around you and explain that on the following day they will make their own soup just as the characters did in the story on Day 1. Talk about soup and about the soups the children like.
   Music Note: "Vegetable Soup Song" from *Piggyback Songs*
2. Give the children plastic vegetables to hold. Discuss the name of each vegetable and its taste. Encourage the children to discuss which vegetables they want to put in their soup, Figure 15-2.

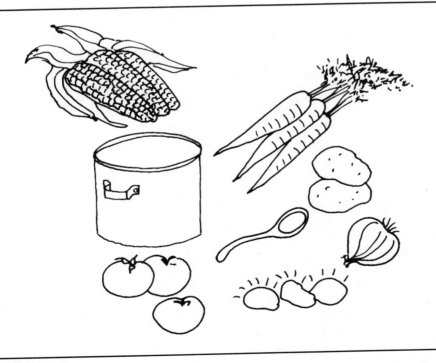

Figure 15-2

3. With the children write a letter to their parents asking for a food contribution to the soup for Day 3. Finalize the letter and then duplicate it. Give each child a letter and an envelope. Ask each child what he or she wants to bring to class for the soup and jot the children's requests on the letters. Then help the children fold their letters and put them into envelopes.
4. Show the children your bag of rocks and invite the children to guess what is in the bag. Encourage the children, one by one, to reach into the bag and find a magic stone. Modify the directions on the stone to meet the needs of the physically challenged child. After each child takes his or her turn, read the direction on the stone and encourage the child to do what is written on the stone.
5. Wash the stones used in Learning Activity 4 and put them into a soup kettle. Discuss the soup the children will make on Day 3.

Day 3: Cooking Soup

Materials

- Storybook from Day 1
- Fresh vegetables from home, aprons, pan(s) of water, a knife, and scrubbing brushes
- Water, soup seasonings, and crock pot or soup kettle and hot plate
- Materials from Day 1 for role-playing
- Bowls, spoons, and napkins

Preparation

Decide where and how you will cook today's soup.

Learning Activities

1. Gather the children around you and reread the story from Day 1. Invite the children's comments.
2. With the children examine the vegetables they brought from home. Put aprons on the children and help them wash and clean the vegetables they brought to class. Cut the vegetables into small pieces so that they will cook more quickly. Invite the children to put the vegetables into a crock pot or a soup kettle along with a clean stone.
3. Add water to the soup and show the children how to season it. Cook the soup until it is done. As the soup cooks, interact with the children by saying things like "I wonder what our soup will taste like," "I like carrots and potatoes," "Doesn't the soup smell good!"
4. While the soup is cooking, encourage the children to play in the kitchen area with stones and other materials and to pretend to make their own soup.
5. When soup is ready, eat and enjoy!

Day 4: Making a Recipe

Materials

- Variety of plastic fruits and vegetables
- Inedible objects like combs, blocks, and balls
- Variety of pebbles, stones, and rocks,
- Cookbook
- Paper and felt-tipped marker or pen

Preparation

Collect a variety of pebbles, stones, and rocks that have different weights and textures.

Learning Activities

1. Show the children the plastic fruits and vegetables you have collected and invite them to sort these materials. To make this activity more difficult, add some inedible objects and invite the children to sort everything into two groups: what they can eat and what they cannot eat.
2. Show the children all the pebbles, stones, and rocks you have collected. Encourage them to look at and touch the collection. As the children examine the collection, use words like *smooth, rough, pitted,* and *hard.*
3. Show the children a cookbook. Ask the children what some of their favorite dishes are. Tell the children what the word *recipe* means. If possible find recipes for these dishes in the cookbook. Read out loud the ingredients in the recipes.
4. Ask the children to help you write the recipe for the soup they made on Day 3. Tell the children that they will get to take this recipe home to their parents so that they can make the soup, too. On a sheet of paper, print each child's name and what he or she brought to class for the soup. Encourage the children to recall what they had to do to make the soup and write these steps on the recipe.
5. Duplicate the classroom soup recipe and encourage the children to take it home to their parents.

Additional Activities

1. Rock hunt. Take the children outside to collect rocks. Come back to the room and let the children wash their rocks and mount them on a piece of cardboard.
2. Painting rocks. Give each child a smooth rock. Invite the children to make each rock into something else by painting it. Ask the children to share with the class what their rock has become.
3. Field trip. Go to the grocery store to buy fruits and vegetables.
4. Visit a vegetable garden.

#16   Brown Bear, Brown Bear

Objective

By responding to the storybook *Brown Bear, Brown Bear, What Do You See?*, the children will sharpen their ability to visually discriminate colors and to match objects.

Day 1: Introducing Brown Bear
Materials

- Storybook *Brown Bear, Brown Bear, What Do You See?*
- Construction paper

Preparation

Find a copy of *Brown Bear, Brown Bear, What Do You See?* (See the bibliography in Section III.) Prepare to read the story out loud with expression.

From colored construction paper, cut out animals to represent all the characters in the story.

Practice the action rhyme "Teddy Bear, Teddy Bear, Turn Around." (See "Action Rhymes" in Section III.)

Learning Activities

1. Gather the children around you and read *Brown Bear, Brown Bear, What Do You See?* Invite the children's comments.
   Note: Keep the storybook for use on Days 2 and 3.
2. Give the children the paper animals you made to represent the characters in the story. Invite the children to manipulate the paper animals as you read the story a second time. As you come to each character in the story, invite the child who is holding that character to show it to the other children. Say something like "I wonder who yellow duck will see?" When you ask questions, remember to give the children several seconds to think before answering.
3. Invite the children to stand and act out the rhyme "Teddy Bear, Teddy Bear, Turn Around."
   Note: Assist children who are physically challenged to make some of the movements to this rhyme.

Day 2: Discovering Bears

Materials

- Storybook from Day 1
- Construction paper, scissors, and envelopes (two per child)
- Many sheets of typing paper and glue sticks or paste
- Stapler and staples

Preparation

Practice the action rhyme "Let's Go on a Bear Hunt." (See "Action Rhymes" in Section III.)

Cut out many small bears from brown construction paper. Hide these in your classroom—under, behind, over, and by other objects.

Make patterns of the characters in the storybook. Then using these patterns, make two sets of characters for each child. Put each set into an envelope so that you have two envelopes per child—one for Day 2 and one for Day 3.

Learning Activities

1. Gather the children around you and reread the story from Day 1. You may want the children to read it. Invite the children's comments and questions.
   Note: Keep the storybook for use on Day 3.
2. Invite the children to do the action rhyme "Let's Go on a Bear Hunt." Encourage the children to perform all the motions in the rhyme as they move around the room on their bear hunt.
3. Show the children a paper bear and tell them that you have hidden many of these small bears in the room. Invite them to find these bears. As the children search, comment on what they are doing by using the words

under, by, over and *behind.* For instance, you might say something like "Maria, you are looking *under* the table," "Antonio, you are looking *behind* the book," and "Lia, you are looking *by* the wall."

4. Give each child an envelope containing a set of construction-paper animals. Provide the children with glue sticks and as many sheets of paper as there are animals in a set. Invite the children to glue one animal to each sheet of paper so that they will have their own storybook. As the children work, reread the story to them. When the children complete their work, staple each set of pages together to make an animal book for each child, Figure 16-1.

Figure 16-1

Note: Keep the second set of envelopes you prepared for use on Day 3.

5. As closure, invite the children to read along with you as you read the story again.

Day 3: Role-Playing

Materials

- Storybook from Day 1
- Set of animals in envelopes prepared on Day 2
- Music box, tape, and sheet of brown construction paper
- Stuffed animals
- Lengths of string and small pieces of sheeting (one per child)

Preparation

Before class obtain a music box. Cut out a bear from brown construction paper and tape it to the music box.

Read Learning Activity 4. Then use pieces of sheeting and string to make a play parachute for each child.

Learning Activities

1. Gather the children around you. Invite the children to read the story with you. Discuss some of the animals in the story and what color they probably really are.

2. Give each child an envelope containing a set of animal characters. Invite the children to use their animal sets to role-play the story as you reread it.

3. Explain to the children that they are going to use both their eyes and their ears as they hunt for bears today. Show them the music box you prepared. Ask the children to close their eyes while you hide the box. Before hiding the box, wind it up. Then invite the children to take turns following the music to find the bear. Give each child an opportunity to find the bear, Figure 16-2.

Figure 16-2

Note: Visually-impaired children can listen for the music box. Hearing-impaired children may need some clues, as to the general area where the bear is hidden.

4. Invite the children to choose a stuffed animal from those in the classroom. Then give each child a small parachute. Invite the children to think of what they can do with the parachute and their stuffed animals.

Day 4: Matching Colored Bears

Materials

* Varied colors of construction paper
* Furniture and boxes
* Ingredients for pudding, mixing utensils, utensils for eating

Preparation

Before class cut two sets of small bears from many colors of construction paper.

Using furniture, boxes, and other classroom materials, set up an obstacle course in your room.

Learning Activities

1. Gather the children around you and show them your two sets of bears. Spread out one set of bears on the floor. Then give each child a bear or bears from the second set. Invite the children to match their bears to the bears on the floor. If the children have difficulty with this matching activity, talk about the different colors on the floor. For instance, say something like "I have a blue bear by my foot" or "I like red bears." While you make each statement, touch the appropriate bear on the floor with one of your feet.
2. Invite the children to pretend that they are bears. Set up an obstacle course for the children to go through.
   Note: Physically challenged children will need assistance. Also visually-impaired children can be guided through the obstacle course.
3. Have the children go to the snack table and make pudding bears. (See "Recipes" in Section III.)

Additional Activities

1. Storybook. Read the children the story of *Goldilocks and the Three Bears.* (See the bibliography in Section III.) Invite the children to act out the story.
2. Cotton bears. Cut out a bear pattern and trace around it to make a picture for each child. Then invite the children to glue cotton balls on their bear.
3. Circle bears. Using only circles, invite the children to make a circle bear, Figure 16-3. (See "Patterns" in Section III.)

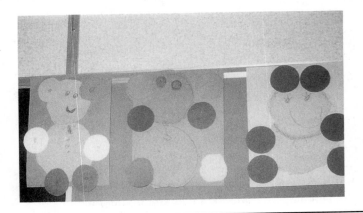

Figure 16-3

17   The Gingerbread Boy

Objective

By responding to the story *The Gingerbread Boy*, the children will develop the concepts *on* and *under* and build their fine-motor skills.

Day 1: Making Gingerbread Cookies

Materials

- Storybook *The Gingerbread Boy*
- Video of *The Gingerbread Boy* by Golden Books (optional)

- Ingredients for gingerbread cookie recipe
- Bowls, mixing utensils, gingerbread-people cookie cutters, and cookie sheets
- Real oven and timer or play oven and timer
- Color Bingo game

Preparation

Find a copy of *The Gingerbread Boy*. (See the bibliography in Section III.) Prepare to read the story out loud with expression. If possible rent or buy a video of *The Gingerbread Boy*.

Assemble the ingredients and utensils for making gingerbread cookies. (See "Recipes" in Section III.) Prime your aide to surreptitiously remove the gingerbread cookies from the oven after you and the children put them there at the end of Learning Activity 3.

Prepare to play Color Bingo.

Learning Activities

1. Gather the children around you and read *The Gingerbread Boy*. If possible show them the video of the story. Encourage the children to talk about the story.
2. Ask the children if they would like to help you make gingerbread boys and girls. Gather the children in the cooking area and point out the assembled ingredients, cookie cutters, and utensils. Invite the children to help you make the cookie dough. Read the recipe out loud, step-by-step, as you and the children add the ingredients to the mixing bowl.
3. When the dough is ready ask the children if they want to make one large gingerbread boy and one large gingerbread girl or if they want to make an individual gingerbread cookie for each of them. Using cookie cutters, cut out the gingerbread people, Figure 17-1. Put the cookies on sheets to bake. If you do not have an oven available to do the baking, put the cookies into a pretend oven. Set a timer and explain to the children what you are doing and what its ringing sound will mean.
   Note: If the cookies are actually baking in your room, set the timer for a little longer than the actual baking time so that your assistant can remove the cookies before the timer rings and you bring the children to the kitchen area.
   Keep the cookies for eating on Day 3.
4. Take the children to another area of the room to play a game of Color Bingo.
5. When the timer sounds, take the children to the oven. Act surprised when the gingerbread cookies are gone. With the children, look around the room for the gingerbread girls and boys and call for them. Invite the children to look on and under things. As you search together, talk about what you are doing and invite the children's comments. After searching for a while, tell the children that all of them will search again on the next day.

Day 2: Painting Gingerbread Children

Materials

- Painting shirts or smocks, easels, painting paper, brushes, and paint
- Modeling clay/dough, rolling pins, gingerbread-people cookie cutters.

Preparation

Tell the other teachers and personnel in the building that the children are going to come looking for their gingerbread cookies today. Ask these other adults to make up stories about the cookies and to tell the children where they saw the gingerbread children.

Prepare for each child a sheet of painting paper on which you have drawn the outline of a gingerbread girl or boy.

Buy or make colored modeling clay/dough. (See "Recipes" in Section III.)

Learning Activities

1. Gather the children around you and tell them that the gingerbread boys and girls did not come back. Continue the hunt for the gingerbread children. Again stress the concepts *on* and *under*. Talk about what you are doing as you search. Stay away from the *who*, *where*, and *why* questions.
2. Take the children out of the classroom to ask others if they have seen the gingerbread children. When the children are unable to locate the cookies, call off the search and tell the children that all of them will search for the gingerbread children again the next day.
3. Help the children put on their painting shirts or smocks. Give each child his or her painting paper and equipment and invite the children to paint a gingerbread child, Figure 17-1.

Figure 17-1

4. Invite the children to use the modeling clay/dough to make gingerbread cookies.

Day 3: Making Gingerbread Puppets

Materials

*   Cookies from Day 1 and real oven or play oven
*   Construction paper or felt, hole punch, and white yarn
*   Felt-tipped markers and crayons
*   Gingerbread cookies from Day 1, milk, and paper cups

Preparation

Place the baked cookies from Day 1 in the oven in your kitchen area.

Read through Learning Activity 2 and decide if you will use felt or construction paper to make the gingerbread-puppet shapes. Make an outline of a gingerbread person. Using this outline, make two shapes for each child. Then hold each set of shapes together and punch holes along the outline of the shapes. (Remember not to punch holes at the bottom of the shapes because this is where the children will put their hand to use the shapes as a puppet.) Prepare yarn for stringing by cutting it into lengths that will go around the gingerbread person. Then knot one end of each length of yarn and put glue or tape at the other end for easier lacing.

Following the directions for Learning Activity 2, make a sample gingerbread-person puppet.

Learning Activities

1. Tell the children that the gingerbread children have not returned and that they will need to search for them again today. Explain that before they go on their hunt, they are going to make gingerbread puppets to take with them. Show the children the puppet you made and encourage them to feel it and put it on their hands. Then put the sample away so that the children do not imitate it as they make their own.
2. Give each child two gingerbread shapes and a length of prepared yarn. Show the children how to lace the two shapes together to make a puppet. Provide time for the children to lace their shapes together. Then invite the children to use felt-tipped markers or crayons to add features to the puppet faces.
    Note: Be aware that you will need to provide assistance to children with physical involvement as they try to make their puppets.
    Keep the puppets for Day 4.
3. Have the children put their puppets on their hand and look for the gingerbread cookies. Conclude the search by the oven in your kitchen area. Invite the children to open the oven and with them be surprised to find the gingerbread children from Day 1 there.
4. Take the gingerbread cookies out of the oven and enjoy them with the children. Invite them to drink milk with their cookies.

Day 4: Making Gingerbread Selves

Materials

- Gingerbread puppets made on Day 3
- Long strips of paper
- Painting shirts or smocks, brushes or sponges, and brown paint
- Gumdrops (three per child)
- Tape
- Audiotape or record of music that the children can dance to and cassette player or phonograph

Preparation

Following the directions for Learning Activities 3 and 4, make a gingerbread self. Hang this in the classroom so the children can see it when they come to school.

Learning Activities

1. Invite the children to use their gingerbread puppets from Day 3 to retell the story of *The Gingerbread Boy.*
2. Tell the children that today they are going to make themselves into gingerbread people. Point out the gingerbread self you made before class and invite the children's comments.
3. Put long strips of paper on the floor and invite each child to lay down on a strip. Outline the body of each child, Figure 17-2.

Figure 17-2

Note: Place children in wheelchairs on the paper also and outline their bodies. Invite the other children to help them paint their outlines.

4. Have the children put on paint smocks and use brown paint to sponge or brush the gingerbread outline. Show them how to decorate the face with two gumdrop eyes and one gumdrop nose. Print each child's name on his or her gingerbread self. Then hang the outlines around the room.

5. Afterward play some music and invite the children to dance for their gingerbread guests.

Additional Activities

1. Follow the Leader. Be the leader in the game and invite the children to do a variety of things like jumping, turning around, touching their head, and so on. Throughout this activity say to the children, "Run, run as fast as you can" and let them run around the room. Have someone available to push any children in wheelchairs.

2. Markers. Let the children use smelly markers to draw and color different things. Look carefully before the children leave the classroom to see if they have left coloring under their noses. Watch the children carefully as they work and caution them not to put the markers in their mouths.

3. Role-Playing. Invite the children to role-play the story from this unit of study.

#18   Hansel and Gretel

Objective

By responding to the story *Hansel and Gretel*, the children will develop their fine-motor skills.

Day 1: Leaving a Trail

Materials

- Storybook *Hansel and Gretel*
- Bits of colored paper (one color per child)
- Envelopes (one per child)
- Extra large box
- Painting and decorating materials

Preparation

Find a copy of *Hansel and Gretel*. (See the bibliography in Section III.) Prepare to read the story out loud with expression.

Plan the route you and the children will take for your walk during Learning Activity 2. If possible plan a walk outside the classroom.

Cut out one-inch squares of colored construction paper (one color per child) so that the children can drop these paper bits behind them to leave a trail during their walk. Put each child's pile of paper squares in an envelope so that the child can hold them easily.

Also have ready a large box, such as that used to pack a refrigerator, washer, or dryer, that the children can make into a gingerbread house. Draw the outline of a door and windows on the box.

Learning Activities

1. Gather the children around you and read them the story of *Hansel and Gretel*. Afterward invite the children's comments and questions.
   Note: Keep the storybook for use on Days 2 and 3.
2. Invite the children to take a walk just as Hansel and Gretel did. Give each child an envelope containing bits of colored paper. Encourage the children to drop these pieces behind them as they walk so as to leave a trail just like Hansel and Gretel. Then walk with the children. As you return to the classroom, encourage the children to try to follow their trail of paper back to the room.
3. When you return to the room, show the children the large cardboard box you have ready for them to decorate as a gingerbread house. Provide decorating materials and paints and invite the children to make their "Hansel and Gretel" house.
   Note: Do not expect the children to complete their "Hansel and Gretel" house in one day. Note that they may need to work on it all week.

Note: Look ahead to Day 2, Learning Activity 2. Prepare the individual graham cracker houses sometime today for use on Day 2.

Day 2: Making a Gingerbread House

Materials

- Storybook from Day 1
- Graham crackers, frosting, candy, utensils for spreading frosting
- Decorating materials, paints, and "Hansel and Gretel" house from Day 1

Preparation

The day before this class prepare each child a graham cracker house and mix a quantity of frosting for the children to use as they decorate their houses. (See "Patterns" in Section III for instructions on how to assemble the houses. Rather than make frosting, you may wish to buy it already prepared.) You will want to prepare the graham cracker houses on Day 1 so that they can sit overnight.

Also have decorating materials and paints available from Day 1 so that the children can continue to work on their "Hansel and Gretel" house.

Learning Activities

1. Gather the children around you and reread the story from Day 1. Afterward talk about what was on the gingerbread house in the story, what it looked like, and what they think it would taste like.
2. Invite the children to make their own gingerbread houses. Gather the children by tables in the work area and place a house before each child. Provide the frosting, candy, and spreading utensils and be ready to give plenty of help as the children decorate their houses.
   Note: Be aware that this activity requires close supervision by you and your assistants because children tend to put too much frosting on their houses. If this project seems too extensive for your group, consider making one large graham-cracker or gingerbread house for the entire group to decorate.
3. As the children finish their houses, invite them to continue to paint and decorate their "Hansel and Gretel" house, which they began on Day 1.

Day 3: Playing Hansel and Gretel

Materials

- Storybook from Day 1
- Video of the storybook by Golden Books (optional)
- Objects for an obstacle course (large tube, something to step over, something to step on, something to crawl under, low balance beam, small slide, box to step into)

- Several mats
- Colored construction paper and scissors

Preparation

Prepare an obstacle course. Have a large tube that the children can crawl *through*, something for them to step *over*, something to step *on*, something to crawl *under*, a low balance beam to walk *across*, a small slide to climb *up* and *down*, and a box for the children to step *into* and *out of*. Along the course place some mats to change the surface of the course and to improve balance.

Make a foot pattern and cut footsteps from construction paper. Tape these footprints along the obstacle course.

Learning Activities

1. Gather the children around you and reread the story from Day 1 or show the videotape of the story.
2. Show the children the obstacle course and point out the footprints. Tell the children that these are Hansel's and Gretel's footprints and that they are at the end of the course.
3. Invite two volunteers to be Hansel and Gretel. Have them go to the end of the obstacle course and stand there to greet the other children. Then invite the rest of the children to follow the course so that they can meet Hansel and Gretel.
4. As the children walk the obstacle course (Figure 18-1), stand along the side and encourage them by using concept words that describe what they are doing. For example, "Maria, you are going *through* the tube!" "Jon, I like the way you step *over* the book." "Timothy, you can certainly climb *up* the ladder in a safe way." "Sophia, you are walking *across* the balance beam like a model."

   Note: Provide help so that the children in wheelchairs can experience some of the obstacle course. Physically challenged and visually-impaired children will also need guidance through the obstacle course.
5. After all the children have completed the obstacle course, invite them to play a game with Hansel and Gretel.

Day 4: Playing in the House

Materials

- Dolls, blankets, chairs, and other furnishings for the "Hansel and Gretel" house from Day 1
- Gingerbread cookies, milk, paper plates, and cups
- Ingredients for making gingerbread cookies (optional)
- Frosting and spreading tools (optional)

Figure 18-1

Preparation

Decide if you want to make gingerbread cookies with or for the children to eat during Learning Activity 2 or if you simply want to buy gingerbread cookies. (See "Recipes" in Section III.) Decide if you want the children to frost the gingerbread cookies in class.

Figure 18-2

Learning Activities

1. Invite the children to play inside their "Hansel and Gretel" house, Figures 18-2 and 18-3. Encourage them to make themselves at home in the house. Follow their lead as to what they want to do with the house: act out the story, play house, or make up other stories to act out. As they play, you may want to emphasize the concepts *in the house* and *out of the house*. You may also want to talk about what the children bring into the house to play with.
2. Afterward invite the children to a snack of gingerbread cookies and milk.
   Note: Consider allowing the children to make and frost the gingerbread cookies in class.

Additional Activities

1. Ornaments. Cut out paper ornaments and invite the children to decorate them with a variety of materials, like cotton, yarn, felt, cloth, glitter, and so on.

Figure 18-3

Figure 18-4

2. Making cookies. Make some modeling dough for the children. (See "Recipes" in Section III.) Have rolling pins and cookie cutters available and invite the children to make their own play cookies.
3. Building houses. Provide blocks, logs, and other building materials and invite the children to make their own playhouses, Figure 18-4.

part six
Holidays

Speech/Language, Developmentally Delayed, and Mentally Handicapped

- Encourage, but do not pressure the child to dress up.
- Playing a group game in the Halloween unit is a good time to reinforce rules.
- You can use other stringing objects like cereal and macaroni for variety.
- Children with fine-motor difficulties may just tear the paper for the turkey mosaic, rather than cutting it.
- Glue sticks provide better fine-motor control.
- Sequencing is reinforced when role-playing the characters on the bed in *The Napping House*. *Big* and *little* can also be reinforced.
- Sewing cards offer good reinforcement at the learning stations.
- Review of steps in the process of baking cookies is good recall.

Multihandicapped and Orthopedically Impaired

- Pumpkins and eggs should be hidden at the wheelchair level.
- Help the child in the wheelchair when ghost painting by bringing the paper to the chair and helping the child apply pressure for the print.
- Because of their spasticity, children with cerebral palsy may need assistance to help them relax their hand when doing handprints in clay.
- Large stockings may be needed for lacing.
- Consider substitutes for some of the snacks for the child with feeding problems.
- Position the child at the table for beating the eggs.
- Assist the child with the movements to the song "The Bunny Hop."

Emotionally Disturbed

- Too much sugar may cause hyperactivity. Snacks should be watched.
- Emphasize that the marbles stay in the cereal box when marble painting.
- Plan ahead and discuss what will happen to eggs if they were to fall on the table or the floor.

Other Health Impaired
* Care should be exercised with children with allergies if animals are brought to the room or if the class visits a pet store.

Blind and Visually Impaired
* Let the child explore the real pumpkins.
* Let the child hold the bunny and have the teacher describe what it looks like.

Deaf and Hearing Impaired
* Direct the child to the illustrations in *The Napping House* or give the child his/her own copy to follow.
* Help the child feel the vibrations of the musical instruments.

#19   Halloween

Objective

By decorating both real and paper pumpkins, preparing food, and inviting their parents to a party, the children will celebrate Halloween.

Day 1: Passing the Pumpkin

Materials

* Storybook *Clifford's Halloween*

- Pumpkin(s)
- Orange construction paper
- Rhythm instruments

Preparation

Find a copy of *Clifford's Halloween*. (See the bibliography in Section III.) Prepare to read the story out loud with expression.

Cut a variety of pumpkins of different sizes from orange construction paper and hide them around the classroom. Keep count of how many paper pumpkins you hide.

Practice the song "Pass the Beanbag."

Learning Activities

1. Gather the children around you and read *Clifford's Halloween*. Afterward invite the children's comments and questions. Children may be so excited about the story that they may interrupt while you are reading.
2. Show the children the pumpkin(s) you have brought to class. Invite the children to touch and lift the pumpkin(s). Invite the children's comments and questions.
3. Show the children a paper pumpkin. Explain that you have hidden many of these paper pumpkins in the classroom. Invite the children to go on a Pumpkin Treasure Hunt and find all the paper pumpkins.
4. After the children have discovered all the paper pumpkins, invite them to sit on the floor in a circle. Play "Pass the Pumpkin" with a real pumpkin. As you play, use the song "Pass the Beanbag" and substitute the word *pumpkin* for *beanbag*.
5. After the children become accustomed to the music for "Pass the Pumpkin," give them rhythm instruments and encourage them to accompany the song.

> *Note:* The "Pass the Pumpkin" activity involves following the directions *fast*, *slow*, *high*, and *low*.
>
> Early this week, call and invite the children's parents to come to the Halloween party of Day 4. Or send an invitation to the parents. Ask the parents to dress their children in a costume for school on Day 4, the day of the party.

Day 2: Making Pumpkins

Materials

- White construction paper (one sheet per child) and scissors
- Saucers or bowls of orange tempera and liquid dishwashing soap
- Spring-type clothespins attached to pieces of sponge
- Yellow tissue paper (1/4 sheet per child) or black construction paper (one

sheet per child) and tape or glue
* Long strip of black paper
* Pan of white tempera and liquid dishwashing soap
* Variety of orange-colored objects, such as plastic oranges and carrots
* Black construction paper (optional)

Preparation

On white construction paper draw the outline of a large pumpkin. Use one sheet per child. Cut out the eyes, nose, and mouth of the pumpkin, Figure 19-1.

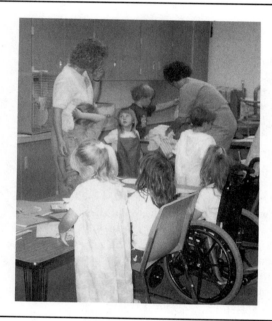

Figure 19-1

Prepare the tempera for the two painting activities by mixing it with dishwashing soap for easier cleanup.

Prepare the paintbrushes by attaching small pieces of sponge to spring-type clothespins (one brush per child).

Learning Activities

1. Give each child a sheet of white construction paper on which you have drawn the outline of a pumpkin and a prepared brush. Point out the saucers of orange tempera and demonstrate how to dip the sponge brush into the tempera and dab the color onto a paper pumpkin. Invite the children to paint their pumpkins.

2. After the pumpkins have dried, show the children how to tape or glue a piece of yellow tissue or black construction paper to the back of the pumpkin so that the color will show through the cut-out eyes, nose, and mouth.

3. Put a long strip of black paper on the floor and show the children the pan of white tempera. Tell the children that they get to be little ghosts and walk across the paper. Divide the children into two groups. Send Group 1 to the play area and invite them to play with the orange-colored objects you collected.

4. One by one, invite the children of Group 2 to step into a pan of white tempera and then to walk across the black paper you put on the floor. After all the children of Group 2 have made footprints, have Group 1 and Group 2 exchange places. After all the children have made their footprints and the paper has dried, display it in the classroom. Tell the children that they were just "ghost walking."

   Note: Physically challenged children should have their feet painted. Then bring the black paper to their feet in their wheelchairs to make the print.

5. If time permits, give each child a piece of black construction paper and invite the children to use the white tempera to make individual ghost footsteps to take home.

Day 3: Making Jack-o'-lanterns

Materials

- Large grocery bags (one per child) and decorating materials, such as Halloween stickers, felt-tipped markers, crayons, scraps of construction paper, and tape or glue
- Chocolate cake, white frosting, black licorice pieces or black jellybeans, and spreading utensils
- Cupcakes, corn candies, licorice bits, chocolate chips (optional)
- One large pumpkin, knife and spoons
- Small pumpkins (one per child) and dark felt-tipped markers

Preparation

Before class make or buy a chocolate cake. Or make cupcakes or cookies. If you provide individual cupcakes or cookies, decide how many you will need for the party on Day 4 when the children's parents will be guests.

Learning Activities

1. Give each child a brown grocery bag. Invite the children to use the decorating materials you have assembled to decorate their bags for trick-or-treating.

2. Help the children use the frosting and black candy to decorate the chocolate cake so that it looks like a ghost face. Or give each child one or more cupcakes and a supply of candy and invite the children to decorate their cupcakes for Halloween. Tell the children that they will get to eat their cake or cupcakes at the Halloween party on Day 4.
   Note: Keep the cake or cupcakes for eating on Day 4.

3. Carve a pumpkin while the children watch. Invite the children to help you scoop out the seeds.
   Fingerplay Fun: "Cut into a Pumpkin" from *Finger Frolics*

4. Encourage each child to decorate his or her own individual pumpkin with felt-tipped markers.

5. Remind the children that on Day 4 they will celebrate Halloween in their classroom. Remind them that their parents are invited to the celebration and that the children can wear costumes to the party, Figure 19-2.

Figure 19-2

Day 4: Celebrating!

Materials

- Large sheet of orange paper, black construction paper, scissors, and tape
- A blindfold
- Tape or record of Halloween music and a cassette player or phonograph
- Rhythm instruments
- Treats from Day 3

Preparation

On a large sheet of paper, draw and color a large jack-o'-lantern. Color the mouth and eyes but leave the nose blank. Cut out a jack-o'-lantern nose for each child from black construction paper. Print the name of the child on his or her pumpkin nose. Place a piece of overlapping tape at the apex of each nose so that the children can tape the nose to the paper jack-o'-lantern. Have seats available for the guests.

Learning Activities

1. As the children arrive, give each child the time to model and tell about his/her costume, Figure 19-3. Invite the parents and other guests to take seats in the classroom and enjoy the celebration and their children's antics.

Figure 19-3

2. When everyone is ready, gather the children around you and invite them to role-play the character they are dressed to be. Encourage the guests to clap and compliment the children on their play.
3. Invite the children to play Tape the Nose on the Jack-o'-lantern. Tape the paper jack-o'-lantern you prepared to the wall. Invite the children to discover what facial feature is missing from the jack-o'-lantern, Figure 19-4. Then give each child his or her jack-o'-lantern nose. Blindfold the players, one by one, and invite them to try to find the center of the jack-o'-lantern and tape the nose on it.

Figure 19-4

> *Note:* Some of the children may be afraid to put on a blindfold. Do not force them to play the game if they do not want to. Children sometimes need to just observe, and that's all right to do.

4. Play some Halloween music and invite the children to use rhythm instruments to accompany the music.
5. At the end of the celebration bring out the treats made on Day 3 and invite everyone to eat and enjoy!

Additional Activities

1. Tasting. Invite the children to taste food that is orange, e.g., oranges, orange juice, carrots, corn candy, and so on.
2. Field trip. Take the children on a field trip to a pumpkin patch and invite each of them to pick out a pumpkin.
3. Sugar cookies. Make dough for sugar cookies and have a number of pumpkin cookie cutters. Invite the children to cut out a pumpkin cookie. After baking the cookies, invite the children to decorate them with orange frosting.
4. Pumpkin patch. For easier cleanup, mix liquid dishwashing soap with orange tempera. Invite the children to use their fingers to make small pumpkins on a sheet of white paper. Use a brush and green tempera to connect the pumpkins so that each picture looks like a pumpkin patch.

#20 Thanksgiving

Objective

By making varied kinds of turkeys, the children will learn the color brown, work on fine-motor skills, and cooperatively complete a class project.

Day 1: Making Hand Turkeys

Materials

- Storybook *Little Bear's Thanksgiving* or any book about Thanksgiving
- Brown construction paper (one sheet per child), felt-tipped markers, crayons, feathers, and tape
- Instant chocolate pudding, shakers or egg beaters, and bowls
- Ingredients for chocolate milk (optional)

Preparation

Find a copy of *Little Bear's Thanksgiving*. (See the bibliography in Section III.) Or choose a Thanksgiving storybook that you especially like. Prepare to read the story out loud with expression.

Following the directions in Learning Activity 3, make a sample turkey.

Learning Activities

1. Gather the children around you and read *Little Bear's Thanksgiving*. As you read, give the children many opportunities to interact with you by saying things like "I wonder what will happen next," "I think the bear must feel like laughing," and so on.
2. Direct the children to the art area. Explain that the children will use one of their hands to make a Thanksgiving turkey, Figure 20-1. Show the children the turkey you made but put the sample away so that the children do not imitate it.

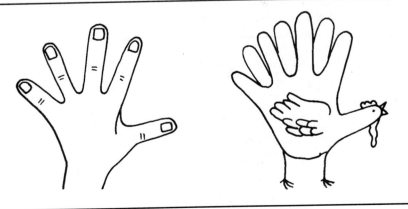

Figure 20-1

3. Give each child a sheet of construction paper and a felt-tipped marker or crayon. Show the children how to spread their hand on the paper so that their fingers become feathers, their palm becomes the turkey's body, and their thumb becomes its head. Help the children outline their hands onto paper. Provide the children with feathers, felt-tipped markers, and crayons for decorating their turkeys.
4. Gather the children together to play the game Turkey, Turkey, Goose. Play the game like Duck, Duck, Gray Duck. (See "Games" in Section III.)
5. Invite the children to make chocolate instant pudding by shaking the mix or by using an egg beater.
    Note: If some children have feeding problems or cannot tolerate the texture of the pudding have them shake up their own chocolate milk.

Day 2: Making Necklaces

Materials

*   Shoelaces or lengths of yarn (one per child), plastic containers, and beads
*   Brown construction paper or grocery bags
*   White construction paper (one sheet per child), felt-tipped markers, and paste or tape

Preparation

If you are using yarn for stringing, knot one end of each length of yarn and tape or glue the other end for easier stringing. Have many sizes, shapes, and colors of beads available for stringing. Sort the beads in plastic containers.

Cut out a variety of turkeys of different sizes and shapes from brown construction paper or grocery bags. Hide these paper turkeys in the classroom.

Learning Activities

1. Gather the children around you and tell them that today they get to make necklaces to wear for Thanksgiving. Show the children the containers of beads and invite them to string a necklace, Figure 20-2. Help children

Figure 20-2

who have difficulty stringing. Allow the children to take their necklaces home.
Note: For children who have difficulty with stringing, you will want to have a number of large beads.
2. Show the children one of the turkeys you cut before class. Invite them to go on a turkey hunt to find all the turkeys you have hidden in the classroom.
3. Invite the children to make a collage of the turkeys they found. Provide sheets of paper, paste or tape, and crayons or felt-tipped markers.
Music Note: "Gobble, Gobble Turkey" from Songs for the Nursery School

Day 3: Creating Mosaic Turkeys
Materials

- Large sheet of white paper
- Scraps of construction paper and paste or glue
- White construction paper
- Blunt-edged scissors (optional)

Preparation

Trace the outline of a large turkey on a sheet of white paper. Look at Learning Activity 2 and decide if you want the children to make individual turkey mosaics. If you do, trace the outline of a large turkey on a sheet of white construction paper (one sheet per child).

Learning Activities

1. Show the children the large turkey outline you prepared. Put the sheet of paper on the floor or tape it to the wall at a level at which the children can work on it. Invite the children to paste or tape scraps of construction paper on the turkey to decorate it.
2. Invite the children to make their own individual turkey mosaics. Give each child a sheet of paper with a turkey outline, scraps of construction paper, and paste or glue. Afterward encourage the children to take their turkey mosaics home for Thanksgiving.
Note: For the children who are able to do so, you may want to invite them to cut or tear the construction paper into pieces to use on their mosaic.

Additional Activities

1. Vegetable printing. Provide the children with printing stamps made from peppers and potatoes. Cut the peppers in half and cut designs in the potatoes, Figure 20-3. Then show the children how to use the stamps and tem-

pera to print. Use tempera paint mixed with dishwasher liquid for easier cleanup afterwards.

Figure 20-3

2. Pine cone turkeys. Using large pine cones, invite the children to make turkeys by attaching feathers and a construction-paper head. Use pipe cleaners for the feet.
3. Paper bag turkeys. Invite the children to stuff lunch bags with crumpled paper or cotton. Show them how to tie the open end of the bag and attach feathers for a tail and a construction-paper head. Provide decorating materials for the children to use.

#21 Christmas

This unit revolves around the Christian holiday of Christmas. The activities can be easily adapted to other celebrations at this time of the year.

Hanukkah and Christmas around the World, give the children the opportunity to learn about other children and their celebrations.

Objective

By making Christmas counting chains, gifts, ornaments, and wrapping paper, and having a party, the children will develop their fine-motor skills, interact with adults and peers, and celebrate Christmas.

Day 1: Making a Christmas Counting Chain

Materials

- Storybook about Christmas
- Red and green construction paper and scissors
- Tape, glue, or stapler and staples
- Self-sticking commercial strips (optional)

Preparation

Count the number of days until Christmas. Use this number to prepare a set of construction paper strips for each child. In each set have as many strips as there are days remaining until Christmas. Following the directions in Learning Activity 3, make a sample counting chain.

On a sheet of paper prepare a letter to send home to parents. On the sheet, print the six-line verse given in Learning Activity 4. At the bottom of the sheet explain to the parents how the children are to use their Christmas counting chain to count down the days until Santa comes. Duplicate one copy of this verse and letter for each child to take home.

Learning Activities

1. Gather the children around you and read the storybook you have chosen. Afterward invite the children's comments and questions.
2. Show the children the Christmas counting chain you made, Figure 21-1. Explain that each day you are going to remove one link from the chain. Explain that when the chain is "all gone," Santa will come! Invite the children to hold the chain, then put it away so that the children do not imitate it. *Note:* This chain could be easily adapted for the Hanukkah celebrations.
3. Invite each child to make a Christmas counting chain. Give each child enough paper strips to make a chain. Demonstrate how to make a counting chain by gluing, taping or stapling the first strip into a circle: slipping a second strip through the circle and then gluing, taping, or stapling its ends together; and continuing to do the same with each strip. Provide as much help as the children need.
   Note: If a number of the children have trouble gluing paper together, you might want to consider purchasing commercial self-sticking strips for the first activity.

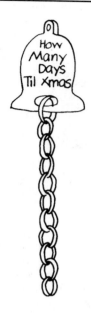

Figure 21-1

4. When the children have completed their chains, read the following verse out loud:

How many days 'til XMAS?
It's very hard to tell.
Take a link off every night
Until you reach the bell.
Then XMAS will be here;
Your favorite time of year!

Note: The words can be changed to include other celebrations.
Read the verse several times and then give each child a duplicated letter containing this verse to take home with his or her counting chain.

5. Play "Santa's in the Shop" to the tune of "The Farmer in the Dell."

Day 2: Role-Playing a Story

Materials

- Storybooks *The Napping House* and *The Night before Christmas*
- Plastic or paper bag, dolls, stuffed animals, toy cradle
- Sheet of typing paper and pen
- Felt-tipped markers or crayons
- Christmas stickers (optional)

Preparation

Find copies of the storybooks. (See the bibliography in Section III.) Prepare to read the stories out loud with expression.

If you do not have a plastic bag to use for role-playing in Learning Activity 2, make a bag out of black construction paper.

Learning Activities

1. Gather the children around you and read *The Napping House*. Afterward invite their comments and questions.
2. Show the children the dolls, cradle, bag, and stuffed animals you have collected and invite them to act out the story, Figure 21-2. You may want to reread the story to help the children sequence the introduction of the characters.

Figure 21-2

Note: Do not expect much verbal output, especially at first, when the children act out the first storybook. If they do the actions without verbalizing, you may want to verbalize for them. Note that this provides the children with a good model for information.

3. Gather the children around you and read *The Night before Christmas*. Invite the children's comments and questions.

   Note: Keep the storybook *The Night before Christmas* for use on Day 3.

4. Tell the children that on Day 8 they are going to have a Christmas party that their parents can attend. Compose an invitation with the children. Write the invitation on a sheet of typing paper and duplicate the original for each child to take home.

Note: In the invitation you and the children might want to invite the parents to bring treats to the party on Day 4.

5. Give each child a copy of the invitation. Invite the children to use felt-tipped markers or crayons to decorate their parents' invitation. Or provide Christmas stickers for the children to use in decorating. Be sure each child takes the invitation home.

Day 3: Visiting with Santa or Mrs. Claus

Materials

- Storybook *The Night before Christmas*
- Treat
- Art dough, Christmas cookie cutters, and lengths of string or yarn (one per child)

Preparation

Find someone to visit the room as Santa, Mrs. Claus, or one of Santa's elves. Be sure this person knows that some children may initially be afraid of this grown-up and will be too shy to sit on the visitor's lap. Tell the person to be careful when reaching out to these shy children. Be sure to tell the visitor the exact time you want him or her to arrive at the classroom door. Also provide the visitor with Christmas treats to give to the children.

Prepare the art dough. (See "Recipes" in Section III.) Following the directions in Learning Activity 4, make your own art-dough ornament.

Learning Activities

1. Gather the children around you and reread *The Night before Christmas.*
2. Act surprised when Santa, Mrs. Claus, or one of Santa's elves comes to visit the room. During the visit invite the children to sit on the visitor's lap, Figure 21-3. Encourage them to thank the visitor for the treat they receive.

Figure 21-3

3. After the Christmas visitor leaves, invite the children to make ornaments in the art area. Show the children the art-dough ornament you made. Then put your ornament away so that the children do not imitate it.
4. Provide the children with the prepared art dough and with cookie cutters. Put a hole in the top of each ornament and attach a string or piece of yarn for hanging. On the back of each ornament print the child's name and the year. Provide time for the ornaments to dry before sending them home.

Day 4: Making Christmas Gifts

Material

- Storybook *Santa's Toy Shop*
- Tape or record of popular commercial Christmas music and cassette or phonograph
- Pan of black tempera mixed with liquid dishwashing soap
- Quantity of quick-hardening clay

Preparation

On a sheet of paper print the poem "My Handprint." (See "Poems" in Section III.) At the bottom of the poem, print the word *Love* and put a line for a name and a line for a date. Duplicate one copy of this page for each child.

Prepare the tempera paint by mixing it with liquid dishwashing soap for easier cleanup.

Learning Activities

1. Gather the children around you and read *Santa's Toy Shop*. Afterward invite the children's comments and questions.
2. With the children, listen to some Christmas music, such as "Rudolph, the Red-Nosed Reindeer," "Up on the Rooftop," and "Jingle Bells." Encourage the children to sing along.
3. Give each child one of the sheets of paper on which you have duplicated the poem "My Handprint." Show the children how to dip one of their hands in tempera and how to make a handprint on the sheet of paper. Afterward go around the room and print each child's name and the date on his or her paper. Wash and dry the children's hands.
4. Tell the children that today they get to make a Christmas gift for their parents. Show them how to make a handprint in clay that hardens quickly, Figure 21-4. Provide each child with clay and give help as needed as the children make handprints. Tell the children that in a few days they will make gift-wrapping paper to wrap their two gifts for their parents.
   Note: Keep the two gifts—the clay handprints and the sheets with the poem and handprints—for wrapping on Day 7.

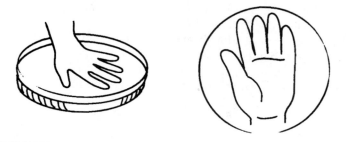

Figure 21-4

Day 5: Making Ornaments

Materials

- Empty cereal boxes (one per child), tape, and white construction paper
- Marbles, spoons, saucers or bowls of red and green tempera, and liquid dishwashing soap
- Colored construction paper (two sheets per child); decorating materials, such as felt-tipped markers, crayons, scraps of construction paper, tape or paste, Christmas stickers, and so on
- Blunt-edged scissors
- Hole punch

Preparation

Prepare for Learning Activities 1 and 2 by cutting Christmas ornaments from white construction paper (one ornament per child). Tape each ornament into the bottom of a cereal box (one ornament per box). Prepare the dishes of red and green tempera by mixing liquid dishwashing soap with the paint for easier cleanup.

Make a pattern for a Christmas stocking and then use this pattern to prepare two sheets of construction paper for each child. Use one sheet of red and one sheet of green paper for each child.

Learning Activities

1. Gather the children around you and show them one of the prepared cereal boxes. Point out the Christmas ornament taped inside the bottom of the box. Using several marbles, show the children how to make a marble painting by dipping the marbles in tempera, taking the marbles out of the tempera with a spoon, dropping the marbles into the cereal box, and then rolling them back and forth across the bottom of the box, Figure 21-5. Remove the ornament from the bottom of your cereal box and show the children how the marbles colored the Christmas decoration.

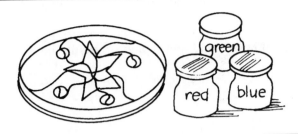

Figure 21-5

2. Invite the children to put marbles into tempera paint and make their own marble painting. Encourage the children to roll their cereal boxes back and forth so that the marbles will roll across the white ornament. Talk about what the marbles are doing and the motion of going back and forth. Afterward let the marble paintings dry. Tell the children that they will use these paper ornaments as they wrap gifts for their parents on Day 7.

3. Play "Santa's in the Shop," the song you introduced on Day 1.

   Note: Remember that repetition is good for children this age. They enjoy doing an activity with which they are familiar and they enjoy recalling past experiences that were fun for them.

4. Invite the children to make their own paper stockings for Christmas. Give each child two sheets of colored construction paper (one red and one green) and point out the decorating materials. Invite the children to decorate their stockings.

5. Help the children cut out their paper stockings. Punch holes around the edge of the stockings for lacing and tell the children that they will lace their stockings on Day 6.

   Note: For the children who may have fine-motor difficulties, remember to modify with a plastic needle or yarn that is taped on the end.

   Note: Keep the paper stockings for use on Day 6.

Day 6: Making Christmas Stockings

Materials

- Paper stockings from Day 5, prepared yarn (one length per child) or shoelaces (one per child), cotton balls, glue or paste, and glitter
- Long sheets of white paper (one sheet per child) holiday cookie cutters, saucers of tempera, and liquid dishwashing soap

Preparation

Prepare an area of the room for making stockings and one for making wrapping paper. Note that Learning Activities 1 and 2 will be going on at the same time. Be sure to have an aide prepared to conduct one of the activities while you monitor the other.

If you are using yarn instead of shoelaces for lacing in Learning Activity 1, prepare the yarn by knotting one end and taping or gluing the other end.

Prepare several colors of tempera by mixing liquid dishwashing soap with each color for easier cleanup.

Learning Activities

1. Split the class into two groups. Have an assistant take Group 2 to the area of the room you have set aside for making wrapping paper. Then give each child in Group 1 a shoelace or a piece of prepared yarn with which to lace their stockings from Day 5. Help the children lace their stockings together and print their names on them. Afterward invite the children to glue cotton along the top of their stockings. Then help them print their name on the stocking with glue and sprinkle glitter over the glue. Let the glue dry and then display the paper stockings in the classroom. After about twenty minutes have Group 1 and Group 2 switch activities.
    Note: Keep the laced stockings for the party on Day 8.
2. While Group 1 works on making stockings, have an aide help the children in Group 2 make wrapping paper. Show the children how to dip Christmas cookie cutters into saucers of tempera and print on long sheets of paper. Provide time for the children's wrapping paper to dry.
    Note: Keep wrapping paper for use on Day 7.
3. Invite the children to gather around you and sing holiday songs.

Day 7: Wrapping Gifts

Materials

*   Rhythm instruments (one per child)
*   Tape or record of holiday music and cassette recorder or phonograph
*   Clay handprint and poem sheet the children made on Day 4
*   Wrapping paper the children made on Day 6
*   Boxes (one per child) and tape or glue
*   Paper ornaments the children made on Day 5
*   Refrigerated dough for cookies, holiday cookie cutters, oven
*   Christmas storybook (optional)
*   Colored sugar, candies, frosting, and spreading utensils
*   Prepared red and green finger gelatin and holiday cookie cutters

Preparation

For each child, find a box large enough for him/her to put the clay gift made on Day 4 into it.

Plan on how you will bake the Christmas sugar cookies in Learning Activity 3.

Prepare sheets of gelatin for the children to cut into holiday shapes for eating.

Prepare duplicated notes reminding parents of the party on Day 8.

Learning Activities

1. Sing some holiday songs with the children. After singing for a while, provide the children with rhythm instruments and invite them to accompany the singing. Then play a tape or record of holiday music and invite the children to accompany the music with their instruments.
2. Give each child a box in which he or she can put the clay handprint made on Day 4. Tape the poem from Day 4 to the top of the box. Then help the children use the wrapping paper they made on Day 6 to wrap the two gifts they made on Day 4. Help the children tape or glue the paper ornaments they made on Day 5 to the wrapped box. Tell the children that they will give the gifts to their parents at the Christmas party on Day 8.
    Note: Let the children wrap the gifts as independently as possible because the parents will enjoy their efforts.
3. Invite the children to make Christmas sugar cookies from refrigerated dough. Provide cookie cutters and encourage the children to cut out their cookies.
    Note: If baking sugar cookies in the classroom is a problem, purchase the cookies and invite the children to decorate them.
4. While the cookies bake, sing Christmas songs or read the children a Christmas story.
5. When the cookies are baked, provide the children with edible decorating materials and invite the children to decorate the cookies. Tell the children that they will get to eat these cookies with their parents at the party on Day 8.
6. Using cookie cutters, cut the prepared finger gelatin into holiday shapes and invite the children to enjoy, Figure 21-6.

Figure 21-6

7. Send home a note reminding the parents that they are invited to a party on Day 8 in their child's classroom.

Note: Keep the wrapped gift and the cookies for the party on Day 8.

Day 8: Celebrating!

Materials

- Rhythm instruments and bells
- Holiday cookie cutters and modeling clay/dough
- Storybooks
- Easels, painting shirts or smocks, paper, and finger paint
- Shaving cream and red or green coloring
- Rice table equipped with sand and small red and green objects
- Wrapped gifts from Day 7
- Cookies from Day 7
- Laced stockings the children made on Day 6

Preparation

Set up a series of five stations as indicated in "Learning Activities."

In the Cutting Station put cookie cutters and commercial or homemade modeling clay/dough. (See "Recipes" in Section III.)

In the Reading Station put a variety of storybooks that the children can "read" to their parents or the parents can read to the children, Figure 21-7.

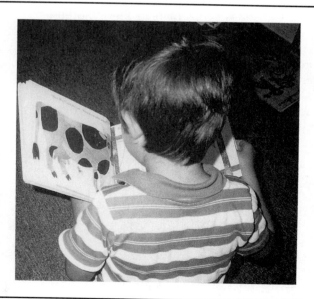

Figure 21-7

In the Painting Station put all the equipment necessary for finger painting.

In the Touching Station put shaving cream that is colored red or green, Figure 21-8.

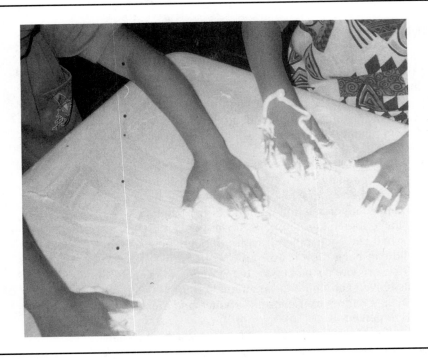

Figure 21-8

In the Finding Treasures Station prepare a rice table in which you have hidden very small objects that are colored red and green.

Learning Activities

1. Invite parents to interact with their children. Then gather the children and their parents in a circle and sing holiday songs. Bring out the rhythm instruments. If possible, have bells available for the singing of "Jingle Bells."

2. Invite the children and their parents to visit the following play stations you have prepared: 1) Cutting; 2) Reading; 3) Painting; 4) Touching; and 5) Finding Treasures. Encourage the parents and children to enjoy as many of these activities as they like.

3. Afterward encourage the children to get their wrapped presents from Day 7 and give them to their parents. Invite the parents to open the presents.

4. While the parents are at the stations and opening gifts, put out the treats—the cookies the children prepared on Day 7 and any snacks the parents

brought to class. Invite the parents to come up with their children for their snacks. Allow the children and their parents to sit anywhere in the room.

5. At the end of the party, invite the parents to take home the stockings the children made on Day 6.

Additional Activities

1. Storybook. Read the children the storybook *Rudolph, the Red-Nosed Reindeer*. (See the bibliography in Section III.)

2. Christmas cards. Invite the children to make Christmas cards to give to their parents. Fold a sheet of paper for each child and have ready pictures from old Christmas cards, Christmas shapes made from scraps of construction paper, and stickers for the children to add to their cards. Help the children write a message on their cards.

3. Finger painting. Invite the children to use either green or red finger paint on white paper. After the paintings have dried, give each child a black marker and invite the children to draw ornaments on their paper. Print each child's name and the date on the bottom of his or her painting.

4. Wooden ornaments. Invite the children to paint small wooden ornaments that you purchased or had cut. Lace a piece of yarn through the top of the ornament, so the child can hang it on his or her Christmas tree at home. When the ornaments are dry, put a small photo of the child in the center.

5. Sponge art ornaments. Give each child an ornament cut from white construction paper. Invite the children to use a small sponge and dab red and green tempera on the ornament.

6. Making a Santa. Help the children make Santa's face by attaching a triangle of red construction paper to a paper plate to make a hat. Then have the children make eyes with a felt-tipped marker. Use a pom-pom for the nose. Then use some curled strips of paper for the beard or use cotton balls.

7. Field trip. Arrange for the children to go to a local shopping center or a holiday display. Make sure to take along lots of helpers, as the holiday crowds can be a problem.

#22   Valentine's Day

Objective

By participating in a series of valentine activities, the children will celebrate their valentine joy and learn more about interacting appropriately with peers and adults in a social situation.

Day 1: Making Valentines and Valentine Boxes

Materials

- Storybook *Charlie Brown in Love* or another storybook about Valentine's Day
- White construction paper
- Small boxes (one per child), crayons, heart stickers, doilies, cotton balls, felt-tipped markers, and glue
- Camera that can produce instant pictures
- Parent notes and class list

Preparation

Find a copy of *Charlie Brown in Love*. (See the bibliography in Section III.) Or find another valentine story the children might enjoy. Prepare to read the story out loud with expression.

After reading Learning Activities 2 and 3, decide how you will go about making valentines and prepare the appropriate materials.

Duplicate a parent note inviting the parents to the valentine party on Day 4. Duplicate the class list of children's names.

Learning Activities

1. Gather the children around you and read them a story about Valentine's Day. Invite the children's comments on the story and on Valentine's Day.
2. Show the children the piece of white paper on which you have drawn a large, red heart. As you print the words "What is love?" above the heart on the paper, read the question to the children. Ask the children what they think love is. If the children are too young to understand the question, invite them to color on the heart. Print their names next to the part they colored.
3. If you want the children to make individual valentines in which they say what love means to them, provide each child with a sheet of white construction paper on which you have drawn a heart and printed the question "What is love?" Ask each child what love is and print the child's response on the paper. Then invite the children to color their valentines. Encourage the children to take their valentines home at the end of the day and to give them to their parents.
4. Tell the children that they will have a Valentine's Party on Day 4. Invite the children to make their own individual valentine boxes for the party. Tell the children that everyone in the room will put valentines in their boxes. Provide a variety of decorating materials and encourage the children to make their boxes beautiful. As the children work, take individual photos of them and tape or glue each child's picture to his or her valentine box. Next to each picture, print the child's name.
   Note: Keep the individual valentine boxes in the classroom for use on Day 4.
5. At the end of the day, send a note home with the children inviting their parents to the party on Day 4. Include with your note a list of the children in the room so that the parents can help their children prepare a valentine for each classmate.

Day 2: Making Valentine People and Tasting Red

Materials

- Red construction paper and scissors
- Envelopes (one per child)
- Felt-tipped markers or crayons
- Lengths of strings (one string per child)
- Samples of "red" food—strawberries, raspberries, apples, tomatoes, cherries, licorice, candy, and so on
- Blunt-edged scissors (optional)

Preparation

Cut hearts and strips from red construction paper so that each child can make a valentine person. For each child you will need a large heart for the body, a smaller heart for the head, four smaller hearts for the two hands and two feet, and four red strips for the arms and legs. Put each child's set of materials in an envelope.

Following the directions in Learning Activity 2, make your own valentine person.

Learning Activities

1. Gather the children around you and show them the valentine person you made, Figure 22-1. After the children have examined it, put the sample away so that the children do not imitate it too closely.

Figure 22-1

2. Give each child an envelope containing the parts for a valentine person. Provide glue or tape and show the children how to attach the two larger hearts together to make the body and the head. Then attach the four strips of red paper to make the arms and legs. Finally, attach a small heart to each strip to make the hands and feet. After the children have made the valentine people, encourage them to draw a face on their valentine person. As they work, talk about facial features—eyes, nose, mouth. Finally, attach a string to the head of each valentine person and hang the art form from the ceiling.

   Note: Depending on the abilities of the children, you may want to invite them to cut out their own paper hearts to make the valentine person.

3. Gather the children around a table and invite them to taste red food. Provide the various foods you've gathered and encourage the children's comments as they taste the food. Things like apples, beets, gelatin desserts, cranberries, tomatoes, etc. Make the necessary modifications for children with feeding problems or allergies.

Note: Before planning the tasting activity of this lesson, be sure to find out which children have allergies to the foods you've selected. Also be aware of the children with feeding problems. Prepare special red food for them.

Note: To enhance the red color of the day, let the children drink from a red straw, have red placemats at the table, decorate with red flowers or fruit, and use red napkins.

Day 3: Discovering Red

Materials

- Red objects
- Prepared red gelatin in shallow pans and cookie cutters
- Empty cereal boxes (one per child), tape, and red construction paper
- Painting shirts or smocks, marbles, spoons, saucers or bowls of pink and white tempera, and liquid dishwashing soap
- Plastic bibs; water table; red coloring; objects for dipping, pouring, pumping, and squeezing water
- Ingredients for baking cookies (optional)

Preparation

Place many red objects around the classroom.

Prepare red gelatin in shallow pans so that the children can use cookie cutters to cut edible shapes for the party on Day 4.

Prepare for marble painting in Learning Activities 3 and 4 by cutting hearts from red construction paper (one heart per child). Tape each heart into the bottom of a cereal box (one heart per box). Prepare the dishes of tempera (pink and white) by mixing liquid dishwashing soap with the paint for easier cleanup.

Prepare the water table by adding red coloring to the water.

Decide if you will bake cookies in class or if you will order them from a bakery.

Learning Activities

1. Gather the children around you and invite them to search the room for all the red objects in it. If the children cannot identify red, point out red things and tell them not only the color but what the object is. For instance, you might say, "I see a red wagon by the shelf" or "There are some red dishes in the kitchen area."
   Music Note: "If Your Clothes Have Any Red" or "Mary Wore Her Red Dress" from *Piggyback Songs for Infants and Toddlers*
2. Invite the children to use cookie cutters to make edible shapes from the red gelatin you prepared in shallow pans. Tell the children that they will

get to eat their red gelatin at the party on Day 4.

3. Show the children how to make a marble painting by dipping marbles in white or pink tempera, taking the marbles out of the paint with a spoon, dropping the marbles into a cereal box, and then rolling them back and forth across the bottom of the box. Untape the valentine from the bottom of your cereal box and show the children how the marbles colored the heart.

4. Invite the children to put marbles into tempera paint and make their own marble painting. Encourage the children to roll their cereal box back and forth so that the marbles will roll across the heart. Talk about what the marbles are doing and the motion of going back and forth. Afterward let the marble paintings dry so that the children can take them home.

5. Put plastic bibs on the children and invite them to play with red water at the water table, Figure 22-2. As they play, talk about the color red; the actions of pouring, floating, squeezing, sinking; and the concepts *full* and *empty*.

Figure 22-2

6. If time permits, bake some heart-shaped sugar cookies for the party on Day 4.
    Note: If there is not enough time to bake cookies purchase them at the bakery or store. Be aware that you sometimes need to place an order for these specially-shaped cookies.

Day 4: Celebrating!

Materials

*   Tape or record of party music and cassette player or phonograph

- Musical and rhythm instruments
- Individual valentine boxes from Day 1
- Heart-shaped sugar cookies
- Red frosting, spreading tools, red sugar sprinkles, and other edible decorating items
- Red gelatin shapes from Day 3
- A red drink, paper cups, and plates
- Storybooks

Preparation

Make the frosting for decorating the cookies.

Select a storybook to read to the children. Prepare to read the story out loud with expression.

Learning Activities

1. Encourage the parents who have come as guests to play with their children in any of the play areas. Play happy music and invite the children and guests to dance, sing, play instruments in accompaniment, and generally enjoy themselves.
2. Direct the guests and children to the individual valentine boxes. Invite the guests and children to put the valentines they have brought to class into the appropriate boxes. After everyone has put cards in the appropriate boxes, invite each child to open his or her box and look at the valentines within it.

    Note: Depending on your group, you may want to have photos on each of the boxes. Another idea is to not have the children put names on the valentines and they can just put them in the boxes.
3. Invite the children and parents to decorate their own heart cookies. Provide edible decorating material.
4. When all is ready, invite the children to help you set out the valentine snack of cookies, a red drink, and the red gelatin from Day 3. Encourage everyone to eat and enjoy!
5. If time permits, read the children a story or invite each parent to read a story to his or her child.

    Note: This party provides a good way for parents to get to know some of their child's classmates.

    Note: You may also want to change the party menu to a more nutritious menu.

Additional Activities

1. Valentine collage. Provide the children with a variety of small red items and invite the children to glue these to a large sheet of paper. Talk about the color red.

2. Printing. Invite the children to print with potato, apple, or green-pepper halves. Use red tempera mixed with liquid dishwashing soap.
3. Hearts. Invite the children to help you make a valentine tree. Put a large branch into a bucket of sand. Attach paper valentines to the large branch with yarn or string.
4. Textures. Add red coloring to shaving cream and invite the children to play with it.
5. Modeling clay/dough. Make some red modeling clay/dough for the children. (See "Recipes" in Section III.) Encourage the children to be creative with their red dough. You may even want to have the modeling clay/dough available for use during the party on Day 4. Invite both the guests and the children to enjoy playing with it.

#23   Saint Patrick's Day

Objective

By looking at green objects, cooking, baking, and making wind socks, the children will learn to identify the color green and will celebrate Saint Patrick's Day.

Day 1: Discovering Green

Materials

- Grocery bag and green objects—such as a shamrock, a plant, a stalk of celery, a green apple, green leaves, pickles, limes, grapes—or pictures of green things, or plastic green things
- Green and black construction paper, scissors, and envelopes (one per child)

- Paste or glue sticks and felt-tipped markers or crayons
- Green-colored drink and paper cups

Preparation

Put some green objects or pictures in a bag, Figure 23-1. Be sure to have other objects colored green around the room.

Figure 23-1

Following the directions in Learning Activity 4, make a shamrock person.

For each child cut out a large green shamrock, four small green shamrocks, four strips of green construction paper, and a black hat. Put each set of materials in an envelope.

Learning Activities

1. Gather the children around you and tell them that today they get to talk about the color green. From your prepared bag, take out—one by one—the green objects. Stress green as you talk about each object. For instance, say something like "This is a green pickle. It tastes so good!" "This is a plant. It has green leaves. I like to watch it grow," and so on.
   Note: Keep the bag of green objects available for use on Day 2.
2. Invite the children to look around the room and discover all the green things in it. If they are unable to identify the color green, just point to green things and give the children the correct information.
3. Gather the children in the art area and show them the shamrock person you made before class. Pass the object around for the children to touch

and play with. Then put the sample away so that the children do not imitate it as they make their own.

4. Give each child an envelope containing a set of materials for making a shamrock person, Figure 23-2. Help the children paste the four green strips to their large shamrock to make arms and legs. Help them paste the four small shamrocks to the "arms" and "legs" to make hands and feet. Show the children how to paste the black hat to their shamrock person and how to use a crayon or felt-tipped marker to add facial features.

Figure 23-2

As the children work on creating their shamrock persons, talk about what they are doing. Say things like "Oh, you are putting on her feet now" or "You put a big smile on your person, I wonder if he's happy." Encourage the children to take their completed shamrock person home or hang the children's work in the classroom.

5. Share with the children a drink that is colored green.

Day 2: Cooking Green

Materials

- Storybook *Green Eggs and Ham*
- Aprons, electric frying pan, knife, mixing bowl, and fork
- Ham, fresh eggs, and green food coloring
- Toaster, bread, butter or margarine, plastic knives and forks, and paper plates
- Large sheet of white paper, felt-tipped green markers and green crayons, paste or glue sticks
- Bag
- Green, textured objects that can be glued to paper

Preparation

Find a copy of *Green Eggs and Ham*. (See the bibliography in Section III.) Prepare to read the story out loud with expression.

Prepare a bag for Learning Activity 4. Fill the bag with objects colored green (pictures, material, scraps of construction paper, leaves, and so on) that children can paste or glue to a sheet of paper. Try to find some objects that are textured.

Prepare the ham for cooking by cutting it into small pieces.

Learning Activities

1. Gather the children around you and read *Green Eggs and Ham*. Afterward invite their comments and questions. Children enjoy the rhyme and rhythm of this book, Figure 23-3.

Figure 23-3

2. Tell the children that today they get to make green eggs. Gather the children in the cooking area and help each child put on an apron. Invite the children to help you crack and beat the eggs in a bowl. Add green food coloring and pieces of ham to the egg mixture. Pour the mixture into an electric frying pan and invite the children to watch as the eggs cook. Talk about how the eggs change as they cook.

Note: This is a good time to reinforce safety rules.

3. While the eggs cook, make toast and invite the children to butter their own piece. When all is ready, eat and enjoy!

   Note: Be sure of food allergies before asking the children to eat the meal they prepared today. Lap boards are good on wheelchairs, so the children can help beat the eggs.

4. After the cooking experience, place a large sheet of white paper on the floor and a bag full of green things. Dump the contents of the bag on the floor and invite the children to make a big green picture. Encourage the children to feel the textured objects as they add them to the picture. Encourage the children to use their felt-tipped markers and crayons to draw on the picture. As necessary, assist the children with pasting and gluing.

   Note: Position children with cerebral palsy to allow for the best learning experience. Invite children with visual handicaps to enjoy feeling different textures before pasting them on the sheet of paper.

Day 3: Eating Green

Materials

- Variety of green food, such as grapes, celery, lettuce, pickles, peas, beans, limes, and apples
- Green baby foods (optional)

Preparation

Wash the food before giving it to the children to sample.

Learning Activities

1. Gather the children at the snack table and show them all the green food you have assembled, Figure 23-4. Invite the children to feel some of the food items and to talk about how they feel. Wash these items before allowing them to taste.

Figure 23-4

2. Encourage the children to sample the food. As they chew, talk about the texture of each food item and also about the sound it makes when the children eat it. Introduce the concepts *sweet* and *sour* during this lesson.
    Note: For children with feeding problems you will want to substitute green baby foods, such as strained peas, strained beans, and thickened green grape juice.

Day 4: Making Green Wind Socks

Materials

*   Aprons, sugar-cookie dough, shamrock cookie cutter, cookie sheets, and oven
*   Wind sock materials
*   Bowls of green frosting and spreading utensils

Preparation

If you have a facility that will allow you to bake cookies, gather the ingredients and utensils for making shamrock sugar cookies. If this is not possible, purchase shamrock sugar cookies for the children to frost and eat during snack time.

Read through Learning Activity 3a and 3b and decide which type of wind sock the children will make. Collect the materials for the wind socks and make one as a sample. Note that whichever method you follow for making a wind sock you will need to prepare materials for the children.

Learning Activities

1. If you are going to make cookies today, gather the children in the cooking area and help each child put on an apron. Then help the children roll out the dough, use the cookie cutters, place the cookies on the cookie sheets, and bake the cookies. Tell the children that they will frost and eat their cookies after they cool.
2. Show the children the wind sock you made before class and talk about what a wind sock is. Invite the children's comments and questions. Then tell them that they get to make a wind sock today.
3. Provide the children with wind sock materials, and using one of the following methods, help the children make their individual wind socks:
    a) Cut three-foot-long sheets of paper from a green roll. Draw a line about one foot from the top of the paper. Then draw lines vertically to the bottom about two inches apart. Give the children scissors and invite them to cut up on the vertical lines to the one-foot line. Then staple the top and encourage the children to attach shamrock stickers or green construction-paper shamrocks to their wind socks. Help the children attach yarn to the top for hanging.

Note: This method of making a wind sock is a good one to use if your group can handle cutting and your objective is to see how well the children can cut.

b)   Cut two-inch strips of green crepe paper for the children to glue to a green construction-paper cylinder that you have glued or stapled for them (one per child). Encourage the children to attach shamrock stickers or construction-paper shamrocks to the outside of the cylinder and attach yarn to the top for hanging.

4.   After the children complete their wind socks, invite the children to come to the cooking area. Provide green frosting and encourage the children to decorate their cooled shamrock cookies. Then eat and enjoy!

5.   Encourage the children to take their wind socks home and hang them outside. Note that the wind socks will not last long in wind and rain.

Additional Activities

1.   Storybook. Gather the children around you and read the story *What Good Luck! What Bad Luck!* (see the bibliography in Section III.) Provide materials so that the children can paint their own individual rainbows or else invite the children to paint one large rainbow for the classroom. Put a small pot of gold at the bottom of the class rainbow.

2.   Match a shamrock. Make a variety of shamrocks with different designs on them. Make two of each design and invite the children to match them.

3.   Parade. Provide materials so that the children can make green hats. Paint a green shamrock on the children's cheeks. Then give the children a rhythm instrument, play some marching music, and invite them to walk in a Saint Patrick's Day parade around the classroom.

#24   Easter

Objective

By making baskets and bonnets, dyeing eggs, and doing other sensory activities, the children will celebrate Easter.

Day 1: Experiencing Sensory Activities

Materials

- Beans, bins, scoops, containers, and shovels
- Shaving cream, bowls, and therapy balls
- Empty liquid-dishwashing containers or empty baby-food jars
- Food and other items that have a distinctive odor, such as peanut butter, cinnamon sticks, coffee, soap crystals, lemon, orange, apple, bubble gum, and potpourri
- Plastic pull-apart eggs and a basket
- Child's plastic wading pool and plastic balls

Preparation

For Learning Activity 1 collect several large bins. Into each bin put a different kind of bean.

For Learning Activity 2 put shaving cream into bowls and rub it onto therapy balls.

For Learning Activity 3 put cotton balls with a fragrance into empty plastic dishwashing containers. Or if you prefer, use empty baby-food jars. Paint the outside of the jars or line them with paper.

For Learning Activity 4 put a variety of plastic pull-apart eggs in a large Easter basket.

For Learning Activity 5 put a variety of plastic balls into a child's wading pool.

Learning Activities

1. Invite the children to play in the bean bins without mixing up the beans. Encourage them to feel the different textures and to note the different sizes.
2. Invite the children to play with the shaving cream in bowls. Then gather them in an area you can easily clean and give them the therapy balls on which you have put shaving cream. Invite the children to rub the balls on their skin.
3. Invite the children to smell the jars you prepared. Encourage all children to guess each smell. Discuss the smells with the children.
4. Invite the children to take apart, play with, and reassemble a collection of plastic eggs.
5. Invite the children to get into the plastic wading pool and roll around on the balls.

Note: When the children play in the wading pool, caution them to be careful of the other children and to keep all the balls in the pool. If possible place children who are normally in wheelchairs into the pool so that they can feel the balls on their bodies.

Day 2: Making Paper Easter Eggs

Materials

- Storybook *Spot's First Easter*
- Easter baskets and colorful plastic eggs
- Tagboard and decorating material, such as Easter stickers, felt-tipped markers, crayons, paint, scraps of construction paper, and glue
- Large sheet of drawing paper

Preparation

Find a copy of *Spot's First Easter*. (See the bibliography in Section III.) Prepare to read the story out loud with expression.

Put the plastic eggs in the Easter baskets. Be sure to have enough eggs for matching.

Cut each child a tagboard egg to decorate. Draw an empty Easter basket on a big sheet of paper. Cut it out and attach it to a large bulletin board.

Learning Activities

1. Gather the children around you and read *Spot's First Easter*. Invite the children's comments and questions.
2. Show the children the baskets into which you have placed plastic eggs. Discuss the eggs with the children. Talk about color or count the eggs or match them.
3. Gather the children in the art area. Give each child a tagboard egg and invite the children to decorate their eggs with the materials you have provided. Afterward print the children's names on their eggs and put them on the bulletin board in the basket you prepared.
   Note: Keep the bulletin board decorated until Day 8 when you will use the tagboard eggs.

Day 3: Hunting for Easter Eggs!

Materials

- Plastic eggs
- Treat (optional)
- Construction paper and scissors (optional)
- Storybook *Peter Cottontail*
- Small baskets (one per child) or small paper bags

- One large basket
- Tape or record of "Here Comes Peter Cottontail" and cassette player or phonograph
- Yellow food, such as bananas, cheese, or lemon finger-gelatin

Preparation

Before the children arrive, hide plastic eggs around the classroom for an egg hunt. Consider putting a treat, such as cookies, in some of them. If you are unable to find a quantity of plastic eggs, make eggs from colorful construction paper.

Learning Activities

1. Gather the children around you and read *Peter Cottontail*. Invite the children's comments and questions.
2. Tell the children that the Easter bunny has hidden eggs all around their classroom for them to find. Give each child a small basket or a paper bag, Figure 24-1. Then encourage the children to search for eggs. As they hunt, talk about looking *up*, *down*, *under*, and *on*.
3. After the Easter egg hunt is over, invite the children to play with their eggs for a while. If you have hidden edible surprises in the eggs, invite the children to eat and enjoy these.

Figure 24-1

4. Ask the children to place all their eggs in a large basket and tell them that during free time they can play with the eggs again.

5. Play the song "Here Comes Peter Cottontail" and invite the children to add gestures and movement to the song.
   Note: Keep the tape or record of "Here Comes Peter Cottontail" for use on Day 4.
6. For a snack, provide a yellow food and use the word *yellow* in speaking of the food. You could serve pineapple, pineapple juice, yellow apple slices, banana, scrambled eggs, custard, or lemon gelatin desserts.

Day 4: Meeting Bunnies

Materials

- Live rabbits
- Small paper plates, white construction paper, scissors, paste or glue sticks, cotton balls, and felt-tipped markers
- Tape or record from Day 3

Preparation

Plan whether you can bring some bunnies to the classroom or if you will need to take a field trip to a pet store to see rabbits.

Following the directions in Learning Activity 3, make a paper bunny to show the children. Cut a pair of bunny ears for each child from white construction paper.

Learning Activities

1. Show the children the bunnies you brought to class or take the children on a field trip to a pet store so that they can note the color of bunnies and see how bunnies eat, how their noses twitch, and how their bodies are formed.
2. Afterward gather the children in the art area. Show the children the bunny you made before class and invite them to pass it around and touch it.
3. Begin to play the tape or record of "Here Comes Peter Cottontail." While the song is playing, give each child a small paper plate and help the children fold the plate in half and glue the edges together. Give each child a set of paper ears and encourage the children to attach their ears to the folded paper plate. Show the children how to attach a cotton ball to one side of the plate for the nose and to the other side for the tail. Encourage the children to use felt-tipped markers to add eyes to the face. Display the bunnies in the classroom.
   Note: Encourage the children to independently do as much of the work as they can.

Day 5: Making Omelets

Materials

- Storybook *Silly Eggs, The Egg Book,* or *Horton Hatches the Egg*
- Aprons, fork, mixing bowl, electric frying pan
- Fresh eggs
- Milk, cheese, mushrooms, bacon bits (optional)
- Toaster, bread, butter or margarine, plastic knives and forks, and paper plates
- Tape or record of "The Bunny Hop" and cassette player or phonograph

Preparation

Find a copy of one of the storybooks. (See the bibliography in Section III.) Prepare to read the story out loud with expression.

Prepare the ham for cooking by cutting it into small pieces.

Find a tape or record of "The Bunny Hop." Practice doing motions to the music.

Learning Activities

1. Gather the children around you and read the chosen story. Afterward invite the children's comments and questions.
2. Show the children the eggs the Easter bunny left for them to make an omelet. Gather the children in the cooking area and help each child put on an apron. Invite the children to help you crack and beat the eggs in a bowl. Add other ingredients. Pour the mixture into an electric frying pan and invite the children to watch as the omelet cooks. Talk about how the eggs change as they cook.
3. While the eggs cook, make toast and invite the children to butter their own piece. When all is ready, eat and enjoy!
4. Play the record or tape of "The Bunny Hop." Encourage the children to hop and dance around. If possible, try to get the children in a line and hop together.
   Note: Invite children in wheelchairs to follow your "bunny hop" line. Or if they are small enough, hold them and hop with them. Physically challenged children will need assistance.

   Note: The day before gathering the ingredients for this class, you might want to ask the children what they would like in their omelets.

Day 6: Making Easter Eggs and Bonnets

Materials

- Commercial egg-dyeing kit or food coloring, spoons, cups, and fresh eggs (one per child)
- Large paper plates (one per child) and ribbons or crepe-paper streamers (two per child)

- Decorating materials, such as cellophane grass, paste or glue sticks, and construction paper
- Tape or record of happy music and cassette player or phonograph
- Rhythm instruments

Preparation

Set up an egg-coloring center with cups of dye, spoons, and a "magic" crayon from a commercial kit.

Set up a bonnet-making center in the room and explain to an aide how to help the children make Easter bonnets. Attach two ribbons or crepe-paper streamers to each paper plate so that the children can tie their bonnet under their chins. Cut out a variety of flowers, bunnies, chicks, and eggs from colorful construction paper for decorating the bonnets. Using these materials, make your own Easter bonnet.

Learning Activities

1. Divide the children into two groups. Invite Group 1 to color eggs. Have Group 2 go with an aide to that part of the room you have set aside for making bonnets. Tell the children that they will all get to do both activities.
2. Gather the children in Group 1 around the table on which you have placed all the materials they will need for coloring eggs. Demonstrate how to color an egg and how to print a name on it. Then invite the children to color their own eggs. Provide help as needed. Be sure to put the children's names on their eggs. Tell the children that the next day they will make Easter baskets into which they can put their eggs.
   Note: Keep the eggs for use on Days 7 and 8.
3. While Group 1 colors eggs, invite Group 2 to make Easter bonnets. Show the children the bonnet you made. Put your bonnet on and model it for the children. Then pass it around for them to touch. Put your bonnet away so that the children do not copy it as they make their own.
4. Give each child a plate prepared with ribbons or streamers. Encourage the children to use the decorating materials to make an Easter bonnet.
   Note: Keep the bonnets for use on Day 8.
5. After each group has completed its project, invite the groups to change places.
6. When everyone has made an egg and a hat, have an Easter parade. Play some happy music, offer rhythm instruments to the children, and encourage them to enjoy their own Easter parade!

Day 7: Making Easter Baskets

Materials

- Empty milk cartons or berry baskets and white construction paper
- Decorating materials, such as Easter stickers, cellophane grass, felt-tipped markers, scraps of construction paper, and crayons

- Colored eggs from Day 6
- Stuffed bunnies or other animals
- Construction paper
- Ribbons (optional)

Preparation

If you use milk cartons to make Easter baskets, cut them down to about four inches and then cover the outside with white construction paper. If you use berry baskets, cover them as well. Decorate your own Easter basket and put cellophane grass in it and the egg you colored on Day 6.

From colorful construction paper, cut out large paper eggs (at least two eggs per color) for the children to match.

For a harder activity, place a design on each egg for the children to match. Be sure to use each design twice.

Learning Activities

1. Invite the children to make their own Easter baskets. Show them the basket you made and let them pass it around and touch it. Then put your basket away so that the children do not copy it.
2. Give each child a prepared milk carton or berry basket. Provide decorating materials and encourage the children to decorate their baskets. Afterward give each child his or her egg from Day 6 and have the children put their eggs in the baskets and set them aside.
3. Give each child a stuffed bunny or small stuffed animal. Then tell the children to use their stuffed animal to follow your directions. Give directions like "Put your animal on your head," "Put your animal on your shoulder," "Put your animal next to your elbow." After giving each direction, model for the children where the stuffed animal should go. Continue to do this, even if all of the children do not know all their body parts.
4. Give the children paper eggs and invite them to match them by color or design.

   Note: You may want to invite older children to weave ribbons through empty berry baskets to make their Easter baskets.

   Keep the Easter baskets and the egg-match game for use on Day 8.

Day 8: Celebrating Easter!

Materials

- Sugar cookies, frosting, food coloring, and plastic knives
- Sheet of white construction paper and scissors
- Sheet of stationery
- Easter baskets from Day 7
- Easter eggs from Day 6

- Easter bonnets from Day 6
- Tagboard eggs from Day 2
- Plastic eggs and candy
- Apple juice, paper cups, paper plates, and napkins
- Tape or record of "The Bunny Hop" and cassette player or phonograph

Preparation

Prepare yellow, pink or white frosting.

On a piece of white construction paper make bunny paw prints. Duplicate this page and cut out the paw prints. Ask your aides to tape the bunny paw prints around the room while you and the children take a walk outside the classroom during Learning Activity 3. Also ask your aides to hide plastic eggs and candy while you and the children go on an Easter parade outdoors or in the school halls.

Write a note to the children from the Easter bunny. In your note compliment the children on all the work they have done in the past two weeks and tell them about the plastic eggs and candy hidden in the room. Ask your aides to put your Easter bunny note in a prominent place when you and the children are walking in your Easter parade.

Learning Activities

1. Gather the children around a table on which you have put sugar cookies, frosting, and knives. Invite the children to frost the cookies.
2. Give the children their Easter baskets from Day 7. Recall with the children that they made the eggs that are in the baskets. Invite the children to put on the bonnets that they made on Day 6.
   Note: If any child chooses not to wear a bonnet in the parade, simply encourage the child to hold it and parade with the rest of the children.
3. Take the children outside of the classroom for an Easter parade.
4. When the children return from their parade, act very surprised when you see the bunny prints. Ask the children to guess who has been to their classroom to visit them. Read the children the note left by the Easter bunny. Then invite the children to go around their room and fill their baskets with the surprises left by the Easter bunny.
   Note: Make sure to have extra treats for any child who is unable to find a treat while hunting.
5. Afterward gather the children at the snack table and invite them to eat their treats. In addition to what was hidden provide the cookies the children frosted and apple juice.
6. If time permits play the song "The Bunny Hop" and bring out the egg-match game from Day 7.
7. At the end of the day send the children home with their bonnets, baskets, dyed egg, and their tagboard egg from Day 2.

Additional Activities

1. Bunny cake. Make two eight-inch round yellow cakes. Use one for the face of a bunny. Cut the other one into ears and a bow tie, Figure 24-2. Have the children frost and use edible decorating materials to make a face on the cake. Or help the children decorate cupcakes for Easter.

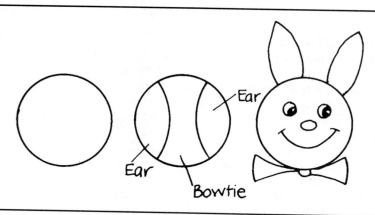

Figure 24-2

2. Marbled eggs. Invite the children to marble paint some white construction-paper eggs. Tape a paper egg in the bottom of a cereal box. (Provide a box for each child.) Dip marbles in tempera paint, spoon them out, and then drop them in the box. Show the children how to roll the marbles back and forth across the bottom of the box. When the paper eggs have dried, remove them from the cereal boxes, print the children's names on them, and encourage the children to take them home.

3. Tissue-paper eggs. Cut out a large egg shape from tagboard. Prepare squares of tissue paper and a mixture of glue and water. Invite the children to place the tissue on the egg shape and brush the water mixture over them. Proceed to do this over the entire egg. Let the egg dry and paste it into a large paper basket on a bulletin board.

part seven
Miscellaneous

Speech/Language, Developmentally Delayed, and Mentally Handicapped

- The concepts *float, sink, shiny,* and *round* can be reinforced by leaving the table out all week.
- Language expansion can occur when using the "Elephant Feely" box by asking "I wonder" statements.
- Have other learning centers during the week revolve around shopping and money.
- Assist the child with fine-motor difficulties to spread the peanut butter on the bread.

Multihandicapped and Orthopedically Impaired

- Positioning the child at the sand and water tables is very important for maximum participation.
- Substitute some of the foods for the child with feeding problems.
- Help the child in a wheelchair onto the blanket for the picnic.
- Attach the backpacks to the back of the wheelchair.

Emotionally Disturbed

- Plan ahead and help the child who may be overstimulated by Circus Day to make some good choices of activities. Make the choices things that you know will be best for the child.
- Sand tables can be relaxing for the child.

Other Health Impaired

- Children with asthma or cystic fibrosis may have difficulty with the blowing activities.
- Diet and allergies must be taken into consideration.

Blind and Vision Impairments

- Let the child experience the feeling of the bubbles on the skin by gently blowing them on him/her.

- Direct the child through the rhymes and chants.

Deaf and Hearing Impairments

- Direct the child to look at the colorful pictures in the books.
- Direct the child to look at the other children to keep in rhythm with the music and rhymes.

#25   Bubbles

Objective

By participating in a series of sensory activities, the children will display their oral-motor development and will celebrate the wonder of water.

Day 1: Blowing Bubbles

Materials

- Water table equipped with a sheet of plastic, pans of water, containers, scoops, jar rings, and an egg beater
- Bubble-blowing mixture and bubble wands

Preparation

Before class set up a water table by putting a sheet of plastic beneath a table. Fill several large and deep pans with water.

Buy a commercial bubble-blowing mixture or make your own solution. (See "Recipes" in Section III.) Buy or make enough solution for use throughout this unit of study. Place the solution by the water table.

Learning Activities

1. Direct the children to the water table and invite them to experiment with the water and to blow bubbles.
2. Encourage the children to experiment with all the equipment at the water table.

Note: Keep the water table assembled for use on Day 2.

Day 2: Learning Concepts

Materials

- Water table assembled for Day 1
- Liquid dishwashing soap
- Ping-Pong balls and small plastic toys and rattles
- Objects that will float in water, such as feathers
- Objects that will sink in water, such as rocks
- Plastic bottles (one per child), bubble-blowing mixture, and bubble wands (one per child)

Preparation

Put some liquid soap in the water at the water table.
Collect a number of items that will sink and items that will float.
Put some bubble-blowing mixture into plastic bottles. Prepare one bottle for each child.
Music Note: "Blowing Bubbles" from *Piggyback Songs*

Learning Activities

1. Gather the children around the water table. Invite them to experiment with the soapy, sudsy water and the array of plastic toys, objects that will float in water, and objects that will sink, that you have provided. As the children play, introduce words such as *float, sink, shiny, round, pop, clean,* and so on.
2. When the children go outside, give each of them a plastic bottle of bubbles and a bubble wand so that they can watch their bubbles in the sunlight. Be sure to have plenty of bubble-blowing mixture available.

Day 3: Using Breath

Materials

- Ping-Pong balls, feathers, facial tissue, leaves, rocks, pencils, and so on

Preparation

Collect a variety of materials that you can use to help the children see what their breath can do when they blow on the objects.

Learning Activities

1. Show the children the materials you have collected for today. Invite them to experiment and see which ones they can move with their breath. Encourage the children to begin by trying to blow a Ping-Pong ball across the floor.
2. Invite the children to blow a feather to a partner. Encourage the partner to blow the feather back.
3. Suggest that the children try to keep a feather in the air by blowing under it, Figure 25-1.

Figure 25-1

4. Invite the children to think of other things in your classroom that might move if blown upon. Suggest that the children experiment with many objects to see which they can get to move with their breath and which they cannot.

> *Note:* If the above activities are not possible with your group, play a guessing game. Hold an object in the palm of your hand and ask the children to predict if it can be blown off your hand. Use a variety of objects.

Day 4: Exploring Taste

Materials

- Peanut butter and tongue depressors
- Pudding and spoons
- Crackers, peas, apples, crunchy cereal, cookies, toast
- Paper plates

Preparation

Prepare the food by slicing the apples, making toast, opening a can of peas, and arranging the food on separate plates.

Learning Activities

1. Gather the children around you and tell them that today will be a tasting day. Give each child a tongue depressor with peanut butter on it and invite the children to lick the tongue depressor clean.
2. Give the children pudding on a spoon and ask them to lick the spoon clean.
3. Invite the children to explore food textures. Encourage them to eat crackers, peas, apple slices, cereal, a cookie, and toast. Have paper plates available so that each child can choose what he or she wishes to eat for a snack. As the children munch away, encourage them to talk about the different textures and how the food feels in their mouths and on their tongues.

   Note: Be aware that children with poor language development and with feeding problems may have some difficulty with these activities. Some of the textures need to be substituted to provide a better consistency.

Additional Activities

1. Straw painting. Cut two or three three-inch circles from white paper for each child. Prepare several dishes of paint and provide each child with a straw. Show the children how to blow colored paint through a straw onto the circles. When the circles are dry, hang them as an array of bubbles.
2. Soap painting. Using Ivory Snow make a paste and invite the children to use it to make pictures on heavy paper.
3. Bubble making. Make a glycerine mixture and invite the children to make large bubbles. Use various sized objects to help the children make the bubbles. For instance, try large commercial bubble wands and coat hangers. Note that large bubbles help the children become aware of their bodies and the gross-motor muscles they use as they try to pop the bubbles.

#26   The Circus

Objective

By participating in activities involving the excitement of a circus, the children will learn more about the sense of touch and will work on color identification.

Day 1: Enjoying a Circus Parade

Materials

- Storybook *Spot Goes to the Circus*
- Tricycles, scooters, and wagons
- Decorating materials, such as crepe paper, tape, balloons, and other decorating materials
- Dress-up clothes
- Stuffed animals and rhythm instruments
- Tape or record of circus music and cassette player or phonograph

Preparation

Set up a route inside and outside the classroom that the children can travel on their parade.

Learning Activities

1. Gather the children around you and read *Spot Goes to the Circus*. Invite the children's comments and questions.

Fingerplay Fun: "Fingerplays Zoo" from *Rhymes for Learning Times*

2. Explain to the children that they get to have a circus parade today. Have the tricycles, scooters, wagons, and a variety of decorating materials ready. Encourage the children to decorate their vehicles.

   Note: Children in wheelchairs can have the other children help them decorate.

3. Provide dress-up clothing for those children who wish to "decorate" themselves.

4. After the children have completed their decorating, invite anyone who wishes to do so to carry stuffed animals and rhythm instruments in the parade, Figure 26-1.

Figure 26-1

5. Play music and invite the children to parade on the route you have set up.

Day 2: Making Friends with Circus Animals

Materials

- Storybook *Big and Little Are Not the Same*
- The "Elephant Feely" box and the Seal
- Plastic food or pictures of food and nonedible items, such as pencils and rulers

Preparation

Find a copy of *Big and Little Are Not the Same*. (See the bibliography in Section III.) Prepare to read the story out loud with expression.

Prepare two animal stations. In one put the "Elephant Feely" box; in the other put the Seal. (See directions for making both in "Classroom Equipment" in Section III.)

Learning Activities

1. Gather the children around you and read *Big and Little Are Not the Same.* Afterward invite the children's comments and questions. Talk about *big* and *little* animals at the circus.
2. Explain to the children that they are going to play with a big and with a small animal today. Direct them to the two animal stations and show them the "Elephant Feely" box and the Seal. Give the children time to wonder about the two animals.
3. Show the children how to use the trunk of the elephant to discover surprise objects in the box. Encourage the children to guess what these objects are. As the children touch the objects, talk about the concepts *soft, hard, smooth, big,* and *little.*
4. Show the children how to feed the Seal and provide them with a variety of items to use as food. Invite the children to put the objects into the Seal's mouth and tell whether the Seal likes to eat the objects.

> *Note:* You will want to encourage the children to go to both animal stations, but do not insist that they do so. Some children will be content to stay in only one area.

Day 3: Creating a Circus Mural and Clowns

Materials

- Large sheet of white paper
- Felt-tipped markers and crayons
- Face paints, brushes, and mirrors

Preparation

Draw a circus mural on a large sheet of paper. Include in your mural the big top, many animals, and clowns. Put this long sheet of paper in one section of the room along with coloring materials.

Learning Activities

1. Gather the children around you and explain that they are each going to do two different circus activities today. Divide the group in half.
2. Direct Group 1 to the circus mural and invite them to use felt-tipped markers or crayons to color it.
   Note: Keep the circus mural for use on Day 4.
3. Direct Group 2 to a table on which you have put face paints. Demonstrate for the children how to paint one's face as a circus clown. Invite the children to paint their own faces so that they will look like circus clowns. As the children work, tell them the name of the colors of the paint and mention the parts of their faces. For instance, you might say, "You're

putting red paint on your nose." Have mirrors available for the children to look into as they paint their faces.

Music Note: "Circus Clown, Parade, Dancing Girls" from *Creative Movement for the Developing Child: A Nursery School Handbook for Non-musicians.*

Note: If some children are frightened by the face painting, invite them to watch the other children for a while. Be ready to paint the faces of the children who ask you to do so. In the demonstration for this activity, paint your face too.

4. After about twenty minutes invite the two groups to switch activities.

Day 4: Celebrating Circus Day!

Materials

- Varied games to play
- Cupcakes and small prizes
- Rope and hula hoops
- Mural from Day 3
- Balloons
- Ice-cream cones or another favored snack

Preparation

Prepare for Circus Day by setting up games such as a cakewalk, beanbag toss, and pick-a-duck. Have cupcakes and small prizes for the children to win. Put a rope on the floor for tightrope walking and place hula hoops around the room for the children to jump through. Display the mural from Day 3. If possible invite a clown or a magician to visit the room to do tricks.

Learning Activities

1. Gather the children around you and give each child a balloon. Invite the children's comments and questions about the circus you have set up in the room.
2. Invite the children to wander around the room and participate in the varied activities.
3. Provide a favored snack for the children to eat at the end of their circus.

    Note: Be ready to reassure any children who seem afraid.

Additional Activities

1. Circus train. Cover shoe boxes with paper. Then invite the children to paste or tape pictures of circus animals to the boxes. Make a circus train by attaching the boxes with yarn or pipe cleaners.
2. Field trip. If there is a circus in town, try to arrange for the children to go.

Figure 26-2

3. Masks. Invite the children to draw and color the face of a circus animal, Figure 26-2. Help the children cut out eye holes. Attach string to the back of the masks and encourage the children to wear them.

#27   Antless Picnic

Objective

By participating in the planning of a picnic and going on a field trip, the children will become more aware of their senses and will celebrate the joy of play.

Day 1: Experiencing the Senses

Materials

- Sand table equipped with plastic sheet and varied containers, funnels, sieves, and shells
- Water table equipped with plastic sheet and varied containers, water pumps, and meat basters

- Magnifying glasses and materials to examine, such as leaves, flowers, pictures, grass, pebbles, and rocks
- Shallow pans, rice, beans, sand, and shaving cream

Preparation

For Learning Activity 1, equip a sand table with materials and place a plastic sheet under it to help with cleanup.

For Learning Activity 2, place a plastic sheet under the water table and equip it with materials.

For Learning Activity 3, collect a variety of interesting items for the children to examine through magnifying glasses.

For Learning Activity 4, prepare texture bins by placing a different material in each shallow pan.

Learning Activities

1. Gather the children around the sand table and invite them to play. While the children experiment, stress the concepts *in/out* and *full/empty*. Encourage the children to enjoy the texture of sand, Figure 27-1.

Figure 27-1

2. Invite the children to enjoy filling containers and pouring from them at a water table. Invite the children to splash the water with their hands and to use the water pumps and meat basters.

3. Give the children large and small magnifying glasses and provide a variety of objects for the children to examine.
4. Help the children take off their shoes and socks. Then invite the children to step into the texture bins with their bare feet.
   Note: This is an especially good activity for the physically challenged child.

Day 2: Playing with a Picnic Basket
Materials

- Storybook *The Picnic Bear*
- Picnic basket equipped with blanket, plates, and utensils
- Plastic food and play stove
- Furnished kitchen area

Preparation

Find a copy of *The Picnic Bear*. (See the bibliography in Section III.) Prepare to read the story out loud with expression.
Prepare a picnic basket. Equip a kitchen area with cooking utensils and tools.

Learning Activities

1. Gather the children around you and read *The Picnic Bear*. Afterward invite the children's comments and questions.
2. Bring out the picnic basket and invite the children to look at the items in it. Encourage them to play with the picnic items in the basket. Help the children spread the blanket on the floor.
3. Give the children the plastic food and invite them to go to the kitchen area and pretend to cook the food. Interact with the children and talk about how they are preparing for the picnic. Afterward encourage the children to put the plastic food on the plates, to sit on the blanket, and to pretend to eat.
4. If time permits, invite the children to retell the story of *The Picnic Bear* as they pretend to enjoy their picnic.

   Note: Keep the assembled picnic basket and the plastic food for use on Day 5.

Day 3: Role-Play Shopping for Groceries
Materials

- Purses, cash register, a variety of pretend food, shopping bags, pretend money, coupons, shopping carts, telephone, and a calculator

Preparation

Set up a grocery store in one area of the room. In the store, display various plastic foodstuffs and other items that one can buy at a grocery store.

Learning Activities

1. Gather the children around you and tell them that today they are going to go to their classroom grocery store to buy things for their picnic. Before beginning the role-playing, provide time for the children to explore the store and its items. As they explore, observe and interact with them when they initiate a conversation with you.
2. After the children have investigated the grocery area, invite them to role-play going to the store, shopping, and buying the things they will need for their classroom picnic. Encourage the children to select different roles to play—shoppers, cashiers, store manager, and baggers.
    Note: Be aware that the children will need time to make up their minds and to organize themselves for their role-playing activity.

Day 4: Playing Picnic Games

Materials

- Plastic or sponge eggs
- Laundry rope or scarves for tying legs
- Plastic horseshoe game, styrofoam baseball bat and ball, ring toss game, and baseball mitts
- Classroom swings, slides, and rocking boat

Preparation

Prepare a space in the classroom where the children can play a variety of games such as are played in parks when people are picnicking.

Learning Activities

1. Gather the children around you and tell them that today they get to play some picnic games. Begin by inviting the children to play a game in which they toss a plastic egg or a sponge egg.
2. Demonstrate for the children a three-legged race by tying one of your legs to the leg of another adult and then hopping around the room. After the children have enjoyed your demonstration, invite them to participate in a three-legged race. Tie their legs loosely and encourage them to go slowly as they run a short distance in the classroom.
3. Bring out the other games you have collected and invite the children to play them.
4. If you have playground equipment such as swings and slides, invite the children to play on them, Figure 27-2.

Figure 27-2

Day 5: Making a Backpack

Materials

- Picnic basket and plastic food from Day 2
- Large grocery sacks (one per child)
- Felt-tipped markers and crayons
- Stapler, staples and construction paper

Preparation

Following the directions in Learning Activities 3 and 4, make your own paper-bag backpack.

Cut two-inch wide strips of construction paper that are long enough to make arm loops for the children to attach to their backpacks.

Learning Activities

1. Gather the children around the items from Day 2. Invite the children to play with these items for a short time.
2. Tell the children that each of them needs a backpack for their picnic lunch and that today they will make their own paper backpacks. Show the children the backpack you made and encourage them to touch it and to put it on. Then put away your backpack so that the children do not copy it as they make their own.

3. Give each child a grocery bag. Invite the children to use felt-tipped markers or crayons to decorate the bags.
4. Help the children make backpacks out of their decorated grocery bags. First fold down the top of the grocery bag. To make loops on the backpacks for the children's arms, staple a wide vertical band of construction paper to the top and bottom of the bag on one side. Staple a second band on the other side. Help the children print their names on their backpacks.
    Note: You will need to help children in wheelchairs attach their backpacks to the back of their wheelchairs.
    Note: Keep the backpacks available for use on Days 7 and 8.

Day 6: Taking a Field Trip

Materials

*   Money for field trip to the grocery store to buy peanut butter, jelly, bread, napkins, small plastic bags, individual juice drinks or a mixable drink, and fruit

Preparation

Enlist the aid of assistants in taking the children on their field trip. Decide exactly what food you will purchase at the grocery store.

Learning Activities

1. Encourage the children to help you make a list of things they will need for their picnic on Day 8. Then take the children on a field trip to the grocery store to purchase the picnic food and other items.
    Note: Keep the food fresh for use on Days 7 and 8. Keep the other items you purchased at the grocery store ready for use on Days 7 and 8.
2. As you shop at the grocery store, talk about all the things you see and smell there. Also talk about the foods you are purchasing and how the children will use them. Point out the cash register and the cashier.
3. When you return to the classroom, invite the children to help you put away the groceries. Once again chat about what the children purchased and how they will use the food and other items. For example, you might say, "Here is the bread for the peanut butter and jelly sandwiches."

Day 7: Making Sandwiches

Materials

*   Storybook *What's for Lunch?*.
*   Food and other items from the field trip of Day 6
*   Backpacks from Day 5

Preparation

Find a copy of *What's for Lunch?* (See the bibliography in Section III.) Prepare to read the story out loud with expression.

Determine where you will keep the sandwiches the children make today so that they will be fresh on Day 8.

Learning Activities

1. Gather the children around you and read them *What's for Lunch?* Afterward invite the children's comments and questions.
2. Explain that today the children are going to pack their lunch for their picnic on Day 8. Gather the children around a large table and recall with them all the things they purchased at the grocery store on Day 6. Talk about the grocery store and their purchases.
3. Provide bread, peanut butter, and jelly so that the children can make sandwiches.
4. Help the children put their sandwiches into plastic bags and then into the paper-bag backpacks they made on Day 5. Provide other items for the children to pack, such as napkins, fruit, and so on.
5. When the children have packed their backpacks, lead them to the refrigerator and have them put their backpacks inside. Tell them that on the next day they will enjoy a picnic.

   Note: If you do not have access to a large refrigerator, remove the food items from the children's backpacks after the children leave and take the sandwiches and other perishables home with you for refrigeration.

Day 8: Enjoying a Picnic

Materials

- Blanket
- Backpacks from Day 5
- Food from Day 7
- Individual juice drinks or paper cups and a mixable drink in a container

Preparation

Decide where in the room you and the children will have your picnic. Pick out a route through the school halls that you and the children can walk on your way to your classroom picnic.

Learning Activities

1. Gather the children around you and tell them that today they are going on a picnic. Have a large blanket ready to take to the picnic so that the chil-

dren can sit on it. Bring out the children's backpacks and help them put them on. If you did not bring individual juice drinks, have a container ready in which to mix a drink.

2. Pretend to go to a park for a picnic by taking the children for a short walk in the room or outside in the hall.

3. Bring the children back to the room and lead them to the designated picnic area. Tell the children that this is a good spot for a picnic. Spread the blanket on the floor and invite the children to sit down. Help them take off their backpacks. Encourage the children to pretend to see many things from their picnic blanket.

4. Invite the children to open their backpacks and to eat their lunch.

5. After eating, help the children clean up the area. Then put their backpacks on again and take a short hike outside the room.

6. Bring the children back to the room and talk about what a picnic is like.

> *Note:* You may want to keep the backpacks for use in the unit entitled "Summer." However, if the children want to take them home, the "Summer" unit provides instructions and time for making backpacks a second time.

Additional Activities

1. Field trip. Take the children to a local park for their picnic. Take along the games from Day 4 and invite the children to play them, Figure 27-3.

Figure 27-3

2. Pretend beach. Read the children the story *Spot Goes to the Beach.* (See the bibliography in Section III.) Invite the children to play at a sand table. Provide beach balls, rings, shovels, and pails. Spread a blanket on the floor and put the picnic things on it. Invite the children to pretend that they are at the beach.

   Music Note: "To the Beach" from *Piggyback Songs*

3. Water play. Spread a plastic sheet on the floor and then put a plastic play pool on top of it. Fill the pool with warm water and let the children play with toys in it. Put plastic ducks in the water and invite the children to pretend to feed them.

4. Guests. Invite parents and grandparents to the children's picnic. Encourage them to play the games from Day 4 with the children.

Section III

Resources

part one
Stories

The Mitten

One cold morning, long, long ago, a little boy named Ivan pulled on his favorite yellow mittens, waved good-bye to his grandparents, and went out to gather wood. He trudged through the new-fallen snow, pulling his little sled behind him.

In the forest, Ivan found a spot where twigs and branches had fallen off the trees. He gathered so much wood that it kept rolling off his sled. As he bent to pick up a stick, Ivan dropped one of his yellow mittens. Little Ivan trudged back home, pulling his sled full of wood behind him, not knowing that he had lost one of his favorite mittens.

Meanwhile in the forest, a little mouse found the mitten and crawled in to keep warm. Soon, a frog came by and asked the mouse if he could come in, too. "Sure. Come in before you freeze," the mouse said. Then an owl flew down and asked if he could come into the mitten."Sure," said the mouse. "If you have good manners you can join us."

A rabbit came hopping by and said, "Is there room for me? The night is so cold."

"Sure," said the mouse. And all four animals huddled closer together.

But then a fox came and pushed his way into the mitten without even asking if he could come in! To make things even worse, a gray wolf squeezed in. Next, a wild boar came by. The other animals were beginning to get anxious, but the wild boar promised he would climb in ever so carefully. Then a great, big grizzly bear walked by, sniffed the air, and caught sight of the animals huddled in the mitten.

"Oh, go away!" cried the group. "We have no more room!"

"Nonsense," said the bear, and he jostled his way in.

Just then the seams of the mitten began to tear. And along came a tiny cricket. "I'm freezing, and the mitten looks so warm and inviting. Surely you'll let me in," he chirped. But as soon as the little cricket put his tiny, little leg in, the mitten split wide open, sending all the animals flying out in the snow!

At just that moment, Ivan realized he had lost his mitten. He ran back to the forest, but alas, all that was left of his mitten were shreds of yellow wool. And how strange! Out of the corner of his eye Ivan imagined he saw a tiny mouse in a yellow hat peeking out from behind a bush.

Ivan walked home, feeling very sad until he saw his grandmother standing by the door. Ivan's sad face broke into a big smile. In his grandmother's hands were a new pair of mittens she had knitted for him while he was gone.

Ivan and his grandparents never did find out what really happened to his other yellow mitten.

part two
Action Rhymes

Act Like an Animal

Can you hop like a rabbit?
Can you jump like a frog?
Can you walk like a duck?
Can you run like a dog?
Can you fly like a bird?
Can you swim like a fish?
Can you sit very still
As still as you wish?

Itsy Bitsy Spider

The itsy bitsy spider
climbed up the water spout.

(Hold one arm straight up for the water spout. For the spider, walk the fingers of your other hand up the spout.)

Down came the rain,

(Starting from up above your head, drop your hands and wiggle your fingers to imitate raindrops.)

and washed the spider out.
Out came the sun,

(Raise your arms overhead in a circle with your fingertips touching.)

and dried up all the rain.
Now the itsy bitsy spider climbed up the spout again.

(Repeat the first action of the rhyme.)

Elephant in the Spider's Web

One little elephant went out to play,
in a spider's web one day.

(Hold up one finger.)

He had such enormous fun,
that he asked someone else to come.

(Continue with the next verse, but this time say two elephants and then three, four, and so on. Even though the children may not know how to count, hold up the right number of fingers for each number given in the verse.)

Let's Go on a Bear Hunt

Let's go on a bear hunt?
All right, let's go.

(Tap hands on thighs like walking.)

Oh look, I see a wheat field.
Can't go around it,
Can't go under it,
Let's go through it.
All right, let's go.
Swish, swish, swish.

(Rub hands together like swishing.)

Oh look, I see a swamp.
Can't go around it,
Can't go under it,
Let's swim through it.
All right, let's go.

(Pretend to swim.)

Oh look, I see a bridge.
Can't go around it,
Can't go under it,
Let's cross over it.
All right, let's go.

(Make tongue clicking noise and stamping feet.)

Oh look, I see a cave.
Can't go around it,
Can't go under it,
Let's go in it.
All right, let's go.

(Clapping with cupped hands.)

O look, I see something.
I think—it's a bear.

(Louder)

IT IS A BEAR!
Let's go!

(Run away and then wipe forehead.)

WHEW!! WE MADE IT!

Roly-Poly Caterpillar

Roly-poly caterpillar into a corner crept,

(Walk fingers along arm or floor.)

spun himself a blanket
and for a long time slept.

(Rest head on hands.)

Roly-poly caterpillar wakened by and by,

(Stretch and yawn.)

found himself with beautiful wings

(Move arms up and down as if moving wings.)

changed to a butterfly!

(Run around with arms/wings flapping.)

The Hungry Caterpillar

Great to serve at your next children's party. With a 3-inch round cookie cutter, cut a circle from each of 12 slices white bread and 12 slices whole wheat bread. Spread one side of each circle lightly with mayonnaise. Spread 1/4 cup egg salad on each of 6 white bread circles. Cover with remaining white bread circles, mayonnaise side down. Spread 1/4 cup tuna salad on each of 6 whole wheat circles. Cover with remaining whole wheat circles, mayonnaise side down. (Or use 1 tablespoon peanut butter and 1 tablespoon jam in each sandwich.) Beginning with an egg salad sandwich, stand alternating tuna and egg salad sandwiches upright on a serving platter. To decorate the head: Spread first sandwich with mayonnaise. Add 2 stuffed-olive slices for eyes, fresh dill for eyelashes, a carrot tip for nose and a red pepper slice for mouth. Attach a radish top with a toothpick to a cucumber slice for hat and place on top of head. Garnish with celery leaves for hair. Insert 3-inch-long carrot and celery sticks into sandwiches for legs. Makes 12 sandwiches. Remove toothpick before eating.

Sound Like an Animal

Can you moo like a cow?
Can you neigh like a horse?
Can you oink like a pig?
Can you quack like a duck?
Can you gobble like a turkey?
Can you peep like a chick?
Can you maa like a goat?
Can you baa like a sheep?
Can you sit very still,
As still as you wish?

Teddy Bear, Teddy Bear, Turn Around

Teddy Bear, Teddy Bear, turn around.
Teddy Bear, Teddy Bear, touch the ground.
Teddy Bear, Teddy Bear, show your shoe.
Teddy Bear, Teddy Bear, that will do.
Teddy Bear, Teddy Bear, go upstairs.
Teddy Bear, Teddy Bear, say your prayers.
Teddy Bear, Teddy Bear, turn out the light.
Teddy Bear, Teddy Bear, say "Good-night!"

part three
Bibliography

Big and Little Are Not the Same. Bob Ottum. Golden Books, Western Publishing, 1972.

The Boy with a Drum. David L. Harrison. Golden Press, 1969.

Brown Bear, Brown Bear, What Do You See? Bill Martin, Jr. New York: H Holt and Co., 1983.

Charlie Brown in Love. Charles Schultz. World Publishers, 1968.

Clifford's Halloween, Norman Bridwell. New York: Scholastic Inc., 1989.

Curious George Flies a Kite. Margaret and H.A. Rey. Boston: Houghton Mifflin Co., 1977.

Frosty the Snowman. Annie N. Bedford. New York: Western Publishing (Golden Books), 1985.

The Gingerbread Boy. Paul Galdone. Boston: Houghton Mifflin Co., 1983.

Goldilocks and the Three Bears. James Marshall. New York: Dial Books for Young Readers, 1988.

Green Eggs and Ham. Dr. Seuss. New York: Random House, 1987.

The Grouchy Ladybug. Eric Carle. New York: Harper Junior, 1977.

Hansel and Gretel. Carol North. New York: Western Publishing (Golden Books), 1990.

Just LIke Daddy. Frank Asch. New York: Simon and Schuster, 1984.

Little Bear's Thanksgiving. Janice. New York: Lothrop, Lee and Shepard, 1967.

The Little Mouse, The Red Ripe Strawberry, and the Big Hungry Bear. Don Wood. Sudbury, MA: Playspaces, 1990.

The Mitten. Macmillan Early Skills Program, 1982. MacMillan Publishing Co.

Monkey Face. Reproduced from *The Everything Book.*

The Napping House. Audrey Wood. San Diego, CA: Harcourt Brace Jovanovich, Inc., 1984.

The Night before Christmas. Clement C. Moore. New York: Western Publishing (Golden Books), 1986.

The Old Lady Who Swallowed a Fly. Child's Play, 1973.

Peter Cottontail. Illustrated by Patrick McRae. Nashville, TN: Ideals Publishing Corp., 1986.

Rudolph the Red-Nosed Reindeer. Barbara S. Hazen. New York: Western Publishing (Golden Books), 1985.

Santa's Toy Shop. Adapted by Al Dempster. New York: Western Publishing, 1950.

The Snow Parade. Barbara Brenner. New York: Crown Publisers, 1984.

Snowy Day. Ezra J. Keats. New York: Viking Penguin, 1962.

Spot's First Easter. Eric Hill. Putnam Publishing Group, 1988.

Spot Goes to the Beach. Eric Hill. Putnam Publishing Group, 1985.

Spot Goes to the Circus. Eric Hill. Putnam Publishing Group, 1986.

Stone Soup. Marcia Brown. New York: Macmillan, 1986.

Too Much Noise. Ann McGovern. Boston: Houghton Co., 1967.

The Very Busy Spider. Eric Carle. New York: Putnam Publishing Group, 1989.

What's for Lunch? Eric Carle. New York: Putnam Publishing Group, 1982.

Did I Ever Tell You How Lucky You Are? Dr. Seuss. Random House, 1973.

Peter Rabbit. Beatrix Potter. Wonder Books, 1947.

The Very Hungry Caterpillar. Eric Carle. Philomel Books, 1984.

Where the Wild Things Are. Maurice Sendak. Harper-Row Publishers, 1988.

Zoo Animals. Michele Chopin Roosevelt. Random House, 1983.

part four
Classroom Equipment

Elephant Feely Box

To make the feely box, place several objects of different sizes and textures in a large box for the children to feel. Be sure that the children will be able to recognize through touch what each object is. (For instance, you might use a comb, an apple, a ball, a small stuffed animal, and so on.)

Make the body of an elephant by covering the box with gray paper. Then cut a hole in the side of the box. To make the elephant's trunk, attach a sleeve from an old sweat shirt to the hole. Add eyes and ears to the elephant's face. On the opposite side of the box, make a tail.

Seal

Draw the outline of a three-foot-high seal on a long sheet of black paper. Place a second sheet of black paper behind the first and cut out two seals. Staple the two seals together around the edge and leave an opening for the mouth.

part five
Games

Duck, Duck, Gray Duck

The players sit in a circle on the floor. One child becomes *IT*. *IT* walks around the outside of the circle and touches the other players on the head saying "Duck" each time he or she touches another child. Eventually *IT* must touch someone and say "Gray Duck." The child (Gray Duck) whom *IT* has just touched immediately rises and chases *IT* around the circle.

IT runs around the circle, trying to get *Gray Duck's* place before being tagged by *Gray Duck*. If *IT* gets to this place safely, *Gray Duck* becomes *IT* and the game proceeds as before. If *IT* is tagged, *Gray Duck* still becomes the new *IT*, but the first *IT* must sit in the center of the circle.

When the next chase begins, the first *IT* must try to get the new *Gray Duck's* place. If he or she gets the open place, the child who was trying to reach it must go to the center.

In another version of this game, no one every goes to the center of the circle. If *IT* gets tagged, *Gray Duck* returns to the circle and *IT* is *IT* again.

part six
Poems

My Handprint

Sometimes you get discouraged
because I am so small

and always leave my fingerprints
on furniture and walls.
But everyday I'm growing;
I'll be grown up someday,
and all those tiny handprints
will surely fade away.
So here's a final handprint
just so you can recall
exactly how my fingers looked
when I was very small!

part seven
Recipes

Bubble Blowing Mixture

10 cups water
1 cup liquid dishwashing detergent
1 tablespoon glycerine

Mix the water and detergent. For making very large bubbles, add glycerine. *Note:* The detergent Joy is especially good for making a bubble mixture.

Graham Cracker House

1 (16-ounce) box Honey Maid Graham Crackers
2 (21-ounce) cans fluffy white frosting
12 (1 1/2-ounce) packages assorted Life Savers Candy
1 package Licorice

Lay two whole NABISCO Graham Crackers, side by side, making a 5-inch square. Spread white frosting between crackers where they meet. Make five sets of connected pairs. Using one set as floor and four as walls, assemble house, sealing all seams with white frosting.

For roof of house, lay 3 whole graham crackers, side by side, making an 8 x 5-inch rectangle. Spread white frosting between crackers where they meet. Repeat to make 2 sides for roof. Lean against each other forming "V" shape. Attach base of roof to top of house, sealing seams with white frosting.

Cut out centers of 9 graham crackers. Fill centers of crackers with crushed Life Savers Candies. Bake on wax paper lined cookie sheets at 350°F. for 5 minutes, or until candy melts. Cool. Attach with frosting for windows. Decorate a whole cookie for a door. Tint frosting if desired.

Spread thin layer of frosting over roof and sprinkle with assorted crushed Life Savers Candies. Decorate edge of roof with licorice and peak with Life Savers, attaching with frosting.

Store house in dry place.

NABISCO BRANDS, East Hanover, New Jersey 07936.
All recipes kitchen tested by NABISCO Food and Nutrition Center
COPYRIGHT © 1984 NABISCO • PRINTED IN U.S.A.
HONEY MAID is a registered trademark of NABISCO, Inc.

Snow Sculptures or Snow Wash

Use a box of Ivory Snow. Pour the amount you think you may need into a large bowl or pan. Slowly, pour water into the flakes. For the sculptures, it will need to be very thick, so that the children can shape it into something. For the snow wash, the mixture needs to be thin, so that it can be washed onto a sheet of blue paper with a brush.

Art Dough

Clay Recipe for Christmas Ornaments
(oven drying method)

Mix well in a large bowl:
   4 cups flour
   1 cup salt
   1 teaspoon powdered alum
   1 1/2 cups water

If the dough is too dry, work in another tablespoon of water with your hands.

Dough can be colored by dividing it into several parts and kneading a drop or two of food coloring into each part. Roll or mold as desired.

To Roll: Roll dough 1/8" thick on lightly floured board. Cut with cookie cutters dipped in flour. Make a hole in the top, 1/4 inch down, for hanging, by using the end of a plastic straw dipped in flour. Shake the dots of clay from the straw and press on as decorations.

To Mold: Shape dough no more than 1/2" thick into figures such as flowers, fruits, animals, etc. Insert a fine wire in each for hanging.

Bake ornaments on ungreased cookie sheet for about 30 minutes in a 250° oven. Turn and bake another 1 1/2 hours till hard and dry. Remove and cool. When done, sand lightly with fine sandpaper till smooth. Paint with plastic-based poster, acrylic paint or markers. Paint both sides. Allow paint to dry and seal with clear shellac, spray plastic, or clear nail polish.

This recipe makes about 5 dozen 2 1/2" ornaments.

#1 *Play Dough*
(no-cooking recipe)

Mix:
   1 cup flour
   1/2 cup salt

2 tablespoons vegetable oil
1 teaspoon alum (if you can't find it at the grocery store, it is available at the drugstore.)

Add a small amount of water at a time until consistency of bread dough. It will not be more than $1/2$ cup. Add food coloring, preferably to the water before mixing. You can make colors not available, such as purple, by creatively mixing colors. Store in an airtight container or plastic bag. It lasts a long time.

#2 *Play Dough a la Peanut Butter*

Mix:
 1 jar of peanut butter (18 ounces)
 6 tablespoons honey
   non-fat dry milk or milk plus flour to the right consistency.
   (Optional: cocoa for chocolate flavor)
   Shape . . . Decorate (raisins?) . . . and Edible!

#3 *Play Dough*
(stove top recipe)

Mix in a medium pot:
 1 cup flour
 $1/2$ cup salt
 2 tablespoons cream of tartar
 Add: 1 cup water
     2 teaspoons vegetable food coloring

Cook over medium heat and stir (about 3–5 minutes). It will look like a "globby" mess and you'll be sure it's not turning out . . . but it will. Store in an airtight container or plastic bag.
 Edible but not as tasty as recipe #2!
 When using play dough, don't neglect those necessary pieces of equipment: cookie cutters, rolling pins (real or play), plastic knives, bottle caps, extra flour, uncooked spaghetti or macaroni, etc.

Modeling Clay/Dough

Ingredients:
 3 cups flour
 1 cup salt
 1 tablespoon alum (optional)
 1 cup water with coloring in it
 1 tablespoon vegetable oil

Mix the dry ingredients together. Gradually add liquids. If dough is too stiff, add more water; if dough is too sticky, add more flour. Note that alum is a preservative that is unessential in a cool climate. Store modeling dough in an airtight container.

Gingerbread Boys

Children—always so eager to help—love to decorate their own ginger-bread boys. But have plenty of extra raisins for nibbling.

1/2	cup shortening
1/2	cup sugar
1/2	cup dark molasses
1/4	cup water
2 1/2	cups all-purpose flour*
3/4	teaspoon salt
1/2	teaspoon soda
3/4	teaspoon ginger
1/4	teaspoon nutmeg
1/8	teaspoon allspice
	Raisins
	Candied cherries or red gumdrops
	Citron
	String licorice

Cream shortening and sugar. Blend in molasses, water, flour, salt, soda, ginger, nutmeg and allspice. Cover; chill 2 to 3 hours.

Heat over to 375°. Roll dough 1/4 inch thick on lightly floured cloth-covered board. Cut with gingerbread boy cutter; place on ungreased baking sheet.

Press raisins into dough for eyes, nose, and buttons. Use bits of candied cherries and strips of citron and string licorice for other trims. Bake 10 to 12 minutes. Immediately remove from baking sheet. Cool. Trim with icing.

ABOUT FIFTEEN 4-INCH COOKIES.

If using self-rising flour, omit salt and soda. If using quick-mixing flour, add 3 tablespoons milk.

Note: For crisper cookies, roll dough 1/8 inch thick. Bake 8 minutes.

ABOUT 2 DOZEN COOKIES.

Bird Nest Clusters

Here's what you need
(Take out all items before beginning)

1	package (12 ounces or 1 1/2 cups) semi-sweet chocolate chips
1/2	cup peanut butter ("chunky" is better if you have a choice)
4	cups chow mein noodles (or a 6-ounce bag)
	Colored candies (optional)

large glass bowl
waxed paper
mixing spoon or fork
2 *cookie trays*

Here's what you do
(First, read steps 1–6)

1. Put the chocolate chips and peanut butter into large glass or microwave-proof bowl. Set the timer for 1 minute. Or melt them in the oven in a cooking pan at 350 degrees Fahrenheit.
2. Remove the mixture and stir. Place it back in the oven for 1 1/2 minutes or until chocolate chips are completely melted.
3. Add the chow mein noodles.
4. Mix the noodles by using one or two forks or spoons as though you were tossing a salad to get them evenly coated with the chocolate/peanut butter mixture.
5. Lay a piece of waxed paper over two cookie sheets.
6. Drop golf-ball size clusters on the covered cookie sheet to cool and set. Add a few colored candies as "eggs" to the nests!

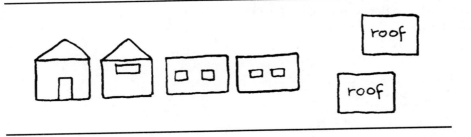

Gingerbread House

This is one of those nifty ideas that will really delight your kids regardless of the fact that it lacks greatly in the nutrition department. This is a super simplified recipe that does not take a great deal of time.

To one Gingerbread Mix, add 1/3 cup water. Mix well and roll out into 1/2" thickness. It will work best if you take the time to make a cardboard pattern, but for a guideline, the base of the house will be about 4" x 6" and 3 1/2" high to the eave line. You will need six sections.

Cut the door and windows before baking, but do not remove pieces until after baking. Extra dough can be molded into little cookie people. Bake on a greased sheet for maximum hardness, but without allowing the edges to get burnt (approximately 15 minutes). The house is "glued" together with frosting. Use toothpicks when or where necessary. Use the frosting to hold e to the plate so that it will stand. Let the frame dry before

: Sprinkle coconut around house, or use cotton.

..th icing and cover with mini-marshmallows, coconut,

..cors, and candied fruit slices, halved.

rath: A group of any small circle candies such as M&Ms or Life Savers, or sliced gumdrops, etc.

Chimney: A pile of 2 or 3 hard circle candies or sugar cubes cemented with frosting.

Trees: Green gumdrops; lollys; pine cones or inverted sugar cones; tree cookies.

Snow Men: From leftover frosting, shape 2 balls and let dry. Attach with frosting.

Pudding Bears

Mix package of instant chocolate pudding as directed on the box. Place in shaker container.

Have the children take turns shaking the pudding mixture.

When ready, put a spoonful in each child's bowl.

Give each child 2 wafer-type cookies for the ears, and use aerosol whipped cream for the eyes.

Section IV

Glossary

Activity time—time in which children can select from a variety of activities independently

adaptive equipment—equipment used to position children for maximum learning

Alternative strategy—teaching a skill in a different way than a typical teaching strategy

articulation—the ability to speak distinctly and clearly

assessment—tests and observations to determine a child's ability level

At risk children—children who may be at risk for developmental delays because of adverse environmental factors

autism—a socio-emotional disorder of unknown origin in which the child's social interactions, language, and other behaviors are delayed and inappropriate

behavior—a person's actions

bolster—long, narrow cushion or pillow for good positioning

cerebral palsy—central nervous system dysfunction affecting motor coordination and unusual ways of moving

Classification—ability to sort and group objects by common properties like size and color

Cognition—process of mental development

Communication devices—equipment used by a child to express ideas and needs through pointing or electronic switches

Congenital—occurring at birth

cooperative play—children playing together in a shared activity

corner chair—chair shaped at a 90° angle to help position a child; one type of adaptive equipment

Creative playground—outdoor play area which includes swings, climbing apparatus, tires, etc.

curriculum—philosophy and master plan of the program

data—information gathered about a particular subject

development delay—a child's development occurring significantly below his/her peers

developmental milestone—behavior that most children do at a particular time like sitting up, walking, talking, etc.

DIAL (R)—Developmental Indicator for the Assessment of Learning (Revised) which is a screening test for motor, concept and language development

Down syndrome—a chromosomal disorder of the twenty-first chromosome pair, usually causing some degree of mental retardation

Dramatic play—play involving the use of objects to represent something imaginary

Early Childhood Education—a developmentally appropriate program that serves children from birth to seven years of age

early childhood special education—combination of the skills of early childhood teachers and special educators to meet the needs of handicapped preschoolers

environment—surroundings

etiology—cause of disorder or disease

expansion—listener responds with a corrected and expanded version of what the child said

Expressive language—form of communication, usually through speech, that allows expression of thoughts

Eye-hand coordination—integrated use of hands guided by the eye

fine-motor development—use of small muscles in the fingers and hands to write and draw

flexible—able to change or be changed easily in a productive and creative way

Gross-motor development—use of large muscles in arms, legs and back to run, jump and climb

Handling techniques—methods of holding children with physical handicaps or motor delays

Home visit—one-on-one interaction in the child's home with parent participation

imitate—copy someone else

integrated curriculum—focuses on all aspects of a child's development

Large group time—time in which the children come together to do a common activity

learning centers—various materials and equipment that are set up around common activities for the children to explore and manipulate

least restrictive environment—a provision in PL 94-142 whereby children with disabilities are placed in an environment that is similar to the environment of children without disabilities while still addressing their special needs

mainstreaming—the integration of handicapped and nonhandicapped children in school programs

Manipulatives—toys and materials that the children can handle like blocks, beads and puzzles

Mildly mentally handicapped—a child with significant delays in cognition, language and social skills

modeling—the process of showing proper behaviors to be imitated

nonverbal cues—cues that involve the use of gestures to get the desired behaviors

Objective—specific teaching techniques to meet general goals of the child

Observable Behavior—actions that can be seen through a series of observation

occupational therapist—professional trained to work with children and adults with their self-help skills, fine-motor activities, visual motor activities, and activities of daily living

open-ended materials—materials designed to be more flexible rather than structured or having a single way of doing things

Parallel play—play where children play alongside one another but do not interact

paraprofessional—also called aide, helper or assistant teacher; works under the guidance of the classroom teacher

physical therapist—professional trained to work with mobility, ambulation, and gross-motor activities

Planning Time—time in which the staff can plan effectively to meet the needs in their program

positioning—ways to help normalize patterns of movement and improve postural tone

Positive Reinforcement—strategies used to get the desired behavior by children by giving immediate feedback

Pragmatics—rules that govern language

Receptive language—the understanding of what is being communicated

reinforcement—a response that follows a behavior and encourages the child to repeat that behavior

response—the action of a person

Schizophrenia—disorder in which a child may have repetitive or bizarre behaviors, unpredictable mood swings and may not be connected to reality.
Self-esteem—children's perception of their worth
self-help skills—ability to take care of oneself by being able to toilet, dress, feed and groom oneself
Semantics—the understanding and study of the meaning of words
Separation anxiety—difficulty a child may have leaving his/her mother or father
socialization—process by which children learn society's rules and values
Strategy—a plan to do something
Syndrome—symptoms occurring together

tactilely defensive—sensitive to touch

variety—different kinds or an assortment
visual—having to do with sight

wedge—adaptive equipment used for positioning

Section V

Resources for Information on Disabilities

The American Brittle Bone Society
1256 Merrill Drive
West Chester, PA 19380

American Cancer Society, Inc.
77 Third Avenue
New York, NY 10017

American Diabetes Association
2 Park Avenue
New York, NY 10016

American Heart Association
7320 Greenville Avenue
Dallas, TX 75231

American Lung Association
1740 Broadway
New York, NY 10019

The Arthritis Foundation
3400 Peachtree Road N.E.
Atlanta, GA 30326

Cystic Fibrosis Foundation
6000 Executive Boulevard
Suite 309
Rockville, MD 20852

Epilepsy Foundation of America
1828 L. Street N.W.
Washington, D.C. 20036

Muscular Dystrophy Association
810 Seventh Avenue
New York, NY 10019

National Amputation Foundation
1245 105th Street
Whitestone, NY 11357

National Down Syndrome Congress
1800 Dempster Street
Pine Ridge, IL 60068-1146

National Foundation for Asthma, Inc.
P.O. Box 50304
Tucson, AZ 85705

National Hemophilia Foundation
25 W. 39th Street
New York, NY 10018

National Kidney Foundation, Inc.
2 Park Avenue
New York, NY 10016

National Spinal Cord Injury Foundation
369 Elliot Street
Newton Upper Falls, MA 02164

The Scoliosis Association, Inc.
1 Penn Plaza
New York, NY 10001

Spina Bifida Association of America
343 S. Dearborn
Suite 319
Chicago, IL 60604

United Cerebral Palsy Association, Inc.
66 E. 34th Street
New York, NY 10016

Index